POLISH PHRASEBOOK

Krzy

Polish phrasebook
1st edition – April 2001

Published by
Lonely Planet Publications Pty Ltd ABN 36 005 607 983
90 Maribyrnong St, Footscray, Victoria 3011, Australia

Lonely Planet Offices
Australia Locked Bag 1, Footscray, Victoria 3011
USA 150 Linden St, Oakland CA 94607
UK 10a Spring Place, London NW5 3BH
France 1 rue du Dahomey, 75011 Paris

Cover illustration
Riding through the Ski on a diamond studded beer keg, as one does in Poland eh eh eh? by Patrick Marris

ISBN 0 86442 588 0

10 9 8 7 6 5 4 3 2 1

Printed through Colorcraft Ltd, Hong Kong
Printed in China

About the Author

Krzysztof DydyŇski was born and raised in Warsaw, Poland. He travelled extensively in Asia and lived for nearly five years in South America before settling in Australia, where he currently resides and works. He's the author of several Lonely Planet guidebooks, including *Poland*, *Kraków*, *Colombia* and *Venezuela*.

From the Author

Warmest thanks to Angela Melendro, Ela Lis, Beata Wasiak, Basia Meder, Tadek Wysocki, Kuba LeszczyŇski, Majka and Marek Bogatek, and Grażyna and Jacek Wojciechowicz.

From the Publisher

Peter D'Onghia supervised but couldn't keep out of the *bimber*. Vicki Webb, who prefers *jarzębiak*, edited, and Lou Callan proofread and assisted with editing. Patrick Marris, a *żytnia* man, drew the cover illustration, designed and layed out, while Rosie Silva-Guevara illustrated. Fabrice Rocher supervised design and Natasha Velleley, who's partial to a drop of *wiśniówka*, produced the map. Karin Vidstrup Monk didn't need any *wódka* to assist in her inimitable style.

CONTENTS

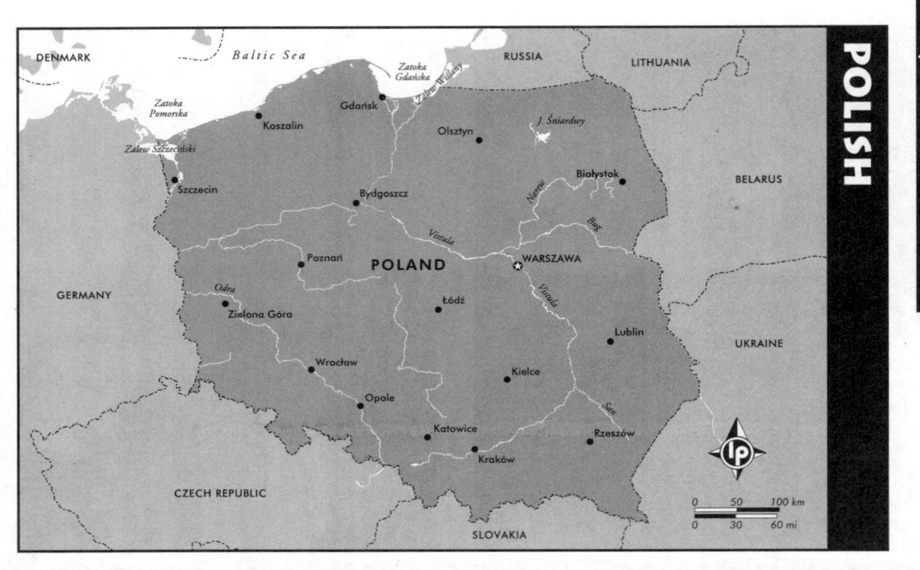
POLISH
DENMARK
Baltic Sea
RUSSIA
LITHUANIA
BELARUS
UKRAINE
GERMANY
CZECH REPUBLIC
SLOVAKIA
POLAND
Zatoka Gdańska
Zalew Wiślany
Zatoka Pomorska
Zalew Szczeciński
J. Śniardwy
Gdańsk
Koszalin
Olsztyn
Szczecin
Bydgoszcz
Białystok
Narew
Bug
Vistula
WARSZAWA
Poznań
Odra
Zielona Góra
Łódź
Lublin
Wrocław
Kielce
Opole
San
Katowice
Rzeszów
Kraków
0 50 100 km
0 30 60 mi

INTRODUCTION

Polish, along with Czech and Slovak, is a western variety of the group of Slavonic languages, which covers a dozen languages spoken in a number of Central and Eastern European countries, including Russia, Ukraine, Bulgaria, Serbia, Croatia, and the Czech and Slovak republics. The group is a branch of the large Indo-European family of languages which includes English, Greek and Latin, and has its distant origins back in ancient Sanskrit.

Although Polish is a language with a long, if obscure, history, its written form didn't actually develop until the Middle Ages. In mediaeval Poland, Latin was the lingua franca and the language used by the Crown's state offices, administration and the Church. The oldest known text in Polish, the song *Bogurodzica,* 'Mother of God', was reputedly written in the 13th century and was the national anthem until the 18th century.

It wasn't until the Renaissance period that the Polish language came into wider use. The invention of printing contributed to the spread of books; the first printed text in Polish was published in 1475. During the course of the 16th century, Latin became largely dominated by Polish in both its spoken and written form. Polish literature began to develop at a remarkable pace and saw its first major achievements, with a range of Polish literature published.

The Latin alphabet was adapted to write the Polish language, but in order to represent the complex sounds of the tongue, a number of consonant clusters and diacritical marks were applied. In effect, the visual appearance of Polish is pretty fearsome for people from outside the Slavic circle, and undoubtedly it's not the easiest language to master. It has a complicated grammar, with word endings changing depending on case, number and gender, and its rules abound in exceptions. Yet, it's not the most difficult language either. Despite its bewildering appearance, Polish script is phonetic, largely consistent, and has a logical structure.

Today, Polish is the official language of Poland and is spoken by over 99 percent of the country's population of 39 million. It's also spoken by roughly up to 10 million Poles scattered all over the world, with the largest Polish emigre community living in the US.

Save for a few tiny areas, Polish has no pronounced regional dialects or variations, and sounds pretty much the same the breadth and width of the country. Understandably, there are some minor regional differences in the language's sound and melody, which locals can distinguish but for outsiders won't be noticeable.

As for Western languages, English and German are the best known in Poland though by no means are they commonly spoken or understood. English is most often heard in larger urban centres among educated youth, while German is largely a heritage of pre-WWII territorial divisions and the war itself. German is mainly spoken by the older generation, particularly in regions which were once German. Taking this as a rough rule, you may have some English conversations in major cities, but when travelling in remote parts of Masuria or Silesia, German will be a better tool for communication than English.

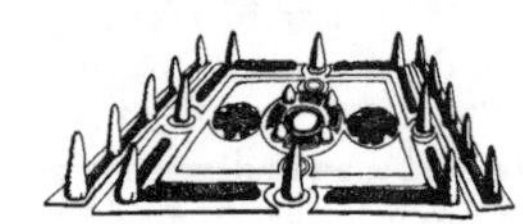

This said, remember that most ordinary Poles don't speak any other language than Polish. This includes attendants of public services such as shops, post offices, banks, bus and train stations, restaurants and hotels (except for some top-end ones), and you may even encounter language problems at tourist offices. It's also true of phone emergency lines, including police, ambulance and the fire brigade.

Ideally, everyone who wants to travel in Poland should know some basic Polish – the more you know the easier your travel is likely to be and the more you'll get out of your time in the country. This phrasebook will help in your travels.

ARTHUR OR MARTHA?

Most nouns in Polish are one of three genders – masculine (m), feminine (f) or neuter (neut).

In this phrasebook, the gender of nouns is indicated in wordlists as well as in the dictionaries.

houses	dom	*dom* (m)
newspaper	ga-*ze*-ta	*gazeta* (f)
sun	*swon*-tse	*słońce* (neut)

Some nouns have both masculine and feminine forms, such as those classifying human gender. In these cases, both nouns are given in full, with the masculine form first:

student	stoo-*den*-tem	*studentem* (m)
	stoo-*dent*-kom	*studentką* (f)

When adjectives have alternative endings, these are separated with a slash:

red	cher-*vo*-ni/a	*czerwony/a* (m/f)

This indicates that the masculine form of the word ends in *-y*, while the feminine form ends in *-a*.

Verb endings that differ according to whether they refer to a masculine or feminine Subject are separated with a slash:

I'm lost.	zgoo-*bee*-wem/ wam she	*Zgubiłem/łam się.* (m/f)

See pages 19-20 for an explanation of gender.

ABBREVIATIONS USED IN THIS BOOK

abb	abbreviation
adj	adjective
adv	adverb
f	feminine
imp	imperfective (see Grammar, page 31)
inf	informal
lit	literally
m	masculine
neut	neuter
perf	perfective (see Grammar, page 31)
pl	plural
pol	polite
sg	singular

HOW TO USE THIS PHRASEBOOK

You *Can* Speak Another Language

It's true – anyone can speak another language. Don't worry if you haven't studied languages before, or that you studied a language at school for years and can't remember any of it. It doesn't even matter if you failed English grammar. After all, that's never affected your ability to speak English! And this is the key to picking up a language in another country. You don't need to sit down and memorise endless grammatical details and you don't need to memorise long lists of vocabulary. You just need to start speaking. Once you start you'll be amazed how many prompts you'll get to help you build on those first words. You'll hear people speaking, pick up sounds from TV, catch a word or two that you think you know from the local radio, see something on a billboard - all these things help to build your understanding.

Plunge In

There's just one thing you need to start speaking another language – courage. Your biggest hurdle is overcoming the fear of saying aloud what may seem to you to be just a bunch of sounds.

The best way to start overcoming your fear is to memorise a few key words. These are the words you know you'll be saying again and again, like 'hello', 'thank you' and 'how much?'. Here's an important hint though – right from the beginning, learn at least one phrase that will be useful but not essential. Such as 'I'm pleased to meet you' or 'I love it here', or even a conversational piece like 'what a lovely day' or 'fortunately it's not raining' (people everywhere love to talk about the weather). Having this extra phrase will enable you to move away from the basics, and when you get a reply and a smile, it'll also boost your confidence. You'll find that people you speak to will like it too, as they'll understand that at least you've tried to learn more of the language than just the usual essential words.

Ways to Remember

There are several ways to learn a language. Most people find they learn from a variety of these, although people usually have a preferred way to remember. Some like to see the written word and remember the sound from what they see. Some like to just hear it spoken in context (if this is you, try talking to yourself in Polish, but do it in the car or somewhere private, to give yourself confidence, and so others don't wonder about your sanity!).

Others, especially the more mathematically inclined, like to analyse the grammar of a language, and piece together words according to the rules of grammar. The very visually inclined like to associate the written word and even sounds with some visual stimulus, such as from illustrations, TV and general things they see in the street. As you learn, you'll discover what works best for you – be aware of what made you really remember a particular word, and if it sticks in your mind, keep using that method.

Kicking Off

Chances are you'll want to learn some of the language before you go. The first thing to do is to memorise those essential phrases and words. Check out the basics (page 43) ... and don't forget your extra phrase. Try the sections on making conversation or greeting people for a phrase you'd like to use. Write some of these words down on a separate piece of paper and stick them up around the place. On the fridge, by the bed, on your computer, as a bookmark - somewhere where you'll see them often. Try putting some words in context - the 'How much is it?' note, for instance, could go in your wallet.

I've Lost my Car Keys

Doesn't seem like the phrase you're going to need? Well in fact, it could be very useful. As are all the phrases in this book, provided you have the courage to mix and match them. We have given specific examples within each section. But the key words remain the same even when the situation changes. So while you may not be planning on any driving during your trip, the first part of the phrase 'I've lost my ġ' could refer to anything else, and there are words in the dictionary that, we hope, will fit your needs. So whether it's your 'ticket', 'credit card' or 'laundry receipt', you'll be able to put the words together to convey your meaning.

Finally

Don't be concerned if you feel you can't memorise words. On the inside front and back covers are the most essential words and phrases you'll need. You could also try tagging a few pages for other key phrases.

PRONUNCIATION

Unlike English, Polish has a consistent relationship between pronunciation and spelling. In other words, a letter or a cluster of letters is always pronounced the same way. For example, Polish *a* has one pronunciation rather than the numerous pronunciations we find in English, such as the 'a' in 'cake', 'art' and 'all'.

POLISH ALPHABET

Polish letters with diacritical marks (*ą*, *ć*, *ę* and so on) are treated as separate letters. The order of letters and their simplified pronunciation, given in blue, are:

a	a	*g*	g/k	*r*	r
ą	on/om	*h*	h	*rz*	zh/sh
b	b/p	*i*	ee	*s*	s
c	ts	*j*	y	*sz*	sh
ć	ch	*k*	k	*ś*	sh
ch	h	*l*	l	*t*	t
cz	ch	*ł*	w	*u*	oo
d	d/t	*m*	m	*v*	v
dz	dz	*n*	n	*w*	v/f
dź	dj	*ń*	n	*y*	i
dż	dj	*o*	o	*x*	ks
e	e	*ó*	oo	*z*	z/s
ę	en/em/e	*p*	p	*ź*	zh
f	f	*q*	k	*ż*	zh

TRANSLITERATIONS

Vowels

Polish vowels are of roughly equal length.

a as the 'u' in 'cut'
e as the 'e' in 'ten'
ee similar to the 'i' in 'marine' but shorter
o as the 'o' in 'not'
oo as the 'u' in 'put'
i as the 'i' in 'bit'

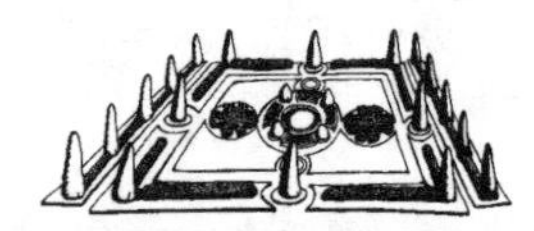

SOUNDING OUT

The letters *u* and *ó* both sound the same, but aren't interchangeable – some words feature *u* and others *ó*. You'll probably have some doubts about which should be used in a particular word, but don't worry too much about it – many Poles have these doubts as well!

The same refers to *ż* and *rz* as well as *h* and *ch*, which also sound the same, and pose eternal problems to even well-educated locals.

Nasal Vowels

em as the 'em' in 'emblem'
en as the 'en' in 'engage'
om as the 'om' in 'tomb'
on as the 'on' in 'bond'

Consonants

Consonants not mentioned here are pronounced as they are in English.

ch	as the 'ch' in 'church'
dj	as the 'j' in 'jam'; as the 'ds' in 'adds up', but softer. Pronounced with the tongue a little further back on the roof of the mouth.
dz	as the 'ds' in 'adds up'
g	as the 'g' in 'get';
h	as the 'ch' in the Scottish 'loch'
n	as the 'ny' in 'canyon'
r	always trilled
s	as the 's' in 'sin'
sh	as the 'sh' in 'show'; as the 'sh' in 'show', but softer
shch	as the 'shch' in 'fresh cheese'
sz	as the 'sz' in 'Paris Zoo', pronounced quickly
ts	as the 'ts' in 'its'
w	as the 'w' in 'wine'
y	as the 'y' in 'yet'
zh	as the 's' in 'pleasure'; as the 's' in 'pleasure', but softer

TONGUE TWISTER

To test your pronunciation skills on, here's the favourite Polish tongue-twister: *W Szczebrzeszynie, chrząszcz brzmi w trzcinie*, which means 'In Szczebrzeszyn (a town in Poland), the cockchafer (a type of beetle) buzzes in the weeds'.

STRESS

As a rule, stress falls on the second-last syllable of a word. In some words of foreign origin (mostly from Latin and Greek), stress falls on the third-last syllable:

music	*moo*-zi-ka	*muzyka*
university	oo-nee-*ver*-si-tet	*uniwersytet*

Despite these quite consistent rules, stressed syllables in the transliteration throughout this phrasebook are given in italics, to help you learn the stress of Polish faster.

Although Polish grammar has a reputation for being complicated, there are rules that will help you speak the language well enough to be understood. This chapter is designed to give you an idea of how Polish phrases are put together, providing you with the basic rules to help you to construct your own sentences.

WORD ORDER

Broadly speaking, the word order of simple sentences is similar to English word order (Subject-Verb-Object). However, since information such as person (I, you, she), case (nominative, accusative), gender (masculine, feminine, neuter), number (singular, plural) and tense (present, past, future) are indicated by the endings of either nouns, verbs or both, the order can be more flexible.

This is particularly true in more complex sentences, where the position of subjects, verbs, adjectives and so on doesn't necessarily have to follow an established pattern. Word order also depends on the context of a sentence, and where the emphasis is intended to go.

ARTICLES

Polish has no articles (the, a, an) before nouns. The context in which a noun has been used usually makes it clear whether it's 'a house' or 'the house'. If not, there are a range of pronouns and adjectives which can be used to avoid ambiguity.

NOUNS

Gender

Nouns in Polish have three genders – masculine, feminine and neuter. Apart from nouns classifying human gender (man, woman), the term 'gender' is purely grammatical and in no way related to a noun's meaning. There's no universal key to determining the gender of a noun, although most follow a general pattern.

- Most masculine nouns end in a consonant:

house	*dom*
table	*stół*

- Most feminine nouns end in *-a*:

newspaper	*gazeta*
monkey	*małpa*

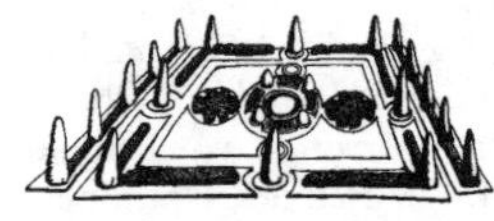

However, there are exceptions to these rules; some masculine nouns end in *-a*, while feminine nouns end in a consonant:

M		F	
artist	*artysta*	journey	*podróż*
man (a male)	*mężczyzna*	help	*pomoc*

- Most neuter nouns end in *-e* or *-o*:

sun	*słońce*
summer	*lato*

- Nouns describing occupations usually have both a masculine and a feminine form, which differ in their endings:

waiter (m)	*kelner*	waiter (f)	*kelnerka*
poet (m)	*poeta*	poet (f)	*poetka*

In this phrasebook, the gender of nouns is indicated in wordlists as well as in the dictionaries:

silk	*yet*-vap	*jedwab* (m)
cotton	ba-*veoo*-na	*bawełna* (f)

Plurals

Plurals of nouns have many different forms, depending on the noun's gender and its final letter. Many plurals take a similar form to their singular counterparts:

shoe	*but*	shoes	*buty*

but some are quite different:

dog	*pies*	dogs	*psy*

In any case, you don't have to worry too much – just use the singular form (which is given in the dictionary), and it's likely you'll be understood.

Noun Case

In English, we're able to recognise the 'role' a noun plays in a sentence – who is peforming an action, to whom, with what and so on – by its position in a sentence and/or by the use of prepositions.

Many other languages, however, including German, Russian and Polish, use what are known as 'cases' to make these distinctions. Different suffixes, called case endings, act as labels to indicate the role of a noun and its relationship to other words in a sentence.

Singular nouns are used in the examples here, but remember that the same case system applies to plurals. As Polish has seven noun cases, a noun can have up to 14 different endings!

Don't panic, though – if you use the nominative form, you'll still be understood. We've included an explanation of how case affects noun endings just so you'll be aware of it when you hear people speak.

Other parts of a sentence, including adjectives and pronouns, also change their endings depending on the case. They have the same number (singular, plural) and gender (masculine, feminine, neuter) as the case ending of the noun to which they refer.

Nominative

The nominative case refers to the Subject of the verb in a sentence. It indicates 'what' or 'who' is performing an action. The noun in this case appears in its nominative, or elementary, form – the one which is given in dictionaries.

My brother reads a lot.	*Mój **brat** dużo czyta.* (lit: my brother much read)
This is my sister.	*To jest moja **siostra**.* (lit: this is my sister)

Accusative

The accusative case refers to the Direct Object. It indicates 'what' or 'whom' the verb refers to. It's only used to refer to the Direct Object of sentences in the affirmative.

Tom often visits his brother.	*Tom często odwiedza swojego **brata**.* (lit: Tom often visit his brother)
I love my sister.	*Kocham moją **siostrę**.* (lit: love-I my sister)

Genitive

The genitive case refers to ownership, possession or association. It answers the questions 'whose', 'of what' and 'of whom'. It's also used to refer to the Direct Object of negative sentences.

This is my brother's dog.	*To jest pies **mojego brata**.* (lit: this is dog my brother)
I don't love my sister.	*Nie kocham **mojej siostry**.* (lit: not love-I my sister)

Dative

The dative case refers to the Indirect Object. It designates the person or object 'to whom' or 'to which' something is given, done, lent and so on.

I gave a book to my brother.	*Dałem* ***bratu*** *książkę.* (lit: gave-I brother book)
Maria helps her sister.	*Maria pomaga swojej* ***siostrze.*** (lit: Maria helps-she her sister)

Instrumental

The instrumental case has several functions. It's used to answer a number of questions, including 'with whom', 'with what', 'by what means', 'how' and 'where'.

Don't argue with your brother.	*Nie kłóć się z twoim* ***bratem.*** (lit: not argue-I self with brother)
I live with my sister.	*Mieszkam z moją* ***siostrą.*** (lit: live-I with my sister)

Locative

The locative case indicates where an action takes place. It's always used with prepositions indicating location, such as 'in', 'on', 'by', 'at', 'about' and so on.

You'd better think about your brother.	*Lepiej pomyśl o swoim* ***bracie.*** (lit: better you-think about your brother)
We often talk about my sister.	*Często rozmawiamy o mojej* ***siostrze.*** (lit: often we-talk about my sister)

Vocative

The vocative case is used when addressing people directly.

Dear brother!	*Drogi* ***bracie!*** (lit: dear brother)
My beloved sister!	*Moja ukochana* ***siostro!*** (lit: my beloved sister)

PERSONAL PRONOUNS

Personal pronouns (I, you, he and so on) are often omitted in Polish because the subject of a sentence is usually indicated in the verb's ending (see Verbs, page 30).

They went to the cinema.	***Oni*** *poszli do kina.* (lit: they-(m+f) went to cinema)
I love you.	*Kocham cię.* (lit: I-love you)

SUBJECT PRONOUNS		
SG		
I	ya	*ja*
you	ti	*ty*
he	on	*on*
she	ona	*ona*
it	ono	*ono*
PL		
we	mi	*my*
you	vi	*wy*
they (m; m+f)	oni	*oni*
they (f; m+f + neut)	one	*one*

The second person singular *ty*,'you', and plural *wy*, are only used in informal situations such as with friends or colleagues. In more formal situations, the pronouns *pan*, 'Mr', *pani*, 'Mrs', are used with the third person form of the verb (he, she, they). See page 44 for more about polite forms of address.

The pronoun 'they' has two forms in Polish – *oni* (used when referring to men and groups including both men and women) and *one* (which refers to women, and animals and things of all three genders).

ADJECTIVES

Adjectives agree in gender, number and case with the nouns which they describe. As in English, adjectives normally appear before a noun, but in some cases they can alternatively be placed after the noun.

When singular, adjectives have three genders, which have the following endings:

M	*-i* or *-y*
F	*-a* or *-ia*
NEUT	*-e* or *-ie*

When plural, adjectives have only two genders, with the following endings:

M PERSONAL *-i* or *-y*

refers to men, and groups of both women and men

GENERAL *-e* or *-ie*

refers to women, animals, and things

Adjectives are given here in the nominative case.

	SG			PL	
	M	F	NEUT	M PERSONAL	GENERAL
old	*star-y*	*star-a*	*star-e*	*starz-y*	*star-e*
nice	*ładn-y*	*ładn-a*	*ładn-e*	*ładn-i*	*ładn-e*
cheap	*tan-i*	*tan-ia*	*tan-ie*	*tan-i*	*tan-ie*

I bought a nice old painting.	*Kupiłem **ładny** stary obraz.* (lit: I-bought nice old painting)

In this phrasebook, alternative endings to adjectives are separated with a slash.

red	cher-*vo*-ni/a	*czerwony/a* (m/f)

Comparatives

Comparatives are usually formed by placing *-sz-* or *-ejsz-* before the last letter of an adjective, though there may be some other letter changes.

M, SG	
older	*star-sz-y*
cheaper	*tań-sz-y*
nicer	*ładni-ejsz-y*

As in English, there are some irregular adjectives whose comparatives are wholly different.

M, SG			
good	*dobry*	better	*lepszy*
bad	*zły*	worse	*gorszy*

Superlatives

Superlatives are formed by adding *naj-* before the comparative.

cheapest	*naj-tańszy*
best	*naj-lepszy*
worst	*naj-gorszy*

The cheapest hotels are far from the centre.	***Najtańsze** hotele są daleko od centrum.* (lit: cheapest hotels are far from centre)

ADVERBS

Adverbs are words that usually derive from adjectives, but describe verbs, not nouns. They're normally formed by removing an adjective's final letter and replacing it with *-ie*, *-io* or *-o*.

nice	*ładny*	nicely	*ładn-ie*
cheap	*tani*	cheaply	*tan-io*

Unlike in English, their position in a sentence is fairly flexible.

I've bought it very cheaply.	*Bardzo* ***tanio*** *to kupiłem.* (lit: very cheaply this I-bought) *Kupiłem to bardzo* ***tanio.*** (lit: I-bought this very cheaply)

POSSESSIVES

As with other adjectives, possessive adjectives (my, your, his and so on) agree in gender, number and case with the noun they describe. In the nominative case, they have the following forms:

	SG			PL	
	M	F	NEUT	M PERSONAL*	GENERAL*
my	*mój*	*moja*	*moje*	*moi*	*moje*
your	*twój*	*twoja*	*twoje*	*twoi*	*twoje*
his/its	*jego*	*jego*	*jego*	*jego*	*jego*
her	*jej*	*jej*	*jej*	*jej*	*jej*
our	*nasz*	*nasza*	*nasze*	*nasi*	*nasze*
your	*wasz*	*wasza*	*wasze*	*wasi*	*wasze*
their	*ich*	*ich*	*ich*	*ich*	*ich*

* See page 25 for an explanation of 'm personal' and 'general'.

GRAMMAR

Possessive pronouns (mine, yours, hers and so on) have the same form in Polish as possessive adjectives, so that *mój* is used to express both 'my' and 'mine'.

This is my house.	*To jest **mój** dom.* (lit: this is my house)
This house is mine.	*Ten dom jest **mój**.* (lit: this house is mine)

DEMONSTRATIVES

Demonstrative adjectives and pronouns (this, that, these, those) agree in gender, number and case with a noun. They have the following forms in the nominative case:

	SG			PL	
	M	F	NEUT	M PERSONAL*	GENERAL
this	*ten*	*ta*	*to*	*ci*	*te*
that	*tamten*	*tamta*	*tamto*	*tamci*	*tamte*

This book is good but that one is better.	*Ta książka jest dobra ale tamta jest lepsza.* (lit: this book is good but that is better)

* See page 25 for an explanation of 'm personal' and 'general'.

PREPOSITIONS

As in English, a preposition appears before the noun it modifies.

about	*o*	
above	*nad*	
after	*po*	
against	*przeciw*	
among	*wśród*	
at	*na*	I'm at the airport. *Jestem* ***na*** *lotnisku.* (lit: I-am at airport)
	przy	Let's sit down at the table. *Usiądźmy* ***przy*** *stole.* (lit: let's-sit at table)
	w	There's nobody at home. *Nie ma nikogo* ***w*** *domu.* (lit: not is nobody at home)
before	*przed*	
behind	*za*	
beside	*obok*	
between	*między*	
beyond	*poza*	
by	*przy*	
for	*dla*	These flowers are for you. *Te kwiaty są* ***dla*** *ciebie.* (lit: these flowers are for you)
	na	I'm saving for my future trip. *Oszczędzam* ***na*** *moją przyszłą podróż.* (lit: I-save for my future trip)
from	*od*	I've got a letter from my mum. *Dostałem list* ***od*** *mojej mamy.* (lit: I-got letter from my mum)
	z	I'm from Australia. *Jestem* ***z*** *Australii.* (lit: I-am from Australia)

in	w	
into	do	Please come into the room. *Proszę wejść **do** pokoju.* (lit: please come into room)
	w	Don't fall into the hole! *Nie wpadnij **w** dziurę!* (lit: not you-fall into hole!)
on	*na*	
through	*przez*	
to	*do*	Let's go to the cinema. *Chodźmy **do** kina.* (lit: let's-go to cinema)
	na	Let's go to the concert. *Chodźmy **na** koncert.* (lit: let's-go to concert)
under	*pod*	
with	*z/ze*	
without	*bez*	

VERBS

Every Polish verb has an infinitive form – the form which appears in dictionaries – which usually ends in *-ć*, or, less commonly, *-c*. The ending of an infinitive changes according to tense, as well as the person, number and gender of its Subject.

Polish verbs have three major tenses – present, past and future. In each tense, they change endings according to the subject of the verb. There are numerous patterns of conjugation as well as a number of irregular verbs which don't follow a pattern.

Verbs may be classed in over a dozen different groups, depending on their conjugation pattern. Each group of infinitives take the same endings, so you can tell which group a verb belongs to by the ending of its infinitive (as well as the first and third person of the present tense).

The endings of the four main verb groups are *-ać*, *-eć*, *-ieć* and *-ować*. There are also a number of irregular verbs which don't follow any pattern, including:

to be	*być*
to be able to	*móc*
to read	*czyt-ać*
to know	*umi-eć*
to see	*widz-ieć*
to work	*prac-ować*

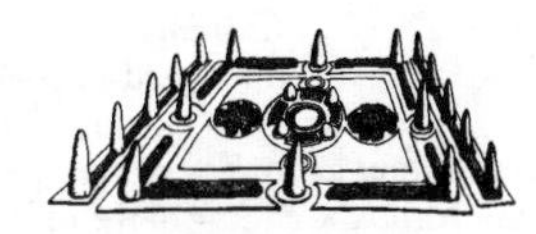

Imperfective & Perfective

Many Polish verbs have two forms, referred to as 'perfective' and 'imperfective'. These forms are known as 'aspect'. The meaning of a sentence can differ depending on which form is used.

Imperfective verbs generally describe actions which are unfinished, continuous or habitual. Perfective verbs generally refer to actions which have already been completed, or which are intended to be completed in the future.

Many infinitives have both imperfective and perfective forms:

	IMP	PERF
to read	*czytać*	*przeczytać*
to see	*widzieć*	*zobaczyć*
to take	*brać*	*wziąć*
to write	*pisać*	*napisać*

I was writing a letter.	***Pisałem** list.* (lit: I-wrote-imp letter)
I've written a letter.	***Napisałem** list.* (lit: I-wrote-perf letter)

Both forms of more verbs can be found in the dictionary in this phrasebook.

Present

The present tense uses the imperfective form of verbs, which describe actions that are repeated or continuous. Whether an action is repeated or continuous is identified from context.

I read a lot.	*Czytam dużo.* (lit: I-read-imp much)
I'm reading a letter.	*Czytam list.* (lit: I-read-imp letter)

Here are words from the four main verb groups (see page 30). To form the present tense, drop the ending of the infinitive (*-ać*, *-eć*, *-ieć* or *-ować*) and add the present-tense ending.

PRESENT TENSE

	czyt-ać (to read)	umi-eć (to know)	widz-ieć (to see)	prac-ować (to work)
I	-am	-em	-ę	-uję
you	-asz	-esz	-isz	-ujesz
he/she/it	-a	-e	-i	-uje
we	-amy	-emy	-imy	-ujemy
you	-acie	-ecie	-icie	-ujecie
they	-ają	-eją	-ą	-ują

They read.	*One czyt-ają.*	(lit: they they-read-imp)
I know.	*Ja umi-em.*	(lit: I I-know-imp)
We see.	*My widz-imy.*	(lit: we we-see-imp)
She works.	*Ona prac-uje.*	(lit: she she-works-imp)

Past

Both imperfective and perfective forms of verbs (see page 31) are used in the past tense. Unlike in the present, their endings change according to the gender of the Subject.

PAST TENSE

czyta-ć (to read – imp)
przeczyta-ć (to read – perf)

	M	F	N
I	*-ałem*	*-ałam*	
you	*-ałeś*	*-ałaś*	
he	*-ał*		
she		*-ała*	
it			*-ało*
we	*-aliśmy*	*-ałyśmy*	
you	*-aliście*	*-ałyście*	
they	*-ali*	*-ały*	

Have you read yesterday's newspaper?	***Przeczyt-ałeś*** *wczorajszą gazetę?* (lit: you-read-perf yesterday newspaper)
No, I didn't read anything yesterday.	*Nie, wczoraj nic nie* ***czyt-ałem****.* (lit: no, yesterday nothing not I-read-imp)

Future

There are two ways of forming the future, depending on whether a future action will be continuous or will be completed.

1. When a future action will be continuous, the future tense of *być*, 'to be' (see page 34) is used. This is followed by the imperfective infinitive of the main verb (see page 31 for an explanation of imperfective and perfective forms of the infinitive).

być + czytać (to be + to read)

Tomorrow I will read all the day.	*Jutro* ***będę czytać*** *cały dzień.* (lit: tomorrow I-will-be read all day)

2. If the action will be completed in the future, the Perfective form of the verb in the present tense is used.

przeczytać (to read)

I	*przeczyt-amy*
you (sg)	*przeczyt-asz*
he/she/it	*przeczyt-a*
we	*przeczyt-amy*
you (pl)	*przeczyt-acie*
they	*przeczyt-ają*

I promise I will read your book before Sunday.	*Przyrzekam że **przeczyt-am** twoją książkę przed niedzielą.* (lit: I-promise that I-will-have-read your book before Sunday)

TO BE

Following are the present, past and future forms of the irregular verb 'to be'.

This verb is also used together with other verbs to form the future tense of imperfective verbs (see page 33).

BYĆ – TO BE

	PRESENT	PAST			FUTURE
		M	F	N	
I	*jestem*	*byłem*	*byłam*		*będę*
you	*jesteś*	*byłeś*	*byłaś*		*będziesz*
he	*jest*	*był*			*będzie*
she	*jest*		*była*		*będzie*
it	*jest*			*było*	*będzie*
we	*jesteśmy*	*byliśmy*	*byłyśmy*		*będziemy*
you	*jesteście*	*byliście*	*byłyście*		*będziecie*
they	*są*	*byli*	*były*		*będą*

TO GO

There are two forms of the verb 'to go' in Polish:

	PERF	IMP
• to go on foot	*iść*	*pójść*
• to go by any means of transport	*jechać*	*pojechać*

Both forms are irregular. The imperfective forms have been given for the present and past tenses, while for the future tense, the perfective forms are more common and have been included here.

IŚĆ – TO GO (ON FOOT)

	PRESENT	PAST			FUTURE
	IMP	IMP	PERF		
		M	F	N	
I	*idę*	*szedłem*	*szłam*		*pójdę*
you	*idziesz*	*szedłeś*	*szłaś*		*pójdziesz*
he	*idzie*	*szedł*			*pójdzie*
she	*idzie*		*szła*		*pójdzie*
it	*idzie*			*szło*	*pójdzie*
we	*idziemy*	*szliśmy*	*szłyśmy*		*pójdziemy*
you	*idziecie*	*szliście*	*szłyście*		*pójdziecie*
they	*idą*	*szli*	*szły*		*pójdą*

JECHAĆ – TO GO (BY TRANSPORT)

I	*jadę*	*jechałem*	*jechałam*		*pojadę*
you	*jedziesz*	*jechałeś*	*jechałaś*		*pojedziesz*
he	*jedzie*	*jechał*			*pojedzie*
she	*jedzie*		*jechała*		*pojedzie*
it	*jedzie*			*jechało*	*pojedzie*
we	*jedziemy*	*jechaliśmy*	*jechałyśmy*		*pojedziemy*
you	*jedziecie*	*jechaliście*	*jechałyście*		*pojedziecie*
they	*jadą*	*jechali*	*jechały*		*pojadą*

TO KNOW

Polish has several verbs for 'to know':

- *znać* — to be acquainted with a person or a place; to have knowledge of something

Do you know Polish?	*Czy **znasz** polski?* (lit: *czy** you-know Polish?)
I don't know anybody here.	*Nie **znam** tu nikogo.* (lit: not I-know here nobody)

- *wiedzieć* — to be aware of or informed about something

I know it's difficult.	***Wiem** że to trudne.* (lit: I-know that this difficult)

- *umieć* — to be able to or have the skills to do something

Do you know how to cook?	*Czy **umiesz** gotować?* z(*czy** you-know-to-cook?)

* *Czy* signifies that the sentence is a question (see page 40).

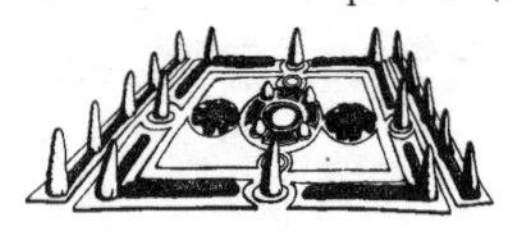

TO LIKE

In Polish, there are two ways to say 'to like something'.

1. *lubić* — The verb 'to like'

I like beer.	***Lubię** piwo.* (lit: I-like beer)
Do you like hot climate?	*Czy **lubisz** gorący klimat?* (lit: *czy** you-like hot climate?)

* *Czy* signifies that the sentence is a question (see page 40).

2. *podobać się* The reflexive verb 'to please oneself'. This is used to give the sense that something pleases you.

I don't like this painting.	*Nie **podoba** mi **się** ten obraz.* (lit: no it-please to-me self this painting)
Did you (pl) like the film?	*Czy **podobał** ci **się** film?* (lit: *czy* you-please to-you selves film?)

There are no hard and fast rules to determine which form is more correct, or sounds better, in a particular situation. In some cases, both forms can be used, for example:

I like this colour.	*Lubię ten kolor.* (lit: I-like this colour) *Podoba mi się ten kolor.* (lit: it-pleases to-me self this colour)

REFLEXIVE VERBS

Reflexive verbs (such as 'to wash oneself') consist of the main verb and the reflexive pronoun *się*, 'self'. Main verbs are conjugated according to their usual patterns reflecting number, gender and tense, but *się* remains unchanged.

I wash myself every day.	***Myję się** codziennie.* (lit: I-wash self every-day)
Don't wash yourself too often!	*Nie **myj się** za często!* (lit: no you-wash self too often!)

The use of reflexive verbs in Polish is more widespread than in English. Many verbs in English which aren't reflexive have reflexive forms in Polish:

to meet	*spotkać się*	(lit: to-meet self)
to happen	*dziać się*	(lit: to-happen self)

I met up with my father yesterday.	*Wczoraj* ***spotkałem się*** *z moim ojcem.* (lit: yesterday I-met self with my father)
What's happening here?	*Co tu się* ***dzieje?*** (lit: what here self it-happens?)

In this phrasebook, verb endings which differ according to whether they refer to a masculine or feminine Subject are separated with a slash:

I'm lost. zgoo-*bee*-wem/wam she *Zgubiłem/łam się.* (m/f)

POLISH OR ENGLISH?

These days, when communication barriers are vanishing and technology is expanding at breakneck speed, the Polish language is increasingly flavoured (purists would prefer to say 'rubbished') with English words.

Terms such as 'top', 'hit', 'supermarket', 'fitness club' and 'burger' have been populating Polish streets and newspapers, long before officially entering Polish dictionaries. Meanwhile, scholars deliberate whether or not to accept a particular word and define its final shape (or invent a Polish counterpart).

In some cases, Polish adopts English words with their original spelling, such as 'jazz' or 'weekend'. More often, however, the spelling of borrowed words is modified to keep the original sound unchanged:

businessman	*biznesmen*
gay	*gej*

In either case, the word usually becomes a victim of Polish grammar, with its complex case and conjugation systems.

KEY VERBS

Following is the list of the verbs you're likely to use frequently. Most are given here in their imperfective form, unless the perfective one is more commonly used.

to be	*być*
to be able	*móc*
to bring	*przynosić*
to buy	*kupować*
to come	*przychodzić*
to cost	*kosztować*
to depart (leave)	*wyjeżdżać*
to do	*robić*
to drink	*pić*
to eat	*jeść*
to give	*dawać*
to go (on foot)	*iść*
to go (by transport)	*jechać*
to have	*mieć*
to know (someone)	*znać*
to know (something)	*umieć*
to like	*lubić*
to live (life)	*żyć*
to live (somewhere)	*mieszkać*
to love	*kochać*
to make	*robić*
to meet	*spotykać*
to need	*potrzebować*
to pay	*płacić*
to prefer	*woleć*
to read	*czytać*
to return	*wracać*
to say	*mówić*
to see	*widzieć*
to stay	*stać*
to take	*brać*
to understand	*rozumieć*
to wait	*czekać*
to want	*chcieć*
to write	*pisać*

QUESTIONS

Word order in questions is generally the same as in affirmative sentences (Subject-Verb-Object), although Polish is reasonably flexible about word order. This word order is used in most questions which begin with an interrogative pronoun such as 'what', 'when' or 'where'.

Yes & No Questions

Many yes/no questions are formed by placing the particle *czy* at the beginning of a sentence. *Czy* has no particular meaning in itself, except to indicate the beginning of a question. It's not essential to use it – the question will be clear by just pronouncing it with rising intonation, yet the particle is frequently used.

Is it far from here?	*Czy to daleko stąd?* (lit: czy this far from-here?)
Can you smoke here?	*Czy tu można palić?* (lit: czy here possible smoke?)

Requests

The verb *prosić* and its perfective form *poprosić* both mean 'to ask for', and are commonly used to make polite requests. Both imperfective and perfective forms are used (see page 31), partly interchangeably. The preposition *o*, meaning 'for', is optional after the verb.

One beer, please.	*Proszę (o) jedno piwo.* (lit: I-ask-for (for) one beer) *Poproszę (o) jedno piwo.* (lit: I-ask-for (for) one beer)

QUESTION WORDS		
What?	*Co?*	What does it mean? ***Co*** *to znaczy?* (lit: what this mean?)
When?	*Kiedy?*	When are you leaving? ***Kiedy*** *wyjeżdżasz?* (lit: when you-leave?)
Where?	*Gdzie?*	Where's the museum? ***Gdzie*** *jest muzeum?* (lit: where is museum?)
Where from?	*Skąd?*	Where do you come from? ***Skąd*** *jesteś?* (lit: from-where you-are?)
Where to?	*Dokąd?*	Where does this road go to? ***Dokąd*** *prowadzi ta droga?* (lit: to-where lead this road?)
Why?	*Dlaczego?*	Why is the bank closed? ***Dlaczego*** *bank jest zamknięty?* (lit: why bank is closed?)
How?	*Jak?*	How far is it from here? ***Jak*** *to daleko stąd?* (lit: how this far from-here?)
How much?	*Ile?*	How much does it cost? ***Ile*** *to kosztuje?* (lit: how-much this cost?)
Who?	*Kto?*	Who is it? ***Kto*** *to jest?* (lit: who this is?)
Which?	*Który/a?*	Which hotel is better? ***Który*** *hotel jest lepszy?* (lit: which hotel is better?)

NEGATIVES

Negative sentences are formed by placing the negative particle *nie* before a verb:

He doesn't understand.	*On **nie** rozumie.* (lit: he not understand)

Unlike in English, double (or more) negatives are acceptable:

He never understands anything.	*On **nigdy nic nie** rozumie.* (lit: he never nothing not understand)

SPOTKANIA Z LUDŹMI — MEETING PEOPLE

If you don't know a single word of Polish, the best point to start is probably by learning some essential greetings and civilities. Expressions such as 'good morning', 'please' and 'thank you' are always useful and welcoming, and often a good first step in getting to know people.

YOU SHOULD KNOW — TO WARTO WIEDZIEĆ

Hello.	djen *do*-bri	*Dzień dobry.*
Goodbye.	do vee-*dze*-nya	*Do widzenia.*
Yes./No.	tak/nye	*Tak./Nie*
Excuse me.	pshe-*pra*-sham	*Przepraszam.*
Please.	*pro*-she	*Proszę.*
Thank you (very much).	djen-*koo*-ye (*bar*-dzo)	*Dziękuję (bardzo).*
You're welcome.	*pro*-she	*Proszę.*
Excuse me; Sorry.	pshe-*pra*-sham	*Przepraszam.*
May I; Do you mind?	chi *mo*-ge?	*Czy mogę?*

GREETINGS & GOODBYES — POWITANIA I POŻEGNANIA

It's a good idea to use greetings whenever you approach someone. *Dzień dobry*, 'good morning/afternoon', is good in any situation, at any time of the day until evening. In more informal encounters with friends and the people you know well, and particularly with young people, *cześć*, 'hi', is commonly used as both a greeting or when saying goodbye.

Good morning/ afternoon.	djen *do*-bri	*Dzień dobry.*
Good evening.	*do*-bri *vye*-choor	*Dobry wieczór.*
Hi.	cheshch	*Cześć.*
Goodbye.	do vee-*dze*-nya	*Do widzenia.*
Goodnight.	do-*bra*-nots	*Dobranoc.*
Bye.	cheshch	*Cześć.*
See you later.	do zo-ba-*che*-nya	*Do zobaczenia.*

WHAT'S NEW?

Polish has a number of expressions roughly equivalent to the English 'how are you?' or 'what's new?'. The following list features some of the most common ones.

They can be used interchangeably, and each is OK in any informal situation. Except for the last expression, they're also suitable for most formal occasions. They don't require any specific answer other than just *Dziękuję, dobrze*, 'fine, thanks'.

tso *swi*-hach?	*Co słychać?*
tso no-*ve*-go?	*Co nowego?*
tso do-*bre*-go?	*Co dobrego?*
yak *zdro*-vye?	*Jak zdrowie?*
yak *ee*-dje?	*Jak idzie?*
yak *le*-chee?	*Jak leci?*

FORMS OF ADDRESS — FORMY ZWRACANIA SIĘ

Poland is still very much a traditional territory where formal forms of address predominate, particularly among strangers. It's best (and safest) to use *pan*, 'Mr/Sir', and *pani*, 'Mrs/Madam', unless you're among friends or hanging around with younger people, where informality is the norm. Both terms can be written with an initial capital letter, depending on context.

The term *panna*, 'Miss', is old-fashioned and has largely been replaced by *pani*, 'Ms', which can be used for all women, regardless of age and marital status.

Mr	pan/pa-*no*-vye	*Pan/Panowie* (sg/pl)
Mrs	*pa*-nee/*pa*-nye	*Pani/Panie* (sg/pl)
Miss	*pan*-na/*pan*-ni	*Panna/Panny* (sg/pl)
Mr & Mrs	*pan*-stfo	*Państwo*
Ladies & Gentlemen	*pan*-stfo	*Państwo*

To strike up a conversation with someone in a formal situation, it's usual to start with *proszę pana* (lit: please, sir) or *proszę pani* (lit: please, madam). To address a group of people, you can say *proszę państwa*, 'ladies and gentlemen'.

If you want to politely attract a stranger's attention (such as when asking for directions), begin with *przepraszam pana/panią*, 'excuse me, sir/madam'.

BODY LANGUAGE — MOWA CIAŁA

Body language in Poland is much the same as in most Western countries, so can be easily understood. For example, 'yes' is commonly indicated by nodding the head down and up, while 'no' is expressed by shaking the head from side to side.

PERFECT HARMONY

Adjectives agree in gender, number and case with the nouns they describe. See Grammar, page 25, for more information.

FIRST ENCOUNTERS — SPOTKANIA

How are you?
- yak she pan/*pa*-nee ma? — *Jak się pan/pani ma?* (pol)
- yak she mash? — *Jak się masz?* (inf)

Fine, thanks. And you?
- djen-*koo*-ye, *do*-bzhe ee pan/*pa*-nee? — *Dziękuję, dobrze. I pan/pani?* (pol)
- djen-*koo*-ye, *do*-bzhe, ee ti? — *Dziękuję, dobrze. I ty?* (inf)

My name's ...
- na-*zi*-vam she ... — *Nazywam się ...* (+ surname; pol)
- mam na *ee*-mye ... — *Mam na imię ...* (+ first name; inf)

I'm pleased to meet you.
- *mee*-wo mee *pa*-na/*pa*-nyom *poz*-nach — *Miło mi pana/panią poznać.* (pol)
- *mee*-wo mee che *poz*-nach — *Miło mi cię poznać.* (inf)

MAKING CONVERSATION — ROZMOWY

Do you live here?
chi pan/*pa*-nee too *myesh*-ka? — *Czy pan/pani tu mieszka?* (pol)
chi too *myesh*-kash? — *Czy tu mieszkasz?* (inf)

Where are you going?
gdje pan/*pa*-nee *ee*-dje? — *Gdzie pan/pani idzie?* (pol)
gdje *ee*-djesh? — *Gdzie idziesz?* (inf)

What are you doing?
tso pan/*pa*-nee *ro*-bee? — *Co pan/pani robi?* (pol)
tso *ro*-beesh? — *Co robisz?* (inf)

What do you think (about ...)?
tso pan/*pa*-nee *mish*-lee (o ...)? — *Co pan/pani myśli (o ...)?* (pol)
tso *mish*-leesh (o ...)? — *Co myślisz (o ...)?* (inf)

PAN-ORAMA

Remember that the terms *pan* and *pani* are polite ways of addressing a man or woman respectively.

What's this called?
yak to she na-*zi*-va? — *Jak to się nazywa?*

Are you here on holiday?
chi pan/*pa*-nee yest too na va-*ka*-tsyah — *Czy pan/pani jest tu na wakacjach?* (pol)
chi *yes*-tesh too na va-*ka*-tsyah? — *Czy jesteś tu na wakacjach?* (inf)

I'm here ...	*yes*-tem too ...	*Jestem tu ...*
for a holiday	na va-*ka*-tsyah	*na wakacjach*
on business	swoozh-*bo*-vo	*służbowo*
to study	na *stoo*-dyah	*na studiach*

How long have you been here?
yak *dwoo*-go pan/*pa*-nee too yest? — *Jak długo pan/pani tu jest?* (pol)
yak *dwoo*-go too *yes*-tesh? — *Jak długo tu jesteś?* (inf)

I've been/We've been here for ... weeks/days.
yes-tem/yes-*tesh*-mi too ... ti-*god*-nee/dnee — *Jestem/Jesteśmy tu ... tygodni/dni.*

How long are you here for?
yak *dwoo*-go pan/*pa*-nee too *ben*-dje? — *Jak długo pan/pani tu będzie?* (pol)
yak *dwoo*-go too *ben*-djesh? — *Jak długo tu będziesz?* (inf)

I'm/We're here for ... weeks/days.
ben-de/ben-*dje*-mi too ... ti-*god*-nee/dnee — *Będę/Będziemy tu ... tygodni/dni.*

Do you like it here?
chi *pa*-noo/*pa*-nee she too po-*do*-ba? — *Czy panu/pani się tu podoba?* (pol)
chi chee she too po-*do*-ba? — *Czy ci się tu podoba?* (inf)

I/We like it here very much.
po-*do*-ba mee/nam she too *bar*-dzo — *Podoba mi/nam się tu bardzo.*

It's very nice here.
yest too *bar*-dzo *wad*-nye — *Jest tu bardzo ładnie.*

PERSONAL PRONOUNS

Personal pronouns such as 'I', 'you' and 'he' are usually omitted in Polish sentences, because a verb's ending clearly indicates the subject. See Verbs, pages 30-39, for details.

Sure.	o-chi-*veesh*-che	*Oczywiście.*
It's OK.	*do*-bzhe	*Dobrze.*
Really?	na-*prav*-de?	*Naprawdę?*
It's true.	to *prav*-da	*To prawda.*
Just a minute.	hfee-*lech*-ke	*Chwileczkę.*
Look!	*pro*-she *spoy*-zhech!	*Proszę spojrzeć!* (pol)
	pach!	*Patrz!* (inf)
Listen (to this)!	*pro*-she po-*swoo*-hach!	*Proszę posłuchać!* (pol)
	swoo-hay!	*Słuchaj!* (inf)
Let's go.	*hoch*-mi	*Chodźmy.*
Wait!	*pro*-she za-*che*-kach!	*Proszę zaczekać!* (pol)
	za-*che*-kay!	*Zaczekaj!* (inf)

Are you ready?

chi yest pan/*pa*-nee go-*to*-vi/a?	*Czy jest pan/pani gotowy/a?* (pol)
chi *yes*-tesh go-*to*-vi/a?	*Czy jesteś gotowy/a?* (inf)

NON-ENTITY

The definite and indefinite articles (the, a, an) don't exist in Polish, but the sense of the noun involved is usually clear from the context of the sentence.

I'm ready.	*yes*-tem go-*to*-vi/a	*Jestem gotowy/a.*
Good luck!	po-vo-*dze*-nya!	*Powodzenia!*
It's (not) important.	to (nye-)*vazh*-ne	*To (nie)ważne.*
It's (not) possible.	to (nye-)mozh-*lee*-ve	*To (nie)możliwe.*
That's strange.	to *djeev*-ne	*To dziwne.*
That's funny. (amusing)	to za-*bav*-ne	*To zabawne.*
It doesn't matter.	to nye-*vazh*-ne	*To nieważne.*

NATIONALITIES — NARODOWOŚCI

Where are you from?
skont pan/*pa*-nee po-*ho*-djee/yest? — *Skąd pan/pani pochodzi/jest?* (pol)
skont po-*ho*-djeesh/*yes*-tesh? — *Skąd pochodzisz/jesteś?* (inf)

I'm from ...	*yes*-tem s ...	*Jestem z ...*
Australia	a-woos-*tra*-lyee	*Australii*
Canada	ka-*na*-di	*Kanady*
England	*an*-glee	*Anglii*
Europe	ew-*ro*-pi	*Europy*
Ireland	eer-*lan*-dyee	*Irlandii*
Japan	ya-*po*-nyee	*Japonii*
the US	*sta*-noof zye-dno-*cho*-nih	*Stanów Zjednoczonych*

I live in/by the ...	*myesh*-kam ...	*Mieszkam ...*
city	*vmyesh*-che	*w mieście*
countryside	na fshee	*na wsi*
mountains	*vgoo*-rah	*w górach*
seaside	nat *mo*-zhem	*nad morzem*

CULTURAL DIFFERENCES — RÓŻNICE KULTURALNE

How do you do this in your country?
yak to she *ro*-bee *vva*-shim *kra*-yoo? — *Jak to się robi w waszym kraju?*

Is this a local or national custom?
chi to yest *zvi*-chay lo-*kal*-ni chi na-ro-*do*-vi? — *Czy to jest zwyczaj lokalny czy narodowy?*

I don't want to offend you.
nye htse *pa*-na/*pa*-nee o-*bra*-zheech — *Nie chcę pana/pani obrazić.*

I'm sorry, it's not common in my country.
pshe-*pra*-sham, to nye yest pof-*sheh*-ne *vmo*-eem *kra*-yoo — *Przepraszam, to nie jest powszechne w moim kraju.*

I don't know this custom.
nye znam *te*-go zvi-*cha*-yoo — *Nie znam tego zwyczaju.*

AGE — WIEK

How old are you?
ee-le ma pan/*pa*-nee lat? — *Ile ma pan/pani lat?* (pol)
ee-le mash lat? — *Ile masz lat?* (inf)

How old is your son/daughter?
ee-le lat ma *pa*-na/*pa*-nee sin/*tsoor*-ka? — *Ile lat ma pana/pani syn/córka?*

I'm ... years old.
mam ... lat — *Mam ... lat.*

(See Numbers & Amounts, page 191, for your age.)

OCCUPATIONS — ZAWODY I ZAJĘCIA

Where do you work?
gdje pan/*pa*-nee pra-*tsoo*-ye? — *Gdzie pan/pani pracuje?*

What's your occupation?
ya-kee yest *pa*-na/*pa*-nee *za*-voot? — *Jaki jest pana/pani zawód?*

OSOBA

Osoba means 'person'. It's a feminine noun per se, but actually refers to people of both sexes.

I'm a/an ...	*yes*-tem ...	*Jestem ...*
artist	ar-*tis*-tom	*artystą* (m)
	ar-*tist*-kom	*artystką* (f)
businessperson	biz-nes-*me*-nem	*biznesmenem* (m)
	biz-nes-*men*-kom	*biznesmenką* (f)
doctor	le-*ka*-zhem	*lekarzem* (m)
	le-*kar*-kom	*lekarką* (f)
engineer	een-zhi-*nye*-rem	*inżynierem*
farmer	rol-*nee*-kyem	*rolnikiem*
journalist	re-por-*te*-rem	*reporterem* (m)
	re-por-*ter*-kom	*reporterką* (f)
lawyer	prav-*nee*-kyem	*prawnikiem* (m)
	prav-*neech*-kom	*prawniczką (f)*
mechanic	me-ha-*nee*-kyem	*mechanikiem*
nurse	pye-leng-*nya*-zhem	*pielęgniarzem* (m)
	pye-leng-*nyar*-kom	*pielęgniarką* (f)
office worker	pra-tsov-*nee*-kyem	*pracownikiem*
	byoo-*ro*-vim;	*biurowym* (m)
	pra-tsov-*nee*-tsom	*pracownicą*
	byoo-*ro*-vom	*biurową* (f)
scientist	na-oo-*kof*-tsem	*naukowcem*
student	stoo-*den*-tem	*studentem* (m)
	stoo-*dent*-kom	*studentką* (f)
teacher	na-oo-chi-*che*-lem	*nauczycielem* (m)
	na-oo-chi-*chel*-kom	*nauczycielką* (f)
waiter	kel-*ne*-rem	*kelnerem* (m)
	kel-*ner*-kom	*kelnerką* (f)
writer	pee-*sa*-zhem	*pisarzem* (m)
	pee-*sar*-kom	*pisarką* (f)

I'm unemployed.
yes-tem bez-ro-*bot*-ni/a *Jestem bezrobotny/a.*

What are you studying?
tso stoo-*dyoo*-yesh? *Co studiujesz?* (inf)

I'm studying ...	stoo-*dyoo*-ye ...	*Studiuję ...*
art	*shtoo*-ke	*sztukę*
arts/humanities	na-*oo*-kee hoo-ma-nees-*tich*-ne	*nauki humanistyczne*
business	*biz*-nes	*biznes*
teaching	pe-da-go-*gee*-ke	*pedagogikę*
engineering	een-zhi-*nye*-rye	*inżynierię*
languages	yen-*zi*-kee	*języki*
law	*pra*-vo	*prawo*
medicine	me-di-*tsi*-ne	*medycynę*
Polish	*yen*-zik *pol*-skee	*język polski*

RELIGION — RELIGIA

What's your religion?

ya-*kye*-go yest pan/*pa*-nee viz-*na*-nya? — *Jakiego jest pan/pani wyznania?* (pol)

ya-*kye*-go *yes*-tesh viz-*na*-nya? — *Jakiego jesteś wyznania?* (inf)

I'm ...	*yes*-tem ...	*Jestem ...*
Buddhist	bood-*dis*-tom	*buddystą* (m)
	bood-*dist*-kom	*buddystką* (f)
Catholic	ka-to-*lee*-kyem	*katolikiem* (m)
	ka-to-*leech*-kom	*katoliczką* (f)
Hindu	heen-doo-*ees*-tom	*hinduistą* (m)
	heen-doo-*eest*-kom	*hinduistką* (f)
Jewish	*zhi*-dem	*żydem* (m)
	zhi-*doof*-kom	*żydówką* (m)
Muslim	moo-zoow-ma-*nee*-nem	*muzułmaninem* (m)
	moo-zoow-*man*-kom	*muzułmanką* (f)

I'm not religious.

yes-tem nye-vye-*zhon*-tsi/a — *Jestem niewierzący/a.*

I'm an atheist.

yes-tem a-te-*ees*-tom/a-te-*eest*-kom — *Jestem ateistą/ateistką.*

I'm (Catholic), but not practising.
yes-tem (ka-to-*lee*-kyem/ ka-to-*leech*-kom) *a*-le nye prak-ti-*koo*-ye — *Jestem (katolikiem/ katoliczką), ale nie praktykuję.*

I (don't) believe in God.
(nye) *vye*-zhe *vbo*-ga — *(Nie) wierzę w Boga.*

I (don't) believe in destiny.
(nye) *vye*-zhe fpshez-na-*che*-nye — *(Nie) wierzę w przeznaczenie.*

I'm interested in astrology/philosophy.
een-te-re-*soo*-ye mnye as-tro-*lo*-gya/fee-lo-*zo*-fya — *Interesuje mnie astrologia/filozofia.*

See also Pilgrimage & Religion, page 183.

FEELINGS — UCZUCIA

I'm sorry. (condolence)	*pshi*-kro mee	*Przykro mi.*
I'm sorry. (regret)	zha-*woo*-ye	*Żałuję.*
I'm afraid.	o-*ba*-vyam she	*Obawiam się.*
I'm cold/hot.	yest mee *zheem*-no/ go-*ron*-tso	*Jest mi zimno/ gorąco.*
I'm in a hurry.	*spye*-she she	*Spieszę się.*
I'm right.	mam *ra*-tsye	*Mam rację.*
I'm well.	*choo*-ye she *do*-bzhe	*Czuję się dobrze.*

I'm ...	*yes*-tem ...	*Jestem ...*
angry	zwi/a	*zły/a*
grateful	*vdjench*-ni/a	*wdzięczny/a*
happy	shchen-*shlee*-vi/a	*szczęśliwy/a*
hungry	*gwod*-ni/a	*głodny/a*
sad	*smoot*-ni/a	*smutny/a*
sleepy	*shpyon*-tsi/a	*śpiący/a*
thirsty	spra-*gnyo*-ni/a	*spragniony/a*
tired	zmen-*cho*-ni/a	*zmęczony/a*
worried	za-nye-po-ko-*yo*-ni/a	*zaniepokojony/a*

BREAKING THE LANGUAGE BARRIER — PRZEŁAMYWANIE BARIERY JĘZYKOWEJ

Do you speak English?
chi pan/*pa*-nee *moo*-vee po an-*gyel*-skoo? — *Czy pan/pani mówi po angielsku?*

Yes, I do.	tak, *moo*-vye	*Tak, mówię.*
No, I don't.	nye, nye *moo*-vye	*Nie, nie mówię.*
I speak a little.	*moo*-vye *swa*-bo	*Mówię słabo.*

Does anyone here speak English?
chi ktosh too *moo*-vee po an-*gyel*-skoo? — *Czy ktoś tu mówi po angielsku?*

Do you understand?
chi pan/*pa*-nee ro-*zoo*-mye? — *Czy pan/pani rozumie?*

I (don't) understand.
(nye) ro-*zoo*-myem — *(Nie) rozumiem.*

Please speak more slowly.
pro-she *moo*-veech *vol*-nyey — *Proszę mówić wolniej.*

Please repeat that.
pro-she to pof-*too*-zhich — *Proszę to powtórzyć.*

Please write it down.
pro-she to na-*pee*-sach — *Proszę to napisać.*

How do you say ...?
yak she *moo*-vee ...? — *Jak się mówi ...?*

What does it mean?
tso to *zna*-chi? — *Co to znaczy?*

KOMUNIKACJA — GETTING AROUND

Sitting in the middle of Europe, Poland has plenty of air and overland transport links with the rest of the continent. Internally too, the country has an array of air, train and bus connections, with train being the main means of intercity transport.

Transport within cities is based on buses and trams, and some cities also have trolleybus lines.

FINDING YOUR WAY — SZUKANIE DROGI

Where's the ...?	gdje yest ...?	*Gdzie jest ...?*
bus station	*dvo*-zhets aw-to-boo-*so*-vi	*dworzec autobusowy*
bus stop	pshis-*ta*-nek aw-to-boo-*so*-vi	*przystanek autobusowy*
city centre	*tsen*-troom	*centrum*
road to ...	*dro*-ga do ...	*droga do ...*
taxi stand	*pos*-tooy tak-*soo*-vek	*postój taksówek*
ticket office	*ka*-sa bee-le-*to*-va	*kasa biletowa*
train station	*dvo*-zhets ko-le-*yo*-vi	*dworzec kolejowy*

How do I get there?
yak she tam *dos*-tach? — *Jak się tam dostać?*

Is it far from here?
chi to da-*le*-ko stont? — *Czy to daleko stąd?*

Please show me (on the map).
pro-she mee po-*ka*-zach (na *ma*-pye) — *Proszę mi pokazać (na mapie).*

Can I walk there?
chi *mozh*-na tam doyshch *pye*-sho? — *Czy można tam dojść pieszo?*

Is there a bus/tram going there?
chi *ho*-djee tam *ya*-keesh aw-*to*-boos/*tram*-vay? — *Czy chodzi tam jakiś autobus/tramwaj?*

DIRECTIONS — WSKAZÓWKI

Go straight ahead.	*pro*-she eeshch *pros*-to	*Proszę iść prosto.*
Turn left/right at the ...	*pro*-she *skren*-cheech *fle*-vo/*fpra*-vo na ...	*Proszę skręcić w lewo/prawo na ...*
end of the street	*kon*-tsoo oo-*lee*-tsi	*końcu ulicy*
next corner	nay-*bleesh*-shim *ro*-goo	*najbliższym rogu*
roundabout	*ron*-dje	*rondzie*
traffic lights	*shfya*-twah	*światłach*

behind	za	*za*
in front of	pshet	*przed*
far	da-*le*-ko	*daleko*
near	*blees*-ko	*blisko*
opposite	na-pshe-*cheef*-ko	*naprzeciwko*
here	too	*tu*
there	tam	*tam*
north	*poow*-nots	*północ* (f)
south	po-*wood*-nye	*południe* (neut)
east	fs-hoot	*wschód* (m)
west	*za*-hoot	*zachód* (m)
avenue	a-*le*-ya	*aleja* (f)
corner	rook	*róg* (m)
intersection	skshi-zho-*va*-nye	*skrzyżowanie* (neut)
roundabout	*ron*-do	*rondo* (neut)
square	plats	*plac* (m)
street	oo-*lee*-tsa	*ulica* (f)

ADDRESSES　　　ADRESY

A Polish address looks something like this:

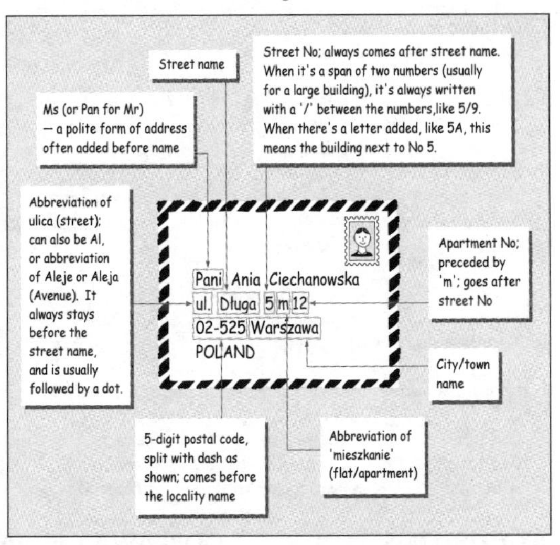

BUYING TICKETS　　　KUPOWANIE BILETÓW

Excuse me, where's the ticket office?
pshe-*pra*-sham, gdje yest *ka*-sa bee-le-*to*-va? — *Przepraszam, gdzie jest kasa biletowa?*

Where can I buy a ticket?
gdje *mo*-ge *koo*-peech *bee*-let? — *Gdzie mogę kupić bilet?*

I want to go to ...
htse po-*ye*-hach do ... — *Chcę pojechać do ...* (bus, train)
htse po-*le*-chech do ... — *Chcę polecieć do ...* (plane)

Do I need to book?
chi *moo*-she re-zer-*vo*-vach? — *Czy muszę rezerwować?*

I'd like to book a seat to ...	htse za-re-zer-*vo*-vach *myey*-stse do ...	*Chcę zarezerwować miejsce do ...*
How much is the ticket?	*ee*-le kosh-*too*-ye *bee*-let?	*Ile kosztuje bilet?*

I'd like ...	po-*pro*-she ...	*Poproszę ...*
a one-way ticket	*bee*-let *fyed*-nom *stro*-ne	*bilet w jedną stronę*
a return ticket	*bee*-let po-*vrot*-ni	*bilet powrotny*
two tickets	dva bee-*le*-ti	*dwa bilety*
a window seat	*myey*-stse pshi *ok*-nye	*miejsce przy oknie*

1st class	*pyer*-fshom *kla*-se	*pierwszą klasę*
2nd class	*droo*-gom *kla*-se	*drugą klasę*
for (non)smokers	dla (nye)pa-*lon*-tsih	*dla (nie)palących*

Is there a discount for ...?	chi yest *zneesh*-ka dla ...?	*Czy jest zniżka dla ...?*
children	*dje*-chee	*dzieci*
pensioners	ren-*chees*-toof	*rencistów*
students	stoo-*den*-toof	*studentów*

AT CUSTOMS — ODPRAWA CELNA

I have nothing to declare.
nye mam neets do zgwo-*she*-nya — *Nie mam nic do zgłoszenia.*

I have something to declare.
mam tsosh do zgwo-*she*-nya — *Mam coś do zgłoszenia.*

Do I have to declare this?
chi *moo*-she to *zgwo*-sheech? — *Czy muszę to zgłosić?*

This is all my luggage.
to yest *tsa*-wi mooy *ba*-gash — *To jest cały mój bagaż.*

I didn't know I had to declare it.
nye vye-*dja*-wem/wam zhe *moo*-she to *zgwo*-sheech — *Nie wiedziałem/łam że muszę to zgłosić.*

AIR — SAMOLOT

Poland's only commercial carrier, *LOT* Polish Airlines, services all domestic routes. It has regular flights from Warsaw, the country's aviation hub, to half a dozen major cities. Tickets can be booked and bought at *LOT* offices and from travel agencies.

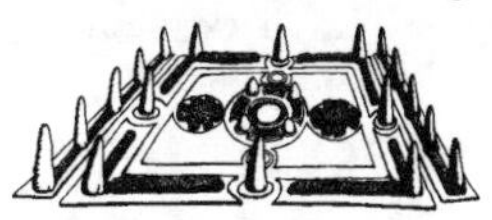

Is there a flight to ...?
    chi yest lot do ...? — *Czy jest lot do ...?*

When's the next flight to ...?
    kye-di yest nas-*temp*-ni lot do ...? — *Kiedy jest następny lot do ...?*

What time does the plane leave/arrive?
    o *ktoo*-rey od-la-*too*-ye/ pshi-la-*too*-ye sa-*mo*-lot? — *O której odlatuje/przylatuje samolot?*

What's the flight number?
    ya-kee yest *noo*-mer *lo*-too? — *Jaki jest numer lotu?*

How long does the flight take?
    ee-le trfa lot? — *Ile trwa lot?*

What time do I have to check in at the airport?
    o *ktoo*-rey *moo*-she bich na lot-*nees*-koo? — *O której muszę być na lotnisku?*

Is there a bus to the airport?
    chi yest *ya*-keesh aw-*to*-bus na lot-*nees*-ko? — *Czy jest jakiś autobus na lotnisko?*

airport	lot-*nees*-ko	*lotnisko* (neut)
airport tax	o-*pwa*-ta lot-nees-*ko*-va	*opłata lotniskowa* (f)
boarding pass	*kar*-ta po-kwa-*do*-va	*karta pokładowa* (f)
flight	lot	*lot* (m)
hand luggage	*ba*-gash pod-*rench*-ni	*bagaż podręczny* (m)
plane	sa-*mo*-lot	*samolot* (m)

BUS — AUTOBUS

Poland's intercity buses are cheap but rather slow. Buses mostly service medium short-distance regional routes. Long-distance travel is faster and more convenient by train.

Most domestic buses are operated by the state bus company commonly known as 'PKS'. Tickets can be bought at the bus terminal or directly from the bus driver.

Where's the bus terminal?
gdje yest *dvo*-zhets aw-to-boo-*so*-vi? — *Gdzie jest dworzec autobusowy?*

Which bus goes to ...?
ktoo-ri aw-*to*-boos *ye*-dje do ...? — *Który autobus jedzie do ...?*

Does this bus go to ...?
chi ten aw-*to*-boos *ye*-dje do ...? — *Czy ten autobus jedzie do ...?*

How often do buses go to ...?
yak *chen*-sto *ho*-dzom aw-to-*boo*-si do ...? — *Jak często chodzą autobusy do ...?*

What time does the bus leave/arrive?
o *ktoo*-rey ot-*ho*-djee/ pshi-*ho*-djee aw-*to*-boos? — *O której odchodzi/ przychodzi autobus?*

Please let me know when we get to ...
pro-she mi po-*vye*-djech gdi do-ye-*dje*-mi do ... — *Proszę mi powiedzieć gdy dojedziemy do ...*

Where do I get the bus for ...?
skont vzhonch aw-*to*-boos do ...? — *Skąd wziąć autobus do ...?*

What time's the ... bus?	o *ktoo*-rey yest ... aw-*to*-boos?	*O której jest ... autobus?*
first	*pyer*-fshi	*pierwszy*
last	os-*tat*-ni	*ostatni*
next	nas-*temp*-ni	*następny*
bus/coach	aw-*to*-boos	*autobus* (m)
conductor	kon-*dook*-tor	*konduktor* (m)
driver	kye-*rof*-tsa	*kierowca* (m)
route	*tra*-sa	*trasa* (f)
bus ...	... aw-to-boo-*so*-vi	... *autobusowy* (m)
station	*dvo*-zhets	*dworzec*
stop	pshis-*ta*-nek	*przystanek*

TRAIN — POCIĄG

Railway network and trains are administered by the Polish State Railways, commonly referred to as *PKP*. Services include EuroCity (EC), InterCity (IC), express (Ex), fast and ordinary.

Almost all trains have seats in two classes – 1st and 2nd – and some night trains carry cars with couchettes and sleepers. Tickets can be purchased at the train stations or from some travel agencies including Orbis.

Where's the train station?
gdje yest *dvo*-zhets ko-le-*yo*-vi? — *Gdzie jest dworzec kolejowy?*

Which platform does the train leave from?
sktoo-*re*-go pe-*ro*-noo ot-*yesh*-dja *po*-chonk? — *Z którego peronu odjeżdża pociąg?*

What station is this?
ya-ka to *sta*-tsya? — *Jaka to stacja?*

What's the next station?
ya-ka yest nas-*temp*-na *sta*-tsya? — *Jaka jest następna stacja?*

Does this train stop at ...?
chi ten *po*-chonk za-tshi-*moo*-ye she f ...? — *Czy ten pociąg zatrzymuje się w ...?*

I want to get off at ...
htse *vi*-shonshch f ... — *Chcę wysiąść w ...*

How long does the trip take?
yak *dwoo*-go trfa *po*-droosh? — *Jak długo trwa podróż?*

Is that seat taken?
chi to *myey*-stse yest za-*yen*-te? — *Czy to miejsce jest zajęte?*

Is this seat free?
chi to *myey*-stse yest *vol*-ne? — *Czy to miejsce jest wolne?*

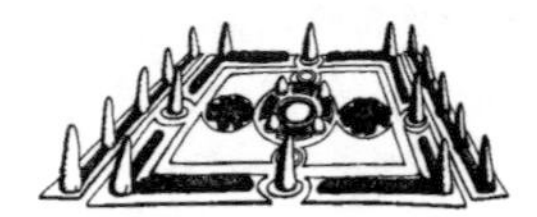

carriage	*va*-gon	*wagon* (m)
compartment	*pshe*-djaw	*przedział* (m)
couchette	koo-*shet*-ka	*kuszetka* (f)
dining car	*va*-gon res-ta-oo-ra-*tsiy*-ni	*wagon restauracyjny* (m)
express	*eks*-pres	*ekspres* (m)
left luggage office	pshe-ho-*val*-nya ba-*ga*-zhoo	*przechowalnia bagażu* (f)
platform	*pe*-ron	*peron* (m)
sleeping car	*va*-gon si-*pyal*-ni	*wagon sypialny* (m)
ticket collector	kon-*tro*-ler	*kontroler* (m)
waiting room	po-che-*kal*-nya	*poczekalnia* (f)

... train	*po*-chonk ...	*pociąg* ... (m)
fast	pos-*pyesh*-ni	*pospieszny*
long-distance	da-le-ko-*byezh*-ni	*dalekobieżny*
slow	o-so-*bo*-vi	*osobowy*
suburban	pod-*myey*-skee	*podmiejski*

TAXI — TAKSÓWKA

Taxis are readily available and reasonably cheap. The number of passengers (usually up to four) and the amount of luggage don't normally affect the fare.

Taxis can be waved down on the street, but it's often faster to go to a taxi rank (there are plenty of them).

Where's the nearest taxi rank?
gdje yest nay-*bleesh*-shi *pos*-tooy tak-*soo*-vek? — *Gdzie jest najbliższy postój taksówek?*

Are you free?
chi yest pan/*pa*-nee *vol*-ni/a? — *Czy jest pan/pani wolny/a?*

How much does it cost to go to ...?
ee-le *ben*-dje kosh-*to*-vach do ...? — *Ile będzie kosztować do ...?*

Please take me to ...	*pro*-she mnye *za*-vyeshch ...	*Proszę mnie zawieźć ...*
the airport	na lot-*nees*-ko	*na lotnisko*
this address	pot ten *a*-dres	*pod ten adres*
the city centre	do *tsen*-troom	*do centrum*
this hotel	do *te*-go ho-*te*-loo	*do tego hotelu*
a cheap hotel	do ta-*nye*-go ho-*te*-loo	*do taniego hotelu*
the train station	na *dvo*-zhets ko-le-*yo*-vi	*na dworzec kolejowy*

How much do I owe you?
ee-le *pwa*-tse? — *Ile płacę?*

Please give me the change.
pro-she mee *vi*-dach *resh*-te — *Proszę mi wydać resztę.*

Please keep the change.
pro-she za-*tshi*-mach *so*-bye *resh*-te — *Proszę zatrzymać sobie resztę.*

Instructions — Wskazówki

Please switch the meter on.
pro-she *vwon*-chich *leech*-neek — *Proszę włączyć licznik.*

Continue straight ahead.
pro-she *ye*-hach *da*-ley *pros*-to — *Proszę jechać dalej prosto.*

The next street to the left/right.
nas-*temp*-na oo-*lee*-tsa na *le*-vo/*pra*-vo — *Następna ulica na lewo/prawo.*

Please slow down.
pro-she *zvol*-neech — *Proszę zwolnić.*

Please wait here.
pro-she too za-*che*-kach — *Proszę tu zaczekać.*

Please stop here.
pro-she she too za-*tshi*-mach — *Proszę się tu zatrzymać.*

Please stop at the corner.
pro-she she za-*tshi*-mach na *ro*-goo — *Proszę się zatrzymać na rogu.*

CAR — SAMOCHÓD

Poland has a dense array of sealed roads. Road rules are similar to those in the rest of continental Europe, and road signs are reasonably clear. Petrol is readily available and cheaper than in Western Europe.

On the other hand, car rental isn't cheap in Poland – the prices are comparable to, or even higher than, full-priced rental in Western Europe – and there are seldom any promotional discounts. It's usually cheaper to book ahead from abroad rather than front up to an agency in Poland.

Where can I rent a car?
gdje *mo*-ge vi-po-*zhi*-chich sa-*mo*-hoot? — *Gdzie mogę wypożyczyć samochód?*

How much is it daily/weekly?
ee-le kosh-*too*-ye *djen*-nye/ti-god-*nyo*-vo? — *Ile kosztuje dziennie/tygodniowo?*

Does that include insurance?
chi oo-bes-pye-*che*-nye yest vlee-*cho*-ne? — *Czy ubezpieczenie jest wliczone?*

Where's the nearest petrol station?
gdje yest nay-*bleesh*-sha *sta*-tsya ben-zi-*no*-va? — *Gdzie jest najbliższa stacja benzynowa?*

Please fill the tank.
pro-she na-*peoo*-neech bak — *Proszę napełnić bak.*

I'd like ... litres.
po-*pro*-she ... *leet*-roof — *Poproszę ... litrów.*

Please check the ...	*pro*-she *sprav*-djeech ...	*Proszę sprawdzić ...*
oil	*o*-ley	*olej*
tyre pressure	cheesh-*nye*-nye fo-*po*-nah	*ciśnienie w oponach*
water	*vo*-de	*wodę*

Can I park here?
chi *mozh*-na too par-*ko*-vach? — *Czy można tu parkować?*

How long can I park here?
yak *dwoo*-go *mozh*-na too par-*ko*-vach? — *Jak długo można tu parkować?*

Does this road lead to ...?
chi ta *dro*-ga pro-*va*-djee do ...? — *Czy ta droga prowadzi do ...?*

air	po-*vyet*-she	*powietrze* (neut)
battery	a-koo-moo-*la*-tor	*akumulator* (m)
brakes	ha-*mool*-tse	*hamulce* (m, pl)
clutch	*spshen*-gwo	*sprzęgło* (neut)
driving licence	*pra*-vo *yaz*-di	*prawo jazdy* (neut)
engine	*sheel*-neek	*silnik* (m)
garage	*var*-shtat	*warsztat* (m)
indicator	kye-roon-*kof*-skas	*kierunkowskaz* (m)
headlights	*shfya*-twa	*światła* (neut, pl)
motorway	aw-to-*stra*-da	*autostrada* (f)
oil	*o*-ley	*olej* (m)
radiator	hwod-*nee*-tsa	*chłodnica* (f)
roadmap	*ma*-pa dro-*go*-va	*mapa drogowa* (f)
seatbelts	*pa*-si bes-pye-*chen*-stfa	*pasy bezpieczeństwa* (m, pl)
self-service	sa-mo-op-*swoo*-ga	*samoobsługa* (f)
speed limit	o-gra-nee-*che*-nye prent-*kosh*-chee	*ograniczenie prędkości* (neut)
tyre	o-*po*-na	*opona* (f)
windscreen	*pshe*-dnya *shi*-ba	*przednia szyba* (f)

... petrol	ben-*zi*-na ...	*benzyna* ... (f)
leaded	o-wo-*vyo*-va	*ołowiowa*
regular	*zvik*-wa	*zwykła*
unleaded	be-so-wo-*vyo*-va	*bezołowiowa*

Car Problems — Kłopoty z Samochodem

I need a mechanic.
pot-she-*boo*-ye me-ha-*nee*-ka — *Potrzebuję mechanika.*

What make is it?
ya-ka to *mar*-ka? — *Jaka to marka?*

The car broke down at ...
sa-*mo*-hoot she *zep*-soow f ... — *Samochód się zepsuł w ...*

The battery's flat.
a-koo-moo-*la*-tor yest roz-wa-do-*va*-ni — *Akumulator jest rozładowany.*

The radiator's leaking.
hwod-*nee*-tsa *chek*-nye — *Chłodnica cieknie.*

I've got a flat tyre.
zwa-*pa*-wem/wam *goo*-me — *Złapałem/łam gumę.*

It's overheating.
pshe-*gzhe*-va she — *Przegrzewa się.*

It's not starting.
nye za-*pa*-la — *Nie zapala.*

Where can I get it fixed?
gdje *mo*-ge go na-*pra*-veech? — *Gdzie mogę go naprawić?*

When will it be ready?
kye-di *ben*-dje go-*to*-vi? — *Kiedy będzie gotowy?*

I've lost my car keys.
zgoo-*bee*-wem/wam kloo-*chi*-kee — *Zgubiłem/łam kluczyki.*

I've run out of petrol.
za-*brak*-wo mee ben-*zi*-ni — *Zabrakło mi benzyny.*

BICYCLE — ROWER

Where can I hire a bike?
gdje *mozh*-na vi-po-*zhi*-chich *ro*-ver? — *Gdzie można wypożyczyć rower?*

I'd like to hire a bike.
htse vi-po-*zhi*-chich *ro*-ver — *Chcę wypożyczyć rower.*

How much is it for an hour/the day?
ee-le kosh-*too*-ye za go-*djee*-ne/djen? — *Ile kosztuje za godzinę/dzień?*

Where can I get my bike fixed?
gdje *mo*-ge na-*pra*-veech *ro*-ver? — *Gdzie mogę naprawić rower?*

Where can I leave my bike?
gdje *mo*-ge zos-*ta*-veech *ro*-ver? — *Gdzie mogę zostawić rower?*

brakes	ha-*mool*-tse	*hamulce* (m, pl)
chain	*wan*-tsooh	*łańcuch* (m)
to cycle	*yezh*-djeech na ro-*ve*-zhe	*jeździć na rowerze*
gearstick	pshe-*zhoot*-ka	*przerzutka* (f)
handlebars	kye-rov-*nee*-tsa	*kierownica* (f)
helmet	kask	*kask* (m)
inner tube	*dent*-ka	*dętka* (f)
lights	*shfya*-twa	*światła* (neut, pl)
padlock	*kwoot*-ka	*kłódka* (f)
pump	*pomp*-ka	*pompka* (f)
saddle	sho-*deoo*-ko	*siodełko* (neut)
tyre	o-*po*-na	*opona* (f)
wheel	*ko*-wo	*koło* (neut)
... bike	*ro*-ver ...	*rower* ... (m)
mountain	*goor*-skee	*górski*
racing	vish-chee-*go*-vi	*wyścigowy*

NOCLEGI ACCOMMODATION

Poland has a range of places to stay, from campsites and youth hostels to international luxury hotels. The choice of accommodation has grown and diversified considerably over recent years, but prices have risen in the process. Yet it's still relatively inexpensive by Western standards.

FINDING ACCOMMODATION — SZUKANIE NOCLEGU

Where can I find a ...?	gdje *mo*-ge *zna*-leshch ...?	*Gdzie mogę znaleźć ...?*
camping ground	*kam*-peenk	*camping*
guesthouse	pen-*syo*-nat	*pensjonat*
hotel	*ho*-tel	*hotel*
motel	*mo*-tel	*motel*
youth hostel	sro-*nees*-ko mwo-dje-*zho*-ve	*schronisko młodzieżowe*
Can you recommend a ...?	chi *mo*-zhe mee pan/ *pa*-n ee po-*le*-cheech ...?	*Czy może mi pan/pani polecić ...?*
cheap hotel	*ta*-nee *ho*-tel	*tani hotel*
clean hotel	*chis*-ti *ho*-tel	*czysty hotel*
good hotel	*do*-bri *ho*-tel	*dobry hotel*
Where's the ... hotel?	gdje yest ... *ho*-tel?	*Gdzie jest ... hotel?*
best	nay-*lep*-shi	*najlepszy*
cheapest	nay-*tan*-shi	*najtańszy*
nearest	nay-*bleesh*-shi	*najbliższy*

What's the address?
ya-kee yest *a*-dres? — *Jaki jest adres?*

Please write down the address.
pro-she na-*pee*-sach *a*-dres — *Proszę napisać adres.*

BOOKING AHEAD — REZERWACJA

I'd like to book a room.
htse za-re-zer-*vo*-vach *po*-kooy — *Chcę zarezerwować pokój.*

For (three) nights.
na (tshi) *no*-tse — *Na (trzy) noce.*

How much does it cost per night?
ee-le kosh-*too*-ye za nots? — *Ile kosztuje za noc?*

We'll be arriving at (two o'clock).
pshi-ye-*dje*-mi o (*droo*-gyey) — *Przyjedziemy o (drugiej).*

My name's ...
na-*zi*-vam she ... — *Nazywam się ...*

SIGNS

BRAK MIEJSC	NO VACANCIES
WOLNE POKOJE	ROOMS AVAILABLE

CHECKING IN — ZAMELDOWANIE

Do you have any rooms available?
chi som *vol*-ne po-*ko*-ye? — *Czy są wolne pokoje?*

I'd like a ... room.	po-*pro*-she o *po*-kooy ...	*Poproszę o pokój ...*
single	yed-no-o-so-*bo*-vi	*jednoosobowy*
double	dvoo-o-so-*bo*-vi	*dwuosobowy*
triple	tshi-o-so-*bo*-vi	*trzyosobowy*

I'd like a ...	po-*pro*-she o ...	*Poproszę o ...*
bed in a dorm	*woosh*-ko *fsa*-lee zbyo-*ro*-vey	*łóżko w sali zbiorowej*
suite	a-par-*ta*-ment	*apartament*

I want a room with a ...	po-*pro*-she o *po*-kooy s ...	*Poproszę o pokój z ...*
bathroom	wa-*zhen*-kom	*łazienką*
double bed	pod-*vooy*-nim *woosh*-kyem	*podwójnym łóżkiem*
phone	te-le-*fo*-nem	*telefonem*
shower	prish-*ni*-tsem/ na-*tris*-kyem	*prysznicem/ natryskiem*
TV	te-le-vee-*zo*-rem	*telewizorem*
twin beds	dvo-ma woosh-*ka*-mi	*dwoma łóżkami*
view	vee-*do*-kyem	*widokiem*
window	*ok*-nem	*oknem*

Can I see it?
chi *mo*-ge go zo-*ba*-chich? — *Czy mogę go zobaczyć?*

Are there any others?
chi som *een*-ne? — *Czy są inne?*

Where's the bathroom?
gdje yest wa-*zhen*-ka? — *Gdzie jest łazienka?*

Is there hot water (all day)?
chi yest *chep*-wa *vo*-da (pshes *tsa*-wi djen)? — *Czy jest ciepła woda (przez cały dzień)?*

How much is the room per night?
ee-le kosh-*too*-ye ten *po*-kooy za nots? — *Ile kosztuje ten pokój za noc?*

Haven't you anything cheaper?
chi nye ma *che*-gosh tan-*she*-go? — *Czy nie ma czegoś tańszego?*

Does it include breakfast?
chi shnya-*da*-nye yest vlee-*cho*-ne? — *Czy śniadanie jest wliczone?*

Is there a discount for children/students?
chi yest *ya*-kash *zneesh*-ka dla *dje*-chee/stoo-*den*-toof? — *Czy jest jakaś zniżka dla dzieci/studentów?*

It's fine. I'll take it.
do-bzhe, *vez*-me go — *Dobrze. Wezmę go.*

REQUESTS & COMPLAINTS — PROŚBY I ZAŻALENIA

Can I deposit my valuables here?
chi *mozh*-na too zde-po-*no*-vach *zhe*-chi var-tosh-*cho*-ve? — *Czy można tu zdeponować rzeczy wartościowe?*

Is there somewhere here to wash clothes?
chi *mozh*-na too *oo*-prach oo-*bra*-nye? — *Czy można tu uprać ubranie?*

Can I use the telephone?
chi *mozh*-na sko-*zhis*-tach ste-le-*fo*-noo? — *Czy można skorzystać z telefonu?*

I don't like this room.
nye po-*do*-ba mee she ten *po*-kooy — *Nie podoba mi się ten pokój.*

It's too ...	yest sbit ...	*Jest zbyt ...*
dark	*chem*-ni	*ciemny*
expensive	*dro*-gee	*drogi*
noisy	*gwosh*-ni	*głośny*
small	*ma*-wi	*mały*

I can't open/close the window/door.
nye *mo*-ge ot-*fo*-zhich/ *zam*-knonch *ok*-na/dzhvee — *Nie mogę otworzyć/ zamknąć okna/drzwi.*

The toilet doesn't flush.
vo-da she nye *spoosh*-cha — *Woda się nie spuszcza.*

The shower doesn't work.
prish-neets nye *dja*-wa — *Prysznic nie działa.*

There's no hot water.
nye ma *chep*-wey *vo*-di — *Nie ma ciepłej wody.*

I want to change to another room.
htse *zmye*-neech *po*-kooy — *Chcę zmienić pokój.*

CHECKING OUT — WYMELDOWANIE

Can I have the bill please?
po-*pro*-she o ra-*hoo*-nek — *Poproszę o rachunek.*

Can I pay by credit card?
chi *mo*-ge za-*pwa*-cheech *kar*-tom kre-di-*to*-vom? — *Czy mogę zapłaciŇ kartą kredytową?*

Can I leave my luggage until tonight?
chi *mo*-ge zos-*ta*-veech mooy *ba*-gash do vye-*cho*-ra? — *Czy mogę zostawiŇ mój bagaż do wieczora.*

air conditioning	klee-ma-ti-*za*-tsya	*klimatyzacja* (f)
bed	*woosh*-ko	*łóżko* (neut)
bedclothes	*posh*-chel	*pościel* (f)
blanket	kots	*koc* (m)
chair	*kshe*-swo	*krzesło* (neut)
key	klooch	*klucz* (m)
lamp	*lam*-pa	*lampa* (f)
light bulb	zha-*roof*-ka	*żarówka* (f)
lock	*za*-mek	*zamek* (m)
mattress	ma-*te*-rats	*materac* (m)
mirror	*loos*-tro	*lustro* (neut)
padlock	*kwoot*-ka	*kłódka* (f)
pillow	po-*doosh*-ka	*poduszka* (f)
soap	*mi*-dwo	*mydło* (neut)
suitcase	va-*lees*-ka	*walizka* (f)
swimming pool	*ba*-sen	*basen* (m)
table	stoow	*stół* (m)
toilet	to-a-*le*-ta	*toaleta* (f)
towel	*rench*-neek	*ręcznik* (m)
washbasin	oo-mi-*val*-ka	*umywalka* (f)
... water	... *vo*-da	... *woda* (f)
cold	*zheem*-na	*zimna*
hot	*chep*-wa	*ciepła*

PAPERWORK — DANE OSOBISTE

address	*a*-dres	*adres*
age	vyek	*wiek*
date of birth	*da*-ta oo-ro-*dze*-nya	*data urodzenia*
date of expiry	*da*-ta vazh-*nosh*-chee	*data ważności*
date of issue	*da*-ta vi-*da*-nya	*data wydania*
driving licence	*pra*-vo *yaz*-di	*prawo jazdy*
given names	ee-*myo*-na	*imiona*
nationality	na-ro-*do*-voshch	*narodowość*
place of birth	*myey*-stse oo-ro-*dze*-nya	*miejsce urodzenia*
profession	*za*-voot	*zawód*
sex	pwech	*płeć*
surname	naz-*vees*-ko	*nazwisko*
marital status	stan tsi-*veel*-ni	*stan cywilny*
divorced	roz-vye-*djo*-ni/a	*rozwiedziony/a*
married	zho-*na*-ti	*żonaty* (m)
	za-*men*-zhna	*zamężna* (f)
single	ka-*va*-ler	*kawaler* (m)
	pan-na	*panna* (f)
	nye-zho-*na*-ti	*nieżonaty* (m)
	nye-za-*men*-zhna	*niezamężna* (f)
widowed	*vdo*-vyets	*wdowiec* (m)
	vdo-va	*wdowa* (f)

YOUTH HOSTELS

Polish Youth Hostels are operated by the *Polskie Towarzystwo Schronisk Młodzieżowych (PTSM).*

THEY MAY SAY ...

yak *dwoo*-go za-*mye*-zha pan/*pa*-nee *zos*-tach?	How long are you going to stay?
ee-le *no*-tsi?	How many nights?
po-*pro*-she o *pash*-port?	Can I see your passport, please?
pro-she vi-*peoo*-neech for-*moo*-lash	Please fill in the form.
nyes-*te*-ti nye ma myeysts	Sorry, we're full.

passport	*pash*-port	*paszport*
passport number	*noo*-mer pash-*por*-too	*numer paszportu*
purpose of visit	tsel vee-*zi*-ti	*cel wizyty*
business	*pra*-tsa	*praca*
tourism	too-ris-*ti*-ka	*turystyka*
signature	*pot*-pees	*podpis*
visa	*vee*-za	*wiza*

W MIEŚCIE AROUND TOWN

LOOKING FOR ... SZUKANIE ...

Where's a/the ...?	gdje yest ...?	*Gdzie jest ...?*
bank	bank	*bank*
city centre	*tsen*-troom	*centrum*
consulate	kon-*soo*-lat	*konsulat*
embassy	am-ba-*sa*-da	*ambasada*
hotel	*ho*-tel	*hotel*
police station	pos-te-*roo*-nek po-*lee*-tsyee; ko-mee-*sa*-ryat	*posterunek policji; komisariat*
post office	*poch*-ta	*poczta*
public telephone	aw-*to*-mat te-le-fo-*neech*-ni	*automat telefoniczny*
public toilet	to-a-*le*-ta poo-*bleech*-na	*toaleta publiczna*
tourist information office	*byoo*-ro een-for-*ma*-tsyee too-ris-*tich*-ney	*biuro informacji turystycznej*

What time does it open/close?
o *ktoo*-rey she ot-*fye*-ra/za-*mi*-ka? *O której się otwiera/zamyka?*

AT THE BANK W BANKU

The usual place to change foreign cash in Poland is the *kantor*, or the private currency-exchange office. They are ubiquitous in cities and towns and change most major currencies. They accept cash only, so if you want to change travellers cheques you'll need a *bank*.

Many major banks will cash travellers cheques, though they'll usually charge a commission. An increasing number of banks have ATMs which accept international credit cards.

Can I exchange money here?
chi *mo*-ge too vi-*mye*-neech pye-*nyon*-dze? — *Czy mogę tu wymienić pieniądze?*

I want to change ...	htse vi-*mye*-neech ...	*Chcę wymienić ...*
cash	go-*toof*-ke	*gotówkę*
Deutschmarks	*mar*-kee nye-*myets*-kye	*marki niemieckie*
foreign currency	*op*-tsom va-*loo*-te	*obcą walutę*
pounds sterling	*foon*-ti bri-*tiy*-skye	*funty brytyjskie*
travellers cheques	*che*-kee po-*droozh*-ne	*czeki podróżne*
US dollars	do-*la*-ri a-me-ri-*kan*-skye	*dolary amerykańskie*

Can I get a cash advance on my credit card?
chi *mo*-ge *dos*-tach za-*leech*-ke na *mo*-yom *kar*-te kre-di-*to*-wom? — *Czy mogę dostać zaliczkę na moją kartę kredytową?*

Can I use my credit card in the ATM?
chi *mo*-ge oo-*zhi*-vach *mo*-yom *kar*-te kre-di-*to*-vom vban-ko-*ma*-che? — *Czy mogę używać moją kartę kredytową w bankomacie?*

The ATM has swallowed my card.
ban-*ko*-mat *powk*-now *mo*-yom *kar*-te — *Bankomat połknął moją kartę.*

Can you give me smaller notes?
po-*pro*-she o *mnyey*-she ban-*kno*-ti — *Poproszę o mniejsze banknoty.*

What's the exchange rate?
ya-kee yest koors vi-*mya*-ni? — *Jaki jest kurs wymiany?*

Is there a commission?
chi yest *ya*-kash pro-*vee*-zya? — *Czy jest jakaś prowizja?*

Can I transfer money here from my bank?
chi *mo*-ge too *pshe*-lach pye-*nyon*-dze zmo-*ye*-go *ban*-koo? — *Czy mogę tu przelać pieniądze z mojego banku?*

How long will it take to arrive?
yak *dwoo*-go *pot*-rfa *za*-neem *pshiy*-dom? — *Jak długo potrwa zanim przyjdą?*

ATM (automatic teller machine)	ban-*ko*-mat	*bankomat* (m)
bank account	ra-*hoo*-nek	*rachunek* (m)
banknote	*ban*-knot	*banknot* (m)
cash	go-*toof*-ka	*gotówka* (f)
cashier	*ka*-syer	*kasjer* (m)
	ka-*syer*-ka	*kasjerka* (f)
cheque	chek	*czek* (m)
coin	mo-*ne*-ta	*moneta* (f)
commission	pro-*vee*-zya	*prowizja* (f)
credit card	*kar*-ta kre-di-*to*-va	*karta kredytowa* (f)
currency	va-*loo*-ta	*waluta* (f)
exchange	vi-*mya*-na	*wymiana* (f)
exchange office	*kan*-tor	*kantor* (m)
exchange rate	koors vi-*mya*-ni	*kurs wymiany* (m)
money	pye-*nyon*-dze	*pieniądze* (pl)
signature	*pot*-pees	*podpis* (m)
transfer	*pshe*-lef	*przelew* (m)
travellers cheque	chek po-*droozh*-ni	*czek podróżny* (m)

AT THE POST OFFICE — NA POCZCIE

In Poland, postal services and telecommunications facilities are usually combined under one roof, in a *poczta*, 'post office'. Large cities have plenty of post offices, of which the *poczta główna*, 'main post office', will usually have the widest range of facilities, including poste restante and fax.

I want to buy ...	htse *koo*-peech ...	*Chcę kupić ...*
postcards	poch-*toof*-kee	*pocztówki*
stamps	*znach*-kee	*znaczki*
I want to send a ...	htse *vi*-swach ...	*Chcę wysłać ...*
letter	leest	*list*
parcel	*pach*-ke	*paczkę*

How much does it cost to send this to ...?
ee-le kosh-*too*-ye vi-*swa*-nye *te*-go do ...?
Ile kosztuje wysłanie tego do ...?

Where can I collect poste restante mail?
gdje *mo*-ge o-*de*-brach post res-tant?
Gdzie mogę odebrać poste restante?

Is there any mail for me?
chi yest *ya*-kash *poch*-ta dla mnye?
Czy jest jakaś poczta dla mnie?

address	*a*-dres	*adres* (m)
airmail	*poch*-ta lot-*nee*-cha	*poczta lotnicza* (f)
envelope	ko-*per*-ta	*koperta* (f)
letter	leest	*list* (m)
mail box	*skshin*-ka poch-*to*-va	*skrzynka pocztowa* (f)
parcel	*pach*-ka	*paczka* (f)
postcard	poch-*toof*-ka	*pocztówka* (f)
postcode	kot poch-*to*-vi	*kod pocztowy* (m)
postal worker	lees-*to*-nosh	*listonosz* (m)
	lees-to-*nosh*-ka	*listonoszka* (f)
post office	*poch*-ta	*poczta* (f)
postage stamp	*zna*-chek poch-*to*-vi	*znaczek pocztowy* (m)
registered letter	leest po-le-*tso*-ni	*list polecony* (m)
sender	na-*daf*-tsa	*nadawca* (m)

TELEPHONE — TELEFON

Could I please use the telephone?
 chi *mo*-ge sko-*zhis*-tach ste-le-*fo*-noo? — *Czy mogę skorzystać z telefonu?*

Can I place a (phone) call?
 chi *mo*-ge za-*moo*-vich roz-*mo*-ve (te-le-fo-*neech*-nom)? — *Czy mogę zamówić rozmowę (telefoniczną)?*

I want to make a call to ...
 htse za-*dzvo*-neech do ... — *Chcę zadzwonić do ...*

The number is ...
 to yest *noo*-mer ... — *To jest numer ...*

I want to speak for (three) minutes.
 htse roz-*ma*-vyach (tshi) mee-*noo*-ti — *Chcę rozmawiać (trzy) minuty.*

How much does a three-minute call cost?
 ee-le kosh-*too*-ye roz-*mo*-va tshi-mee-noo-*to*-va? — *Ile kosztuje rozmowa trzyminutowa?*

Is there a cheaper rate in the evening?
 chi yest *tan*-sha ta-*ri*-fa vye-*cho*-rem? — *Czy jest tańsza taryfa wieczorem?*

I want to make a reverse-charges/collect call.
 htse za-*dzvo*-neech na kosht a-bo-*nen*-ta — *Chcę zadzwonić na koszt abonenta.*

What's the area code for ...?
 ya-kee yest *noo*-mer kye-roon-*ko*-vi do ...? — *Jaki jest numer kierunkowy do ...?*

It's engaged.
 yest za-*yen*-te — *Jest zajęte.*

I've been cut off.
 roz-won-*cho*-no mnye — *Rozłączono mnie.*

operator	te-le-fo-*nees*-ta te-le-fo-*neest*-ka	*telefonista* (m) *telefonistka* (f)
phone book	*kshon*-shka te-le-fo-*neech*-na	*książka telefoniczna* (f)
phonecard	*kar*-ta te-le-fo-*neech*-na	*karta telefoniczna* (f)
public telephone	aw-*to*-mat te-le-fo-*neech*-ni	*automat* *telefoniczny* (m)
telephone	te-*le*-fon	*telefon* (m)
token	*zhe*-ton	*żeton* (m)

OUT & ABOUT

artist	ar-*tis*-ta ar-*tist*-ka	*artysta* (m) *artystka* (f)
beggar	*zheb*-rak zheb-*rach*-ka	*żebrak* (m) *żebraczka* (f)
busker; street performer	ar-*tis*-ta oo-*leech*-ni ar-*tist*-ka oo-*leech*-na	*artysta* *uliczny* (m) *artystka* *uliczna* (f)
magician	cha-*ro*-djey cha-ro-*djey*-ka	*czarodziej* (m) *czarodziejka* (f)
musician	*moo*-zik moo-*zich*-ka	*muzyk* (m) *muzyczka* (f)
street vendor	spshe-*daf*-tsa oo-*leech*-ni spshe-daf-*chi*-nee oo-*leech*-na	*sprzedawca* *uliczny* (m) *sprzedawczyni* *uliczna* (f)

Making a Call — Telefonowanie

Hello. (making a call) *ha*-lo *Halo.*
Hello. (answering a call) *swoo*-ham/*pro*-she *Słucham./Proszę.*

Can you put me through to ...?
  pro-she mnye po-*won*-chich s ... *Proszę mnie połączyŇ z ...*
I want extension ...
  po-*pro*-she vev-*nench*-ni ... *Poproszę wewnętrzny ...*

Who's calling? kto *moo*-vee? *Kto mówi?*
This is ... too *moo*-vee ... *Tu mówi ...*

Can I speak to ...?
  chi *mo*-ge *moo*-veech s ...? *Czy mogę mówiŇ z ...?*
Is ... there?
  chi yest ...? *Czy jest ...?*
Yes, s/he is here.
  tak, yest *Tak, jest.*
One moment, please.
  hfee-*lech*-ke *Chwileczkę.*
I'm sorry, s/he's not here.
  pshi-kro mi, nye ma go/yey too *Przykro mi, nie ma go/jej tu.*
What time will s/he be back?
  o *ktoo*-rey *ben*-dje? *O której będzie?*
Can I leave a message?
  chi *mo*-ge zos-*ta*-veech vya-*do*-moshch? *Czy mogę zostawiŇ wiadomośŇ?*
Please tell him/her I called.
  pro-she pof-*too*-zhich zhe dzvo-*nee*-wem/wam *Proszę powtórzyŇ że dzwoniłem/łam.*
I'll call back later.
  zadz-*vo*-nye *poozh*-nyey *Zadzwonię później.*

INTERNET — INTERNET

Like all over the developed world, there's been a proliferation of cybercafes in Poland in recent years. Most major cities have at least a few, and they're also popping up in smaller localities. The service is reasonably reliable and cheap, but may be slow because of dated equipment and congested phone lines.

Is there an Internet cafe around here?
chi yest too *ya*-kash ka-*vyar*-nya een-ter-ne-*to*-va? — *Czy jest tu jakaś kawiarnia internetowa?*

I want to get access to the Internet.
shoo-kam dos-*tem*-poo do een-ter-*ne*-too — *Szukam dostępu do internetu.*

I want to check my email.
htse *sprav*-djeech *mo*-yom *poch*-te e-lek-tro-*neech*-nom — *Chcę sprawdzić moją pocztę elektroniczną.*

POLISH COMPUTER JARGON

If you use a local computer in Poland, you may discover that the commands on the screen are in Polish, which is the norm for most computer software in the country. Here's some useful Polish cyber-speak:

Drukuj	Print	*Widok*	View
Edycja	Edit	*Wklej*	Paste
Format	Format	*Wstaw*	Insert
Kopiuj	Copy	*Wyczyść*	Clear
Nowy	New	*Wytnij*	Cut
Okno	Window	*Zakładka*	Bookmark
Otwórz	Open	*Zakończ*	Exit
Pełny Ekran	Full Screen	*Zamknij*	Close
Plik	File	*Zapisz*	Save
Pomoc	Help	*Zapisz Jako ...*	Save As ...
Szukaj	Search	*Zaznacz Wszystko*	Select All
Usuń	Delete		

SIGHTSEEING — ZWIEDZANIE

Can I get a guidebook/city map?
chi dos-*ta*-ne pshe-*vod*-neek/ plan *mya*-sta?
Czy dostanę przewodnik/ plan miasta?

What are the tourist attractions here?
ya-kye too som a-*trak*-tsye too-ris-*tich*-ne?
Jakie tu są atrakcje turystyczne?

Are there organised tours?
chi som zor-ga-nee-zo-*va*-ne vi-*chech*-kee?
Czy są zorganizowane wycieczki?

SIGNS

CIĄGNĄĆ	PULL
NIE PALIĆ	NO SMOKING
OTWARTE	OPEN
PCHAĆ	PUSH
TOALETY	TOILETS
WEJŚCIE	ENTRANCE
WSTĘP WOLNY	FREE ADMISSION
WSTĘP WZBRONIONY	NO ENTRY
WYJŚCIE	EXIT
WYJŚCIE AWARYJNE/ BEZPIECZEŃSTWA	EMERGENCY EXIT
WZBRONIONY	PROHIBITED
ZAMKNIĘTE	CLOSED
ZAREZERWOWANY	RESERVED

7
44
7

STREET LIFE

What's this?	tso to yest?	*Co to jest?*
What's happenning?	tso she *dje*-ye?	*Co się dzieje?*
What happened?	tso she *sta*-wo?	*Co się stało?*
What's he/ she doing?	tso on/ *o*-na *ro*-bee?	*Co on/ ona robi?*
festival	fes-*tee*-val	*festiwal* (m)
flea market	phlee targ	*pchli targ* (m)
newspaper kiosk	kyosk sga-ze-*ta*-mee	*kiosk z gazetami* (m)
	kyosk *roo*-hoo	*kiosk Ruchu* (m)
street	oo-*lee*-tsa	*ulica* (f)
street demonstration	de-mon-*stra*-tsya oo-*leech*-na	*demonstracja uliczna* (f)
street market	targ oo-*leech*-ni	*targ uliczny* (m)
street theatre	*te*-atr oo-*leech*-ni	*teatr uliczny* (m)

What's that?
tso to yest? — *Co to jest?*

Can I visit it?
chi *mo*-ge to *zvye*-djeech? — *Czy mogę to zwiedzić?*

Is there an admission charge?
chi *pwa*-chee she za fstemp? — *Czy płaci się za wstęp?*

Can I take photographs?
chi *mo*-ge *ro*-beech *zdyen*-cha? — *Czy mogę robić zdjęcia?*

What's the name of this street/suburb?
yak she na-*zi*-va ta oo-*lee*-tsa/djel-*nee*-tsa? — *Jak się nazywa ta ulica/ dzielnica?*

art gallery	ga-*le*-rya *shtoo*-kee	*galeria sztuki* (f)
botanic gardens	*o*-groot bo-ta-*neech*-ni	*ogród botaniczny* (m)
castle	*za*-mek	*zamek* (m)
cathedral	ka-*te*-dra	*katedra* (f)
cemetery	*tsmen*-tash	*cmentarz* (m)
church	*kosh*-choow	*kościół* (m)
concert hall	*sa*-la kon-tser-*to*-va	*sala koncertowa* (f)
monastery	*klash*-tor	*klasztor* (m)
monument	*pom*-neek	*pomnik* (m)
museum	*moo*-ze-oom	*muzeum* (neut)
old town	*sta*-re *mya*-sto	*stare miasto* (neut)
old town square	*ri*-nek	*rynek* (m)
palace	*pa*-wats	*pałac* (m)
stadium	*sta*-dyon	*stadion* (m)
synagogue	si-na-*go*-ga	*synagoga* (f)
tourist information office	*byoo*-ro een-for-*ma*-tsyee too-ris-*tich*-ney	*biuro informacji turystycznej* (neut)
university	oo-nee-*ver*-si-tet	*uniwersytet* (m)

Are you married?
: chi yest pan zho-*na*-ti? — *Czy jest pan żonaty?* (m)
: chi yest *pa*-nee za-*men*-zhna? — *Czy jest pani zamężna?* (f)

I'm single.
: *yes*-tem ka-va-*le*-rem — *Jestem kawalerem.* (m)
: *yes*-tem *pan*-nom — *Jestem panną.* (f)

I'm married.
: *yes*-tem zho-*na*-ti — *Jestem żonaty.* (m)
: *yes*-tem za-*men*-zhna — *Jestem zamężna.* (f)

How many children do you have?
: *ee*-le pan/*pa*-nee ma *dje*-chee? — *Ile pan/pani ma dzieci?* (pol)
: *ee*-le mash *dje*-chee? — *Ile masz dzieci?* (inf)

We don't have any children.
: nye *ma*-mi *dje*-chee — *Nie mamy dzieci.*

Do you have any brothers/sisters?
: chi ma pan/*pa*-nee *bra*-chee/*shos*-tri? — *Czy ma pan/pani braci/siostry?* (pol)
: chi mash *bra*-chee/*shos*-tri? — *Czy masz braci/siostry?* (inf)

Do you live with your family?
: chi pan/*pa*-nee *myesh*-ka zro-*djee*-nom? — *Czy pan/pani mieszka z rodziną?* (pol)
: chi *myesh*-kash zro-*djee*-nom? — *Czy mieszkasz z rodziną?* (inf)

Do you have a boyfriend?
: chi mash na-zhe-cho-*ne*-go? — *Czy masz narzeczonego?* (inf)

Do you have a girlfriend?
: chi mash na-zhe-*cho*-nom? — *Czy masz narzeczoną?* (inf)

aunt	*chot*-ka	*ciotka* (f)
boy	*hwo*-pyets	*chłopiec* (m)
brother	brat	*brat* (m)
child	*djets*-ko	*dziecko* (neut)
children	*dje*-chee	*dzieci* (pl)
cousin	*koo*-zin	*kuzyn* (m)
	koo-*zin*-ka	*kuzynka* (f)
dad	*ta*-ta	*tata* (m)
daughter	*tsoor*-ka	*córka* (f)
family	ro-*djee*-na	*rodzina* (f)
father	*oy*-chets	*ojciec* (m)
girl	djef-*chi*-na	*dziewczyna* (f)
grandfather	*dja*-dek	*dziadek* (m)
grandmother	*bap*-ka	*babka* (f)
husband	monsh	*mąż* (m)
man	men-*shchiz*-na	*mężczyzna* (m)
mother	*mat*-ka	*matka* (f)
mum	*ma*-ma	*mama* (f)
parents	ro-*djee*-tse	*rodzice* (pl)
sister	*shos*-tra	*siostra* (f)
son	sin	*syn* (m)
uncle	*voo*-yek	*wujek* (m)
wife	*zho*-na	*żona* (f)
woman	ko-*bye*-ta	*kobieta* (f)

TALKING WITH PARENTS — ROZMOWY Z RODZICAMI

When's the baby due?
kye-di spo-*dje*-va she *pa*-nee *djets*-ka?
Kiedy spodziewa się pani dziecka?

Is this your first child?
chi to *pa*-nee *pyer*-fshe *djets*-ko?
Czy to pani pierwsze dziecko?

How many children do you have?
ee-le ma *pa*-nee *dje*-chee?
Ile ma pani dzieci?

How old are your children?
ee-le lat *ma*-yom *pa*-nee *dje*-chee?
Ile lat mają pani dzieci?

I can't believe it! You (pol,f) look too young.
nye *mo*-ge oo-*vye*-zhich! *pa*-nee vig-*lon*-da tak *mwo*-do
Nie mogę uwierzyŇ! Pani wygląda tak młodo.

Does s/he go to school?
chi *ho*-djee do *shko*-wi?
Czy chodzi do szkoły?

Do you have grandchildren?
chi ma pañ/*pa*-nee *vnoo*-kee?
Czy ma pan/pani wnuki?

What's the baby's name?
yak *djets*-ko ma na *ee*-mye?
Jak dziecko ma na imię?

Is it a boy or a girl?
chi to *hwo*-pyets chi djef-*chin*-ka?
Czy to chłopiec czy dziewczynka?

What a beautiful child!
tso za *shleech*-ne *djets*-ko!
Co za śliczne dziecko!

TALKING WITH CHILDREN / ROZMOWY Z DZIEĆMI

What's your name?
yak mash na *ee*-mye?
Jak masz na imię?

How old are you?
ee-le mash lat?
Ile masz lat?

When's your birthday/saint's day?
kye-di mash oo-ro-*djee*-ni/ ee-mye-*nee*-ni?
Kiedy masz urodziny/ imieniny?

Have you got brothers or sisters?
chi mash *bra*-chee *al*-bo *shos*-tri?
Czy masz braci albo siostry?

Do you go to school/kinder?
chi *ho*-djeesh do *shko*-wi/ pshet-*shko*-la?
Czy chodzisz do szkoły/ przedszkola?

Do you like school?
chi *loo*-beesh *shko*-we?
Czy lubisz szkołę?

Do you play sport?
chi oo-*pra*-vyash sport? — *Czy uprawiasz sport?*

What sport do you play?
ya-kee sport oo-*pra*-vyash? — *Jaki sport uprawiasz?*

Do you learn English?
chi *oo*-chish she an-gyel-*skye*-go? — *Czy uczysz się angielskiego?*

I come from far away.
yes-tem zda-le-*kye*-go *kra*-yoo — *Jestem z dalekiego kraju.*

We speak a different language in my country.
fmo-eem *kra*-yoo ros-ma-*vya*-mi *feen*-nim yen-*zi*-koo — *W moim kraju rozmawiamy w innym języku.*

I don't understand you very well.
nye bar-dzo che ro-*zoo*-myem — *Nie bardzo cię rozumiem.*

Do you want to play a game?
chi htsesh *za*-grach? — *Czy chcesz zagrać?*

What shall we play?
ftso za-*gra*-mi? — *W co zagramy?*

ZAINTERESOWANIA
INTERESTS

Poland has long and strong cultural and artistic traditions, especially in music, theatre, cinema and the visual arts. Today, the country has an active and diversified artistic scene, with numerous theatres, concert halls, cinemas and art galleries.

Poles are quite cultured folk, with wide interests in the traditional and contemporary culture and arts. Cinema and popular music are, as almost everywhere, the core of pop culture, particularly among the young. Many Poles, however, pursue some more demanding cultural fare, such as classical music, theatre and opera.

COMMON INTERESTS — WSPÓLNE ZAINTERESOWANIA

What do you do in your spare time?

tso pan/*pa*-nee *ro*-bee *vvol*-nim *cha*-she? — *Co pan/pani robi w wolnym czasie?* (pol)

tso *ro*-beesh *vvol*-nim *cha*-she? — *Co robisz w wolnym czasie?* (inf)

Do you like ...?	chi pan/*pa*-nee *loo*-bee ...?	*Czy pan/pani lubi ...?* (pol)
	chi *loo*-beesh ...?	*Czy lubisz ...?* (inf)
I like ...	*loo*-bye ...	*Lubię ...*
arts	*shtoo*-ke	*sztukę*
film	*kee*-no	*kino*
dance	*ta*-nyets	*taniec*
literature	lee-te-ra-*too*-re	*literaturę*
music	*moo*-zi-ke	*muzykę*
photography	fo-to-*gra*-fye	*fotografię*
sports	sport	*sport*
theatre	*te*-atr	*teatr*
travel	po-*droo*-zhe	*podróże*
TV	te-le-*vee*-zye	*telewizję*

VISUAL ARTS — SZTUKI PLASTYCZNE

I'm interested in contemporary art.
een-te-re-*soo*-ye mnye *shtoo*-ka fspoow-*ches*-na
Interesuje mnie sztuka współczesna.

Where can I go to see traditional Polish painting?
gdje *mo*-ge o-*bey*-zhech *sta*-re ma-*lar*-stfo *pol*-skye?
Gdzie mogę obejrzeć stare malarstwo polskie?

Which gallery has sculpture exhibits?
ktoo-ra ga-*le*-rya vis-*ta*-vya *zhezh*-be?
Która galeria wystawia rzeźbę?

Is there a gallery here showing graphic art?
chi yest too *ya*-kash ga-*le*-rya *gra*-fee-kee?
Czy jest tu jakaś galeria grafiki?

Where can I buy posters?
gdje *mo*-ge *koo*-peech pla-*ka*-ti?
Gdzie mogę kupić plakaty?

art	*shtoo*-ka	*sztuka* (f)
art gallery	ga-*le*-rya *shtoo*-kee	*galeria sztuki* (f)
artist	ar-*tis*-ta	*artysta* (m)
	ar-*tist*-ka	*artystka* (f)
contemporary art	*shtoo*-ka fspoow-*ches*-na	*sztuka współczesna* (f)
graphic art	*gra*-fee-ka	*grafika* (f)
modern art	*shtoo*-ka no-vo-*ches*-na	*sztuka nowoczesna* (f)
painter	*ma*-lash	*malarz* (m)
	ma-*lar*-ka	*malarka* (f)
painting (the art)	ma-*lar*-stfo	*malarstwo* (neut)
painting (picture)	*o*-bras	*obraz* (m)
poster	*pla*-kat	*plakat* (m)
sculptor	*zhezh*-byash	*rzeźbiarz* (m)
	zhezh-*byar*-ka	*rzeźbiarka* (f)
sculpture	*zhezh*-ba	*rzeźba* (f)
watercolor	a-kfa-*re*-la	*akwarela* (f)
work of art	*dje*-wo *shtoo*-kee	*dzieło sztuki* (neut)

MUSIC

MUZYKA

Do you like listening to music?

chi pan/*pa*-nee *loo*-bee *swoo*-hach *moo*-zi-kee? — *Czy pan/pani lubi słuchać muzyki?* (m/f, pol)

chi *loo*-beesh *swoo*-hach *moo*-zi-kee? — *Czy lubisz słuchać muzyki?* (inf)

Do you play a musical instrument?

chi pan/*pa*-nee gra na *ya*-keemsh een-stroo-*men*-che? — *Czy pan/pani gra na jakimś instrumencie?* (m/f, pol)

chi grash na *ya*-keemsh een-stroo-*men*-che? — *Czy grasz na jakimś instrumencie?* (inf)

Which kind of music do you like?

ya-kom *moo*-zi-ke pan/*pa*-nee *loo*-bee? — *Jaką muzykę pan/pani lubi?* (m/f, pol)

ya-kom *moo*-zi-ke *loo*-beesh? — *Jaką muzykę lubisz?* (inf)

ALL THAT JAZZ

Many English terms for musical genres have been adopted by Polish, including blues, rock, disco, jazz, rap and reggae. They're written and pronounced as in English, yet may still follow Polish gramatical rules, with endings being added depending on the case. For example:

I don't like jazz. — *Nie lubię jazzu.*

I don't know anything about jazz. — *Nie znam się na jazzie.*

The language has also created a Polish adjective for 'jazz' according to the local grammar. Thus:

jazz club — *klub jazzowy*

jazz music — *muzyka jazzowa*

Where can you go to hear folk music?		
	gdje too *mozh*-na pos-*woo*-hach *moo*-zi-kee loo-*do*-vey?	*Gdzie tu można posłuchać muzyki ludowej?*
Is there a jazz club around here?		
	chi yest too gdjesh kloop dje-*zo*-vi?	*Czy jest tu gdzieś klub jazzowy?*
I'd like to see this band.		
	htse zo-*ba*-chich ten *zes*-poow	*Chcę zobaczyć ten zespół.*
Let's go to the philharmonic.		
	hoch-mi na *kon*-tsert do feel-har-*mo*-nee	*Chodźmy na koncert do filharmonii.*

band	*groo*-pa/ *zes*-poow	*grupa* (f)/ *zespół* (m)
concert	*kon*-tsert	*koncert* (m)
musician	*moo*-zik	*muzyk* (m)
	moo-*zich*-ka	*muzyczka* (f)
orchestra	or-*kyes*-tra	*orkiestra* (f)
show	*spek*-takl	*spektakl* (m)

MASTERPIECE OR CRAP?

Here are some useful adjectives for expressing opinions:

extraordinary	nad-zvi-*chay*-ni/a	nadzwyczajny/a
amazing	tsoo-*dov*-ni/a	cudowny/a
fantastic	fan-tas-*tich*-ni/a	fantastyczny/a
so-so	*ta*-kee/a *so*-bye	taki/a sobie
average	pshe-*chent*-ni/a	przeciętny/a
nothing special	neets spe-tsyal-*ne*-go	nic specjalnego
poor	*swa*-bi/a	słaby/a
bad	zwi/a	zły/a
dreadful	*strash*-ni/a	straszny/a

CINEMA & THEATRE — KINO I TEATR

Except for children's movies, virtually all foreign films are screened with their original soundtrack and Polish subtitles. The majority of films screened in Poland come from the English-speaking world, particularly the US.

In contrast, theatre is, understandably, performed in Polish, which is obviously an obstacle for non-Polish speakers. It may still be worth going to see some leading productions, if only to see the acting.

I feel like going to a cinema/theatre.
mam o-*ho*-te pooyshch do *kee*-na/te-*a*-troo — *Mam ochotę pójść do kina/teatru.*

What's on tonight?
tso *gra*-yom djeesh vye-*cho*-rem? — *Co grają dziś wieczorem?*

Are there any tickets for ...?
chi som bee-*le*-ti na ...? — *Czy są bilety na ...?*

... film	feelm ...	*film* ... (m)
action	sen-sa-*tsiy*-ni	*sensacyjny*
animated	a-nee-mo-*va*-ni	*animowany*
adventure	pshi-go-*do*-vi	*przygodowy*
short	kroot-ko-me-tra-*zho*-vi	*krótkometrażowy*
war	vo-*yen*-ni	*wojenny*

cinema	*kee*-no	*kino* (neut)
comedy	ko-*me*-dya	*komedia* (f)
documentary film	feelm do-koo-men-*tal*-ni	*film dokumentalny* (m)
drama	*dra*-mat	*dramat* (m)
performance	pshet-sta-*vye*-nye	*przedstawienie* (neut)
(theatre) play	*shtoo*-ka (te-a-*tral*-na)	*sztuka (teatralna)* (f)

BAD POLISH

The meaning and impact of swearwords depend on the context and situation in which they're used – which can be easily determined by locals, but not by outsiders. Improper use can get you into trouble, or at least make you look ridiculous. This said, you'll certainly learn some of these words, as many Poles use them – sometimes far too often. This section is to help you understand what's going on around you.

By far the most common Polish swearword is *kurwa*, which literally means 'bitch' or 'whore', although it's used flexibly and has various meanings including 'shit', 'fuck' and 'damn'.

Some people use the word indiscriminately in virtually every sentence, as a form of punctuation. It forms the stem of other swearwords such as *skurwysyn*, 'son of a bitch' and *wkurwić się*, 'to get fucking mad', both of which are fairly strong.

Other common swearwords and expressions include:

Damn!	ho-*le*-ra!/ *psha*-kref!	*Cholera!/ Psiakrew!*
Fuck off!	*ot*-pyepsh she!	*Odpieprz się!*
Fuck off! (strong)	ot-*pyer*-dol she!	*Odpierdol się!*
Kiss my arse!	po-*tsa*-wooy mnye *vdoo*-pe!	*Pocałuj mnie w dupę!*
Get lost!	*zyezh*-djay!/ *spa*-day!/ *spye*-pshay!	*Zjeżdżaj!/ Spadaj!/ Spieprzaj!*
Shit!	*goov*-no!	*Gówno!*
an idiot	*kre*-tin	*kretyn* (m)
	ee-*dyo*-ta	*idiota* (m)
a fool	*gwoo*-pyets/ *doo*-ren	*głupiec/ dureń*
to fuck	*pyep*-shich	*pieprzyć*
to fuck (strong)	pyer-*do*-leech	*pierdolić*

OPINIONS — OPINIE

Did you like the ...?	chi po-*do*-baw she *pa*-noo/*pa*-nee ...?	*Czy podobał się panu/pani ...?*
concert	*kon*-tsert	*koncert* (m)
film	feelm	*film* (m)

I liked it (a lot).
po-*do*-baw mee she (*bar*-dzo) — *Podobał mi się (bardzo).*

I didn't like it (at all).
nye po-*do*-baw mee she (*ftsa*-le) — *Nie podobał mi się (wcale).*

I thought it was ...	*son*-dze zhe biw ...	*Sądzę że był ...*
boring	*nood*-ni	*nudny*
excellent	dos-ko-*na*-wi	*doskonały*
good	*do*-bri	*dobry*
terrible	nye-*do*-bri	*niedobry*

What a great concert/film!
tso za fspa-*nya*-wi *kon*-tsert/feelm! — *Co za wspaniały koncert/film!*

YES OR NO?

Since opinions are subjective, some of the following expressions might come in handy:

Of course!	o-chi-*veesh*-che!	*Oczywiście!*
Sure!	spev-*nosh*-chom!	*Z pewnością!*
Exactly!	do-*kwad*-nye!	*Dokładnie!*
I agree.	*zga*-dzam she	*Zgadzam się.*
Yes, but ...	tak, *a*-le ...	*Tak, ale ...*
Perhaps.	bich *mo*-zhe	*Być może.*
It's doubtful.	to vont-*plee*-ve	*To wątpliwe.*
I disagree.	nye *zga*-dzam she	*Nie zgadzam się.*
That's not true!	to nye-*prav*-da!	*To nieprawda!*
No way!	vi-kloo-*cho*-ne!	*Wykluczone!*
Never!	*neeg*-di!	*Nigdy!*

POLITICAL & SOCIAL ISSUES — SPRAWY POLITYCZNE I SPOŁECZNE

The fall of communism effectively brought an end to state censorship, and few topics are now taboo. Poles these days openly discuss and criticise diverse social and political issues, including those related to the communist period, Soviet Union, Russia and religion.

What's the government's policy on ...?	
ya-ka yest po-*lee*-ti-ka *zhon*-doo tso do ...?	*Jaka jest polityka rządu co do ...?*
What are the major social problems?	
ya-kye son *gwoov*-ne pro-*ble*-mi spo-*wech*-ne?	*Jakie są główne problemy społeczne?*
What do you think about ...?	
tso pan/*pa*-nee *son*-djee o ...?	*Co pan/pani sądzi o ...?* (pol)
tso *son*-djeesh o ...?	*Co sądzisz o ...?* (inf)
Which party do you support?	
ktoo-rom *par*-tye pan/*pa*-nee po-*pye*-ra?	*Którą partię pan/pani popiera?* (pol)
ktoo-rom *par*-tye po-*pye*-rash?	*Którą partię popierasz?* (inf)
What's its program?	
ya-kee yest yey *pro*-gram?	*Jaki jest jej program?*
Do you agree with ...?	
chi *zga*-dza she pan/*pa*-nees ...?	*Czy zgadza się pan/pani z ...?* (pol)
chi *zga*-dzash she s ...?	*Czy zgadzasz się z ...?* (inf)
Do you support ...?	
chi pan/*pa*-nee po-*pye*-ra ...?	*Czy pan/pani popiera ...?* (pol)
chi po-*pye*-rash ...?	*Czy popierasz ...?* (inf)
Are you in favour or against?	
yest pan/*pa*-nee za chi *pshe*-cheef?	*Jest pan/pani za czy przeciw?* (pol)
yes-tesh za chi *pshe*-cheef?	*Jesteś za czy przeciw?* (inf)

abortion	pshe-ri-*va*-nye *chon*-zhi	*przerywanie ciąży* (neut)
elections	vi-*bo*-ri	*wybory* (m, pl)
employment	za-trood-*nye*-nye	*zatrudnienie* (neut)
environmental ...	... shro-do-*vees*-ka	... *środowiska*
pollution	ska-*zhe*-nye	*skażenie* (neut)
protection	oh-*ro*-na	*ochrona* (f)
government	zhont	*rząd* (m)
policy	po-*lee*-ti-ka	*polityka* (f)
prime minister	*pre*-myer	*premier* (m/f)
privatisation	pri-va-ti-*za*-tsya	*prywatyzacja* (f)
racism	*ra*-sheezm	*rasizm* (m)
strike	strayk	*strajk* (m)
social welfare	o-*pye*-ka spo-*wech*-na	*opieka społeczna* (f)
taxes	po-*dat*-kee	*podatki* (m, pl)
trade union	*zvyon*-zek za-vo-*do*-vi	*związek zawodowy* (m)
unemployment	bez-ro-*bo*-che	*bezrobocie* (neut)

STARS / GWIAZDY

Astrology / Astrologia

When's your birthday?
kye-di son *tfo*-ye oo-ro-*djee*-ni? — *Kiedy są twoje urodziny?* (inf)

What's your star sign?
ya-kee yest tfooy znak zo-*dya*-koo? — *Jaki jest twój znak zodiaku?* (inf)

Capricorn	ko-zho-*ro*-zhets	*Koziorożec* (m)
Aquarius	*vod*-neek	*Wodnik* (m)
Pisces	*ri*-bi	*Ryby* (f, pl)
Aries	*ba*-ran	*Baran* (m)
Taurus	bik	*Byk* (m)
Gemini	bleezh-*nyen*-ta	*Bliźnięta* (neut, pl)
Cancer	rak	*Rak* (m)
Leo	lef	*Lew* (m)
Virgo	*pan*-na	*Panna* (f)
Libra	*va*-ga	*Waga* (f)
Scorpio	*skor*-pyon	*Skorpion* (m)
Sagittarius	*stshe*-lets	*Strzelec* (m)

astrology	as-tro-*lo*-gya	*astrologia* (f)
horoscope	ho-*ros*-kop	*horoskop* (m)
star sign	znak zo-*dya*-koo	*znak zodiaku* (m)

GENDER SPLENDOUR

Although there aren't any hard and fast rules to determine the gender of every Polish noun, there are patterns that can make it easier to recognise. See Gender, pages 19-20, for an explanation.

Astronomy | Astronomia

astronomy	as-tro-*no*-mya	*astronomia* (f)
comet	ko-*me*-ta	*kometa* (f)
constellation	gvyaz-*do*-zbyoor	*gwiazdozbiór* (m)
earth	*zhe*-mya	*ziemia* (f)
full moon	*peoo*-nya kshen-*zhi*-tsa	*pełnia księżyca* (f)
Milky Way	*dro*-ga *mlech*-na	*Droga Mleczna* (f)
moon	*kshen*-zhits	*księżyc* (m)
planet	pla-*ne*-ta	*planeta* (f)
planetarium	pla-ne-*ta*-ryoom	*planetarium* (neut)
sky	*nye*-bo	*niebo* (neut)
star	*gvyaz*-da	*gwiazda* (f)
sun	*swon*-tse	*słońce* (neut)
telescope	te-*les*-kop	*teleskop* (m)
universe	*fsheh*-shfyat	*wszechświat* (m)
world	shfyat	*świat* (m)

WRITING LETTERS | PISANIE LISTÓW

Once you get back home, you may want to drop a line to people you met. Here are a few lines to help you.

WHICH LETTER?

A letter you write to someone is *list*; a letter of the alphabet is *litera*.

Dear ...	*Drogi/ga* ... (m/f)
I'm sorry it's taken me so long to write.	*Przepraszam że tak długo nie pisałem/łam.*
It was great to meet you.	*Cieszę się że pana/panią poznałem/łam.* (pol, m/f) *Cieszę się że cię/was poznałem/łam.* (inf, sg/pl)

Thanks so much for your hospitality. — *Bardzo dziękuję za gościnnośŇ.*

I had a fantastic time in Poland. — *Było fantastycznie w Polsce.*

My favourite place was ... — *Moje ulubione miejsce to ...*

I hope to visit Poland again. — *Mam nadzieję odwiedziŇ Polskę ponownie.*

Say 'hi' to ... for me. — *Proszę pozdrowiŇ ...*

I'd love to see you again. — *Chciałbym/chciałabym pana/panią zobaczyŇ ponownie.* (pol, sg/pl)
Chciałbym/chciałabym cię/was zobaczyŇ ponownie. (inf, sg/pl)

Looking forward to hear from you soon. — *Czekam na szybką odpowiedź.*

Write soon. — *Napisz szybko.* (inf)

Best wishes. — *Najlepsze życzenia.*

Regards. — *Pozdrowienia.*

PAN-ORAMA

If you want to be polite, address a man as *pan* and a woman as *pani*. It's formal, but a safe option.

AKTYWNY WYPOCZYNEK ACTIVITIES

SPORT SPORT

Besides soccer (see page 106), there's no particular sport that drives the nation crazy. Cycling is reasonably popular in some circles, as are basketball, athletics, boxing, tennis and skiing.

Do you like sport?
chi pan/*pa*-nee *loo*-bee sport? — *Czy pan/pani lubi sport?* (pol)
chi *loo*-beesh sport? — *Czy lubisz sport?* (inf)

I play sport.
oo-*pra*-vyam sport — *Uprawiam sport.*

I prefer to watch rather than play sport.
vo-le o-*glon*-dach sport neesh go oo-*pra*-vyach — *Wolę oglądać sport niż go uprawiać.*

Which sport do you like?
ya-kee sport pan/*pa*-nee *loo*-bee? — *Jaki sport pan/pani lubi?* (pol)
ya-kee sport *loo*-beesh? — *Jaki sport lubisz?* (inf)

What sport do you play?
ya-kee sport pan/*pa*-nee oo-*pra*-vya? — *Jaki sport pan/pani uprawia?* (pol)
ya-kee sport oo-*pra*-vyash? — *Jaki sport uprawiasz?* (inf)

athletics	lek-ko-a-tle-*ti*-ka	*lekkoatletyka* (f)
basketball	ko-shi-*koof*-ka	*koszykówka* (f)
boxing	boks	*boks* (m)
diving	noor-ko-*va*-nye	*nurkowanie* (neut)
gymnastics	geem-nas-*ti*-ka	*gimnastyka* (f)
hockey	*ho*-key	*hokej* (m)
horseriding	*yaz*-da *kon*-na	*jazda konna* (f)
horse racing	vish-*chee*-gee *kon*-ne	*wyścigi konne* (m, pl)
soccer	*peew*-ka *nozh*-na	*piłka nożna* (f)
swimming	pwi-*va*-nye	*pływanie* (neut)
tennis	*te*-nees	*tenis* (m)
skiing	nar-*char*-stfo	*narciarstwo* (neut)

Useful Words — Przydatne Słowa

horse stable	sta-*dnee*-na *ko*-nee	*stadnina koni* (f)
soccer field	bo-*ees*-ko peew-*kar*-skye	*boisko piłkarskie* (neut)
stadium	*sta*-dyon	*stadion* (m)
swimming pool	*ba*-sen/ pwi-*val*-nya	*basen* (m)/ *pływalnia* (f)
tennis court	kort te-nee-*so*-vi	*kort tenisowy* (m)

(See also Hiking, page 148.)

SOCCER — PIŁKA NOŻNA

Soccer is Poland's most popular sport. The country had quite a strong national team and brilliant soccer players in the 1970s, but its fortunes have since fallen. National League matches still fill up the stadiums.

Are you interested in soccer?
chi een-te-re-*soo*-yesh she *peew*-kom *nozh*-nom? — *Czy interesujesz się piłką nożną?* (inf)

Who's the best team?
ktoo-ri *zes*-poow yest nay-*lep*-shi? — *Który zespół jest najlepszy?*

Who's at the top of the league?
kto pro-*va*-djee *flee*-dze? — *Kto prowadzi w lidze?*

Who plays for ...?
kto gra v ...? — *Kto gra w ...?*

My favourite player is ...
mooy oo-loo-*byo*-ni za-*vod*-neek to ... — *Mój ulubiony zawodnik to ...*

He's a great player.
to fspa-*nya*-wi za-*vod*-neek — *To wspaniały zawodnik.*

coach	*tre*-ner	*trener* (m)
corner	*kor*-ner; zhoot *rosh*-ni	*korner* (m); *rzut rożny* (m)
fans	kee-*bee*-tse	*kibice* (m, pl)
free kick	zhoot *vol*-ni	*rzut wolny* (m)
foul	*fa*-ool	*faul* (m)
goal	gol	*gol* (m)
goalkeeper	*bram*-kash	*bramkarz* (m)
league	*lee*-ga	*liga* (f)
manager	kye-*rov*-neek	*kierownik* (m)
offside	spa-*lo*-ni	*spalony* (m)
penalty	zhoot *kar*-ni	*rzut karny* (m)
player	za-*vod*-neek	*zawodnik* (m)

AT THE MATCH — NA MECZU

Would you like to go to a match?
chi htsesh pooyshch na mech? — *Czy chcesz pójść na mecz?* (inf)

Where's it being held?
gdje she ot-*bi*-va? — *Gdzie się odbywa?*

How much are the tickets?
ee-le kosh-*too*-yom bee-*le*-ti? — *Ile kosztują bilety?*

What time does it start?
o *ktoo*-rey she za-*chi*-na? — *O której się zaczyna?*

Who's playing?
kto gra? — *Kto gra?*

Who do you think will win?
yak *mish*-leesh kto *vi*-gra? — *Jak myślisz, kto wygra?* (inf)

Who are you supporting?
za keem *jes*-tesh? — *Za kim jesteś?* (inf)

I'm supporting ...
yes-tem za ... — *Jestem za ...*

Who's winning?
kto vi-*gri*-va? — *Kto wygrywa?*

Which team's winning/losing?
ktoo-ri *zes*-poow vi-*gri*-va/pshe-*gri*-va? — *Który zespół wygrywa/przegrywa?*

What's the score?
ya-kee yest *vi*-neek? — *Jaki jest wynik?*

What a ...!	tso za ...!	*Co za ...!*
goal	gol	*gol*
kick	stshaw	*strzał*
pass	po-*da*-nye	*podanie*

What a great match!
tso za fspa-*nya*-vi mech! — *Co za wspaniały mecz!*

How much time is left?
ee-le *cha*-soo zos-*ta*-wo? — *Ile czasu zostało?*

That was a really good game!
to biw na-*prav*-de *do*-bri mech! — *To był naprawdę dobry mecz!*

What a boring game!
tso za *nood*-ni mech! — *Co za nudny mecz!*

What was the final score?
ya-kee biw os-ta-*tech*-ni *vi*-neek? — *Jaki był ostateczny wynik?*

It was a draw.
to biw *re*-mees — *To był remis.*

international championships	mees-*tshos*-tfa myen-dzi-na-ro-*do*-ve	*mistrzostwa międzynarodowe* (neut, pl)
medal	*me*-dal	*medal* (m)
national championships	mees-*tshos*-tfa kra-*yo*-ve	*mistrzostwa krajowe* (neut, pl)
Olympic Games	o-leem-*pya*-da	*olimpiada* (f)
referee	*sen*-dja	*sędzia* (m)
seat	*myey*-stse	*miejsce* (neut)
ticket	*bee*-let	*bilet* (m)
ticket office	*ka*-sa bee-le-*to*-va	*kasa biletowa* (f)

ZAKUPY SHOPPING

The shopping scene in Poland is alive and busy, and you can now buy just about everything from basic food and drink to international cars and fashion. Poland imports a lot of Western products, but many consumer goods are produced locally, and these are usually cheaper.

THEY MAY SAY ...

chim *mo*-ge *swoo*-zhich?	Can I help you?
ee-le?	How much/many?
chi to *fshis*-tko?	Will that be all?
chi tsosh *yesh*-che?	Anything else?
chi za-pa-*ko*-vach?	Would you like it wrapped?
nye ma	There aren't any.

LOOKING FOR ... SZUKANIE ...

Where can I buy ...?
gdje *mo*-ge *koo*-peech ...? *Gdzie mogę kupić ...?*

Where's the ...?	gdje yest ...?	*Gdzie jest ...?*
bakery	pye-*kar*-nya	*piekarnia* (f)
bookshop	kshen-*gar*-nya	*księgarnia* (f)
butcher	sklep *myen*-sni	*sklep mięsny* (m)
cake shop	tsoo-*kyer*-nya	*cukiernia* (f)
chemist	ap-*te*-ka	*apteka* (f)
clothing store	sklep o-dje-*zho*-vi	*sklep odzieżowy* (m)
delicatessen	de-lee-ka-*te*-si	*delikatesy* (pl)
drycleaner	*pral*-nya he-*meech*-na	*pralnia chemiczna* (f)
fishmonger	sklep *rib*-ni	*sklep rybny* (m)
flower shop	kfya-*char*-nya	*kwiaciarnia* (f)
greengrocer	sklep o-vo-*tso*-vo va-*zhiv*-ni	*sklep owocowo-warzywny* (m)
grocer	sklep spo-*zhif*-chi	*sklep spożywczy* (m)
laundry	*pral*-nya	*pralnia* (f)
market	*ba*-zar/targ	*bazar* (m)/ *targ* (m)
pharmacy	ap-*te*-ka	*apteka* (f)
photographic shop	fo-to-*op*-*ti*-ka	*fotooptyka* (f)
shoe shop	sklep o-boo-*vnee*-chi	*sklep obuwniczy* (m)
shopping centre	*tsen*-troom han-*dlo*-ve	*centrum handlowe* (neut)
souvenir shop	sklep spa-myont-*ka*-mee	*sklep z pamiątkami* (m)
stationers	sklep pa-pyer-*nee*-chi	*sklep papierniczy* (m)
travel agency	*byoo*-ro po-*droo*-zhi	*biuro podróży* (neut)

SHOPPING

MAKING A PURCHASE — KUPOWANIE

I'd like to buy ...	htse *koo*-peech ...	*Chcę kupić ...*
Do you have ...?	chi som ...?	*Czy są ...?*

Can I look at it?
chi *mo*-ge to zo-*ba*-chich? — *Czy mogę to zobaczyć?*

I (don't) like it.
(nye) po-*do*-ba mee she — *(Nie) podoba mi się.*

Do you have others?
chi som *een*-ne? — *Czy są inne?*

I'm just looking.
til-ko o-*glon*-dam — *Tylko oglądam.*

How much is this?
ee-le to kosh-*too*-ye? — *Ile to kosztuje?*

Can you write down the price?
pro-she na-*pee*-sach *tse*-ne? — *Proszę napisać cenę.*

Can I pay by credit card?
chi *mo*-ge za-*pwa*-cheech *kar*-tom kre-di-*to*-vom? — *Czy mogę zapłacić kartą kredytową?*

I'll take it.
vez-me to — *Wezmę to.*

Please wrap it.
pro-she to za-pa-*ko*-vach — *Proszę to zapakować.*

BARGAINING — TARGOWANIE

Bargaining isn't common in Poland, and is limited to some informal places such as markets, bazaars and street vendors.

It's expensive.
to yest *dro*-gye — *To jest drogie.*

Do you have anything cheaper?
chi *yest* tsosh tan-*she*-go? — *Czy jest coś tańszego?*

to bargain	tar-*go*-vach she	*targować się*
reduced price	*tse*-na zneesh-*ko*-va	*cena zniżkowa* (f)
sale	vi-*pshe*-dash	*wyprzedaż* (f)
secondhand goods	*zhe*-chi oo-zhi-*va*-ne	*rzeczy używane* (f, pl)
special offer	o-*ka*-zya	*okazja* (f)

ESSENTIAL GROCERIES — ARTYKUŁY PODSTAWOWEGO UŻYTKU

bread	hlep	*chleb* (m)
butter	*ma*-swo	*masło* (neut)
cheese	ser	*ser* (m)
chocolate	che-ko-*la*-da	*czekolada* (f)
eggs	*yay*-ka	*jajka* (neut, pl)
flour	*mon*-ka	*mąka* (f)
fruit	o-*vo*-tse	*owoce* (m, pl)
ham	*shin*-ka	*szynka* (f)
margarine	mar-ga-*ri*-na	*margaryna* (f)
matches	za-*paw*-kee	*zapałki* (f, pl)
milk	*mle*-ko	*mleko* (neut)
salt	sool	*sól* (f)
shampoo	*sham*-pon	*szampon* (m)
soap	*mi*-dwo	*mydło* (neut)
sugar	*tsoo*-kyer	*cukier* (m)
toilet paper	*pa*-pyer to-a-le-*to*-vi	*papier toaletowy* (m)
toothpaste	*pas*-ta do *zem*-boof	*pasta do zębów* (f)
washing powder	*pro*-shek do *pra*-nya	*proszek do prania* (m)
yogurt	*yo*-goort	*jogurt* (m)

SOUVENIRS — UPOMINKI

amber	*boor*-shtin	*bursztyn* (m)
glassware	shkwo	*szkło* (neut)
handicrafts	vi-*ro*-bi shtoo-kee loo-*do*-vey	*wyroby sztuki ludowej* (m, pl)
jewellery	bee-zhoo-*te*-rya	*biżuteria* (f)
posters	pla-*ka*-ti	*plakaty* (m, pl)

CLOTHING — ODZIEŻ

Can I try it on?
chi *mo*-ge to pshi-*mye*-zhich? *Czy mogę to przymierzyć?*

It doesn't fit.
nye pa-*soo*-ye *Nie pasuje.*

It's too ...	yest za ...	*Jest za ...*
big	*doo*-zhi/a	*duży/a*
long	*dwoo*-gee/a	*długi/a*
loose	*loozh*-ni/a	*luźny/a*
short	*kroot*-kee/a	*krótki/a*
small	*ma*-wi/a	*mały/a*
tight	op-*chees*-wi/a	*obcisły/a*

One size smaller/larger, please.
po-*pro*-she o *noo*-mer *mnyey*-shi/*vyenk*-shi *Poproszę o numer mniejszy/większy.*

Do you have it in any other colours?
chi som *een*-ne ko-*lo*-ri? *Czy są inne kolory?*

belt	*pa*-sek	*pasek* (m)
bra	byoos-*to*-nosh	*biustonosz* (m)
clothing	oo-*bra*-nye	*ubranie* (neut)
coat	pwashch	*płaszcz* (m)
dress	soo-*kyen*-ka	*sukienka* (f)
jacket	*koor*-tka	*kurtka* (f)
jumper	*sfe*-ter	*sweter* (m)
shirt	ko-*shoo*-la	*koszula* (f)
shoes	*boo*-ti	*buty* (m, pl)
skirt	spood-*nee*-tsa	*spódnica* (f)
socks	skar-*pet*-kee	*skarpetki* (f, pl)
sweater	*sfe*-ter	*sweter* (m)
trousers	*spod*-nye	*spodnie* (pl)
T-shirt	pot-ko-*shool*-ka	*podkoszulka* (f)
underpants (men's)	*slee*-pi	*slipy* (pl)
underpants (women's)	*fee*-gee	*figi* (pl)

MATERIALS — MATERIAŁY

ceramic	tse-ra-*mee*-ka	*ceramika* (f)
cotton	ba-*veoo*-na	*bawełna* (f)
glass	shkwo	*szkło* (neut)
gold	*zwo*-to	*złoto* (neut)
leather	*skoo*-ra	*skóra* (f)
linen	*pwoot*-no	*płótno* (neut)
silk	*yet*-vap	*jedwab* (m)
silver	*sre*-bro	*srebro* (neut)
wood	*dzhe*-vo	*drzewo* (neut)
wool	*veoo*-na	*wełna* (f)

COLOURS — KOLORY

beige	be-*zho*-vi/a	*beżowy/a*
black	*char*-ni/a	*czarny/a*
blue	nye-*byes*-kee/a	*niebieski/a*
brown	bron-*zo*-vi/a	*brązowy/a*
dark	*chem*-ni/a	*ciemny/a*
green	zhe-*lo*-ni/a	*zielony/a*
grey	*sha*-ri/a	*szary/a*
light	*yas*-ni/a	*jasny/a*
orange	po-ma-ran-*cho*-vi/a	*pomarańczowy/a*
pink	roo-*zho*-vi/a	*różowy/a*
purple	fyo-le-*to*-vi/a	*fioletowy/a*
red	cher-*vo*-ni/a	*czerwony/a*
white	*bya*-wi/a	*biały/a*
yellow	*zhoow*-ti/a	*żółty/a*

SHOPPING

PERFECT HARMONY

Note that adjectives, including colours, agree in gender, number and case with the nouns they describe. Both masculine and feminine endings are given here. See Grammar, page 25, for more information.

TOILETRIES / PRZYBORY TOALETOWE

comb	*gzhe*-byen	*grzebień* (m)
condoms	pre-zer-va-*ti*-vi/ kon-*do*-ni	*prezerwatywy* (f, pl)/ *kondony* (m, pl)
moisturiser	krem na-veel-zha-*yon*-tsi	*krem nawilżający* (m)
razor	ma-*shin*-ka do go-*le*-nya	*maszynka do golenia* (f)
sanitary napkins	pot-*pas*-kee hee-gye-*neech*-ne	*podpaski higieniczne* (f, pl)
shampoo	*sham*-pon	*szampon* (m)
shaving cream	krem do go-*le*-nya	*krem do golenia* (m)
soap	*mi*-dwo	*mydło* (neut)
tampons	tam-*po*-ni	*tampony* (m, pl)
toilet paper	*pa*-pyer to-a-le-*to*-vi	*papier toaletowy* (m)
toothbrush	shcho-*tech*-ka do *zem*-boof	*szczoteczka do zębów* (f)
toothpaste	*pas*-ta do *zem*-boof	*pasta do zębów* (f)

SHOPPING

FOR THE BABY / DLA DZIECKA

baby food	od-*zhif*-ka dla nye-*mov*-lont	*odżywka dla niemowląt* (f)
baby powder	za-*sip*-ka dla nye-*mov*-lont	*zasypka dla niemowląt* (f)
bib	*shlee*-nyak	*śliniak* (m)
dummy/pacifier	*smo*-chek	*smoczek* (m)
feeding bottle	boo-*tel*-ka do kar-*mye*-nya	*butelka do karmienia* (f)
nappy	pye-*loosh*-ka	*pieluszka* (f)
powdered milk	*mle*-ko *fprosh*-koo	*mleko w proszku* (neut)

STATIONERY & PUBLICATIONS — MATERIAŁY PAPIERNICZE I WYDAWNICTWA

Is there an English-language bookshop here?
chi yest too kshen-*gar*-nya an-glo-yen-*zich*-na? — *Czy jest tu księgarnia anglojęzyczna?*

Where's the English-language section?
gdje yest sek-tsya an-glo-yen-*zich*-na? — *Gdzie jest sekcja anglojęzyczna?*

book	*kshon*-shka	*książka* (f)
city map	plan *mya*-sta	*plan miasta* (m)
dictionary	*swov*-neek	*słownik* (m)
envelope	ko-*per*-ta	*koperta* (f)
magazine	ma-*ga*-zin	*magazyn* (m)
map	*ma*-pa	*mapa* (f)
newspaper	ga-*ze*-ta	*gazeta* (f)
notebook	no-*tat*-neek	*notatnik* (m)
paper	*pa*-pyer	*papier* (m)
pen (ballpoint)	dwoo-*go*-pees	*długopis* (m)
pencil	o-*woo*-vek	*ołówek* (m)
postcard	poch-*toof*-ka	*pocztówka* (f)
stamp	*zna*-chek	*znaczek* (m)
weekly	ti-*god*-neek	*tygodnik* (m)

ON THE CASE

Nouns in Polish are subject to a complex case system, and change their endings depending on case. See Grammar, page 21, for an explanation.

SHOPPING

MUSIC — MUZYKA

I'm looking for folk music CDs.
shoo-kam pwit kom-pak-*to*-vih *zmoo*-zi-kom loo-*do*-vom — *Szukam płyt kompaktowych z muzyką ludową.*

Do you have any cassettes with Polish jazz?
chi som *ya*-kyesh ka-*se*-ti *spol*-skeem *dje*-zem? — *Czy są jakieś kasety z polskim jazzem?*

What's the best Polish rock group?
ya-ka yest nay-*lep*-sha *pol*-ska *groo*-pa ro-*ko*-va? — *Jaka jest najlepsza polska grupa rockowa?*

Do you have the latest record by ...?
chi yest nay-*nof*-sha *pwi*-ta ...? — *Czy jest najnowsza płyta ...?*

Can I listen to this CD here?
chi *mo*-ge too pshes-*woo*-hach tem *pwi*-te? — *Czy mogę tu przesłuchać tę płytę?*

I need a blank cassette.
pot-she-*boo*-ye *chis*-tom ka-*se*-te — *Potrzebuję czystą kasetę.*

cassette	ka-*se*-ta	*kaseta* (f)
CD	*pwi*-ta kom-pak-*to*-va	*płyta kompaktowa* (f)
headphones	swoo-*haf*-ki	*słuchawki* (f, pl)

PHOTOGRAPHY — FOTOGRAFIA

Can I have this film processed here?
chi *mo*-ge too vi-*vo*-wach ten feelm? — *Czy mogę tu wywołać ten film?*

How much is it to process this film?
ee-le kosh-*too*-ye vi-vo-*wa*-nye *te*-go *feel*-moo? — *Ile kosztuje wywołanie tego filmu?*

When will it be ready?
kye-di *ben*-dje go-*to*-vi? — *Kiedy będzie gotowy?*

I'd like a set of prints from this film.
po-*pro*-she o *kom*-plet ot-*bee*-tek *ste*-go *feel*-moo — *Poproszę o komplet odbitek z tego filmu.*

I need new batteries for this camera.
pot-she-*boo*-ye *no*-ve ba-*te*-rye do *te*-go a-pa-*ra*-too — *Potrzebuję nowe baterie do tego aparatu.*

My camera doesn't work.
mooy a-*pa*-rat nye *dja*-wa — *Mój aparat nie działa.*

Where can I have it fixed?
gdje go *mo*-ge na-*pra*-veech? — *Gdzie go mogę naprawić?*

battery	ba-*te*-rya	*bateria* (f)
B&W film	feelm char-no-*bya*-wi	*film czarno-biały* (m)
camera	a-*pa*-rat (fo-to-gra-*feech*-ni)	*aparat (fotograficzny)* (m)
colour film	feelm ko-lo-*ro*-vi	*film kolorowy* (m)
enlargement	po-vyenk-*she*-nye	*powiększenie* (neut)
lens	o-*byek*-tiv	*obiektyw* (m)
light meter	shvya-*two*-myesh	*światłomierz* (m)
print	ot-*beet*-ka	*odbitka* (f)
slides	*slay*-di	*slajdy* (m, pl)
videotape	*tash*-ma vee-*de*-o	*taśma video* (f)

SIGNS

CZYNNE OD ... DO ...	OPEN FROM ... TO ...
NIECZYNNE	CLOSED
OTWARTE	OPEN
REMANENT	CLOSED FOR STOCK CONTROL
REMONT	CLOSED FOR REFURBISHMENT
URLOP OD ... DO ...	CLOSED FOR HOLIDAYS FROM ... TO ...
ZAMKNIĘTE	CLOSED
ZARAZ WRACAM	BACK IN A MOMENT

SMOKING — PALENIE

A packet of cigarettes, please.
po-*pro*-she *pach*-ke pa-pye-*ro*-soof — *Poproszę paczkę papierosów.*

Are these cigarettes strong or mild?
chi te pa-pye-*ro*-si som *mots*-ne chi wa-*god*-ne? — *Czy te papierosy są mocne czy łagodne?*

Do you have a light?
chi *mo*-ge *pro*-sheech o *o*-gyen? — *Czy mogę prosić o ogień.*

Please don't smoke here.
pro-she too nye *pa*-leech — *Proszę tu nie palić.*

Can I smoke here?
chi *mo*-ge too *pa*-leech? — *Czy mogę tu palić?*

Do you smoke?
chi pan/*pa*-nee *pa*-lee? — *Czy pan/pani pali?* (pol)
chi *pa*-leesh? — *Czy palisz?* (inf)

I'm trying to give up.
sta-ram she *zhoo*-cheech pa-*le*-nye — *Staram się rzucić palenie.*

I don't smoke anymore.
yoosh nye *pa*-le — *Już nie palę.*

cigarettes	pa-pye-*ro*-si	*papierosy* (m, pl)
cigarette paper	bee-*boow*-ka do pa-pye-*ro*-soof	*bibułka do papierosów* (f)
lighter	za-pal-*neech*-ka	*zapalniczka* (f)
matches	za-*paw*-kee	*zapałki* (f, pl)
pipe	*fay*-ka	*fajka* (f)
tobacco	*ti*-ton	*tytoń* (m)
with filter	*sfeel*-trem	*z filtrem*
without filter	bes *feel*-tra	*bez filtra*

SIZES & COMPARISONS — ROZMIARY I PORÓWNANIA

small	*ma*-wi/a	*mały/a*
big	*doo*-zhi/a	*duży/a*
heavy	*chensh*-kee/a	*ciężki/a*
light	*lek*-kee/a	*lekki/a*
little (amount)	*ma*-wo	*mało*
a little bit	*tro*-he	*trochę*
too little	za *ma*-wo	*za mało*
much/many	*doo*-zho	*dużo*
too much/many	za *doo*-zho	*za dużo*
more	*vyen*-tsey	*więcej*
less	mnyey	*mniej*
enough	vis-*tar*-chi	*wystarczy*
also	*tak*-zhe	*także*

WYŻYWIENIE FOOD

Poland has for centuries been a cosmopolitan country, and its food has been influenced by various cuisines. The Jewish, Lithuanian, Belarusian, Ukrainian, Russian, Hungarian and German traditions have all made their mark. Polish food is hearty and filling – with thick soups and sauces, potatoes and dumplings – and is rich in meat, if not in vegetables.

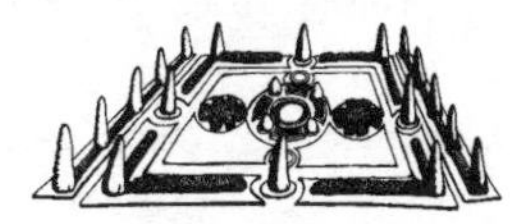

THROUGH THE DAY W CIĄGU DNIA

Poles start off their day with *śniadanie*, 'breakfast', which is roughly similar to its Western counterpart. For some people, the second meal is the *drugie śniadanie* (lit: second breakfast), which is often just a sandwich or other snack eaten somewhere between 10 am and noon. (See page 123 for breakfast foods.)

The most important and substantial meal of the day is the *obiad*, which is normally eaten somewhere between 1 and 5 pm. *Obiad* has no direct equivalent in English – judging by its contents, it's closer to Western dinner, but the timing is closer to lunch. Put simply, it's a dinner at lunch time.

The last meal is *kolacja*, 'supper', which is usually much lighter than the *obiad*. It often consists of foods similar to those eaten at breakfast.

breakfast	shnya-*da*-nye	*śniadanie* (neut)
lunch/dinner	*o*-byat	*obiad* (m)
main course	*droo*-gye *da*-nye	*drugie danie* (neut)
snack	pshe-*kon*-ska	*przekąska* (f)
supper	ko-*la*-tsya	*kolacja* (f)

VEGETARIAN & SPECIAL MEALS — DLA JAROSZY

The overwhelming majority of Poles are avid meat-eaters and don't consider a lunch or dinner a serious meal if it comes without a chunk of meat. This said, vegetarians won't starve in Poland, as most restaurants and cafes offer a selection of vegetarian dishes, called *dania jarskie*, though this isn't always an inspiring choice.

Exclusively vegetarian restaurants are rare, but there will almost always be a cafeteria, bistro, salad bar or other eatery around which will sport some veggie fare. (See page 129 for vegetarian dishes.)

I'm a vegetarian.
yes-tem ya-*ro*-shem/ ya-*rosh*-kom — *Jestem jaroszem/ jaroszką.* (m/f)

I don't eat meat.
nye *ya*-dam *myen*-sa — *Nie jadam mięsa.*

I don't eat chicken or fish.
nye *ya*-dam *dro*-byoo *a*-nee rip — *Nie jadam drobiu ani ryb.*

I can't eat dairy products.
nye *mo*-ge yeshch pro-*dook*-toof *mlech*-nih — *Nie mogę jeść produktów mlecznych.*

Do you have any vegetarian dishes?
chi som *ya*-kyesh *da*-nya *yar*-skye? — *Czy są jakieś dania jarskie?*

Does this dish have meat?
chi to *da*-nye za-*vye*-ra *myen*-so? — *Czy to danie zawiera mięso?*

Can I get this without meat?
chi *mo*-ge to *dos*-tach bes *myen*-sa? — *Czy mogę to dostać bez mięsa?*

Does it contain eggs?
chi to za-*vye*-ra *yay*-ka? — *Czy to zawiera jajka?*

I'm allergic to ...
mam oo-choo-*le*-nye na ... — *Mam uczulenie na ...*

without meat
bez-*myen*-sni/a — *bezmięsny/a*

FOOD

BREAKFAST ŚNIADANIE

Polish breakfast usually includes bread with butter, cheese, jam, and sausage or ham. Eggs are fairly popular, and can be prepared in a variety of guises such as soft-boiled, fried and scrambled. All this is washed down with a glass of tea or a cup of coffee with milk.

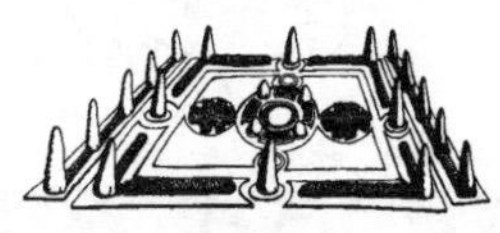

bacon	*bo*-chek	*boczek* (m)
butter	*ma*-swo	*masło* (neut)
cheese	ser	*ser* (m)
coffee	*ka*-va	*kawa* (f)
ham	*shin*-ka	*szynka* (f)
honey	myoot	*miód* (m)
jam	djem	*dżem* (m)
margarine	mar-ga-*ri*-na	*margaryna* (f)
milk	*mle*-ko	*mleko* (neut)
sandwich	ka-*nap*-ka	*kanapka* (f)
sausage	kyew-*ba*-sa	*kiełbasa* (f)
tea	her-*ba*-ta	*herbata* (f)
bread	hlep	*chleb* (m)
bread roll	boo-*wech*-ka	*bułeczka* (f)
dark rye bread	hlep ra-*zo*-vi	*chleb razowy* (m)
white bread	*boow*-ka	*bułka* (f)
toast	*gzhan*-ka	*grzanka* (f)
eggs	*yay*-ka	*jajka* (neut)
with bacon/ ham	na *boch*-koo/ *shin*-tse	*na boczku/ szynce* (neut)
fried eggs	*yay*-ka sa-*dzo*-ne	*jajka sadzone* (neut, pl)
hard-boiled egg	*yay*-ko na *tfar*-do	*jajko na twardo* (neut)
scrambled eggs	ya-yech-*nee*-tsa	*jajecznica* (f)
soft-boiled egg	*yay*-ko na *myenk*-ko	*jajko na miękko* (neut)

EATING OUT — JEDZENIE NA MIEŚCIE

Where's the nearest ...?	gdje yest nay-*bleesh*-shi ...?	*Gdzie jest najbliższy ...?*
coctail bar	*kok*-tail bar	*cocktail bar*
cafe	ka-*vyar*-nya	*kawiarnia*
cafeteria	bar *mlech*-ni	*bar mleczny*
restaurant	res-ta-oo-*ra*-tsya/ yad-*wo*-*day*-nya	*restauracja/ jadłodajnia*

OUT TO EAT

The main place for a meal with table service is the *restauracja*, 'restaurant'. You'll come across many, especially in major cities, which range from unpretentious budget eateries up to a la carte.

Another place to eat is a *kawiarnia*, 'cafe'. Unlike in communist Poland, when cafes provided little apart from sweets and drinks, most now offer meals which may be more attractive and often cheaper than those of some restaurants.

The cheapest place to eat is a *bar mleczny* (lit: milk bar), a sort of no-frills, self-service cafeteria. They were created to provide cheap food for the less affluent, and were once subsidised by the state. The free-market economy forced many to close, but a number have survived. They offer mostly vegetarian fare, including Polish specialities, but also feature a choice of meat dishes. They are no-smoking, no-alcohol territory.

Another type of budget eatery, the *jadłodajnia*, is rougly similar to a *bar mleczny* (self-service, no alcohol, no smoking), though a little more expensive. Many have a family atmosphere and the food usually tastes home-cooked. Some of these places are excellent value.

For a dessert or a sweet snack try a *cocktail bar* which serves not alcohol, but milkshakes (in Polish, *cocktails*, hence the name), ice cream, cakes, pastries, coffee, tea and the like.

Table for (four), please.
po-*pro*-she *sto*-leek dla (*chte*-reh *o*-soop) — *Poproszę stolik dla (czterech osób).*

Can I/we see the menu?
chi *mozh*-na *pro*-sheech o *kar*-te? — *Czy można prosić o kartę?*

What's the speciality here?
ya-ka yest spe-*tsyal*-noshch zak-*wa*-doo? — *Jaka jest specjalność zakładu?*

What do you recommend?
tso pan/*pa*-nee po-*le*-tsa? — *Co pan/pani poleca?*

Are the accompaniments included in the price?
chi do-*dat*-ki som vlee-*cho*-ne *ftse*-ne? — *Czy dodatki są wliczone w cenę.*

Can I have the bill, please?
po-*pro*-she o ra-*hoo*-nek? — *Poproszę o rachunek.*

ashtray	po-pyel-*neech*-ka	*popielniczka* (f)
bill	ra-*hoo*-nek	*rachunek* (m)
cup	fee-lee-*zhan*-ka	*filiżanka* (f)
fork	vee-*de*-lets	*widelec* (m)
glass (for tea, water, soft drinks)	*shklan*-ka	*szklanka* (f)
glass (for wine and spirits)	kye-*lee*-shek	*kieliszek* (m)
knife	noosh	*nóż* (m)
menu	*kar*-ta dan; ya-*dwos*-pees	*karta dań* (f); *jadłospis* (m)
napkin	ser-*vet*-ka	*serwetka* (f)
plate	*ta*-lesh	*talerz* (m)
spices	pshi-*pra*-vi	*przyprawy* (f, pl)
spoon	*wish*-ka	*łyżka* (f)
tablecloth	*o*-broos	*obrus* (m)
teaspoon	wi-*zhech*-ka	*łyżeczka* (f)
tip	na-*pee*-vek	*napiwek* (m)
waiter	*kel*-ner	*kelner* (m)
waitress	kel-*ner*-ka	*kelnerka* (f)

... dish	*da*-nye ...	*danie ...*
buffet	ba-*ro*-ve	*barowe*
fish	*rib*-ne	*rybne*
meat	*myen*-sne	*mięsne*
poultry	*sdro*-byoo	*z drobiu*
vegetarian	*yar*-skye	*jarskie*

POLISH CUISINE — KUCHNIA POLSKA

Poland's most internationally known dishes are *bigos* (sauerkraut cooked with different kinds of meat); *pierogi* (ravioli-like dumplings stuffed with a variety of fillings); and *barszcz* (red beetroot soup).

Favourite ingredients and herbs include dill, marjoram, caraway seeds and wild mushrooms.

Starters & Appetisers — Przekąski

boiled egg in mayonnaise
yay-ko vma-yo-*ne*-zhe — *jajko w majonezie*

carp in aspic
karp vga-la-*re*-che — *karp w galarecie*

herring in oil with onion
shlech vo-*le*-yoo — *śledź w oleju*

herring in sour cream
shlech fshmye-*ta*-nye — *śledź w śmietanie*

jellied pig's knuckles
noosh-kee vga-la-*re*-che — *nóżki w galarecie*

salad made with potato, vegetable and mayonnaise
sa-*wat*-ka ya-zhi-*no*-va — *sałatka jarzynowa*

sirloin, minced and raw
bef-shtik ta-*tar*-skee/*ta*-tar — *befsztyk tatarski/tatar*

smoked eel
ven-gosh ven-*dzo*-ni — *węgorz wędzony*

smoked salmon
wo-sosh ven-*dzo*-ni — *łosoś wędzony*

Soups — Zupy

barley, meat and vegetable soup
kroop-neek — *krupnik*

beef/chicken & noodle soup
ro-soow — *rosół*

dill cucumber soup
zoo-pa o-goor-*ko*-va — *zupa ogórkowa*

fruit soup
zoo-pa o-vo-*tso*-va — *zupa owocowa*

lentil soup
gro-*hoof*-ka — *grochówka*

mushroom soup
zoo-pa gzhi-*bo*-va — *zupa grzybowa*

potato soup
kar-to-*flan*-ka — *kartoflanka*

sauerkraut soup with potatoes
ka-*poosh*-nyak — *kapuśniak*

sorrel soup
zoo-pa shcha-*vyo*-va — *zupa szczawiowa*

tomato soup
zoo-pa po-mee-do-*ro*-va — *zupa pomidorowa*

tripe and vegetable bouillon
fla-kee/flach-kee — *flaki/flaczki*

vegetable soup
zoo-pa ya-zhi-*no*-va — *zupa jarzynowa*

beetroot broth ...	barshch (cher-*vo*-ni) ...	*barszcz (czerwony) ...*
with meat dumplings	zoosh-*ka*-mee	*z uszkami*
with pastry filled with minced meat	spash-te-*chee*-kyem	*z pasztecikiem*
with yogurt and vegetables, served cold	*hwod*-neek	*chłodnik*

Meat Dishes — Dania Mięsne

beef rolls stuffed with mushrooms and/or bacon, in sour cream *zra*-zi za-vee-*ya*-ne	*zrazy zawijane*
boiled beef served with horseradish *shtoo*-ka *myen*-sa	*sztuka mięsa*
boiled pig's knuckle served with horseradish go-*lon*-ka	*golonka*
cabbage leaves stuffed with minced beef and rice go-*womp*-kee	*gołąbki*
pork chop fried in breadcrumbs *kot*-let s-ha-*bo*-vi	*kotlet schabowy*
roasted pork seasoned with prunes s-hap pye-*cho*-ni	*schab pieczony*
sauerkraut, cabbage and meat stew *bee*-gos	*bigos*

OUT OF THE FRYING PAN

baked	pye-cho-ni/a	*pieczony/a*
boiled	go-to-va-ni/a	*gotowany/a*
braised	doo-sho-ni/a	*duszony/a*
fried	sma-zho-ni/a	*smażony/a*
grilled	zroosh-too	*z rusztu*
jellied; in aspic	vga-la-re-che	*w galarecie*
marinated	ma-ri-no-va-ni/a	*marynowany/a*
roasted	pye-cho-ni/a	*pieczony/a*
smoked	ven-dzo-ni/a	*wędzony/a*
spit-roasted	zrozh-na	*z rożna*
steamed	go-to-va-ni/a na pa-zhe	*gotowany/a na parze*
stewed	doo-sho-ni/a	*duszony/a*
stuffed	na-dje-va-ni/a	*nadziewany/a*

Vegetarian Dishes — Dania Jarskie

crepes served with various fillings
na-lesh-*nee*-kee — *naleśniki*

crepes with white, soft cheese
na-lesh-*nee*-kee *sse*-rem — *naleśniki z serem*

dumplings ...	pye-*ro*-gee ...	*pierogi ...*
with blueberries	zya-go-*da*-mee	*z jagodami*
with cottage cheese	*sse*-rem	*z serem*
with sauerkraut and wild mushrooms	ska-*poos*-tom ee gzhi-*ba*-mee	*z kapustą i grzybami*
with soft, white cheese and potatoes	*roos*-kye	*ruskie*

pancakes made with grated potatoes, egg and flour; usually served with sour cream and/or sugar
plats-kee kar-to-*fla*-ne/ zhem-nya-*cha*-ne — *placki kartoflane/ ziemniaczane*

potato dumplings, steamed
pi-zi — *pyzy*

pickled vegetables served raw
boo-kyet *zya*-zhin — *bukiet z jarzyn*

Desserts — Desery

apple cake	shar-*lot*-ka	*szarlotka*
apple strudel	yab-*wech*-neek	*jabłecznik*
biscuits	her-bat-*nee*-kee	*herbatniki*
cheesecake	*ser*-neek	*sernik*
confiture (confection)	kon-fee-*too*-ri	*konfitury*
cream cake	tort; *chas*-tko tor-*to*-ve	*tort; ciastko tortowe*
crepes with jam	na-lesh-*nee*-kee *zdje*-mem	*naleśniki z dżemem*
doughnut	*pon*-chek	*pączek*
dumplings filled with plums/cherries/apples	*kne*-dle	*knedle*
fruit cake	keks	*keks*
fruit compote	*kom*-pot	*kompot*
ginger bread	*pyer*-neek	*piernik*
ice cream	*lo*-di	*lody*
ice cream with fruit and whipped cream	*mel*-ba	*melba*
jelly dessert	*kee*-shel	*kisiel*
marble cake	*bap*-ka	*babka*
milk pudding	*boo*-din	*budyń*
pastry; small cake	*chas*-tko	*ciastko*
poppyseed strudel	ma-*ko*-vyets	*makowiec*
sweets/candy	tsoo-*kye*-rek	*cukierek*
waffles	*gof*-ri	*gofry*
whipped cream	*bee*-ta shme-*ta*-na	*bita śmietana*

MMM ... BEER ...

Local Polish beers include Żywiec, Okocim and EB. Beer's not always served cold in Poland, so if you like your brew chilled, ask for *zimne piwo*.

MENU DECODER

Polish letters with diacritical marks (ą, ć, ę and so on) are treated as separate letters. The order of letters is:

a ą b c ć d e ę f g h i j k l ł m n ń o ó p q r s ś t u v w x y z ź ż

baleron	cooked neck of pork (a kind of ham)
baranina	lamb/mutton
barszcz (czerwony) ...	beetroot broth ...
ukraiński	with beans and potatoes
zabielany	with sour cream
z pasztecikiem	with a savoury pastry filled with minced meat
z uszkami	with small, ravioli-style dumplings stuffed with meat
bażant	pheasant
befsztyk	beef steak
befsztyk tatarski	raw minced sirloin served with onion, raw egg yolk and often chopped dill cucumber
bigos	thick stew made of sauerkraut, cabbage and various kinds of meat and seasonings
bitki wołowe	beef cutlets
bliny	small, thick pancakes
botwinka	summertime soup made from the stems and leaves of baby beetroot; often includes a hard-boiled egg
bryzol	grilled beef steak
bukiet z jarzyn	mixed raw and pickled vegetables
bulion	broth
bułeczka	small bread roll
bułka	white bread
buraczki	grated beetroot
cebula	onion
chleb	bread
chłodnik	baby beetroot soup with yogurt and fresh vegetables, served cold, in summer only
chrzan	horseradish
ciastko	pastry; small cake

MENU DECODER

cielęcina	veal
czosnek	garlic
cynaderki	kidneys
ćwikła	boiled and grated beetroot with horseradish
danie	dish
deser	dessert
dodatki	accompaniments to main courses
dorsz	cod
drożdżówka	brioche; sweet yeast bun
drób	poultry
drugie danie	main course
drugie śniadanie	a light meal between breakfast and lunch
dziczyzna	game
dżem	jam
farsz	stuffing
fasola	beans
fasolka po bretońsku	baked beans in tomato sauce
faszerowany	stuffed
filet cielęcy	veal escalope
flaczki/flaki	seasoned tripe and vegetables cooked in bouillon
flądra	flounder
frytki	chips; French fries
galaretka	jelly
gęś	goose
gęś pieczona	roasted goose
gofry	thick, rectangular waffles served with toppings such as whipped cream, chocolate or jam
golonka	boiled pig's knuckle
gołąbki	cabbage leaves stuffed with minced beef and rice
grahamka	small wholemeal roll
greipfrut	grapefruit
groch	lentils
grochówka	lentil soup, sometimes served with croutons
groszek	green peas
grzanka	toasted bread

MENU DECODER

grzyby (marynowane)	(marinated) wild mushrooms
gulasz	goulash
herbata	tea
homar	lobster
imbir	ginger
indyk	turkey
jadłospis	menu
jagnię	lamb
jajecznica	scrambled eggs
jajka ...	eggs ...
na boczku	with bacon
na szynce	with ham
jajka sadzone	fried eggs
jajko w majonezie	hard boiled egg in mayonnaise
jarski	vegetarian
jarzyny	vegetables
kabanos	thin, dry, smoked pork sausage
kaczka ...	duck ...
pieczona	roasted
z jabłkami	roasted and stuffed with apples
kajzerka	small white round roll
kanapka	sandwich
kapusta	cabbage
kapusta kiszona/ kwaszona	sauerkraut
kapuśniak	sauerkraut soup
karp ...	carp ...
po grecku	served cold in an onion and tomato sauce
w galarecie	in aspic
z wody	boiled
karta dań	menu
karta win	wine list

MENU DECODER

kartofel	potato
kartoflanka	potato soup
kasza gryczana	buckwheat
kasza jęczmienna	pearl barley
kasza manna	semolina
kawa (neska)	(instant) coffee
kawa z ekspresu	espresso
kawa ze śmietanką	coffee with cream
kawior	caviar
kiełbasa ...	... sausage
z rożna	spit-roasted
z rusztu	grilled/barbecued
klopsiki/klopsy	meatballs
kluski	dumplings/noodles
knedle	dumplings stuffed with plums, cherries or apples
kolacja	evening meal
kołduny	dumplings
kopytka	potato dumplings, similar to gnocchi
korniszony	small pickled gherkins
kotlet (cielęcy)	(veal) cutlet/chop
kotlet de volaille	chicken breast fillet fried in breadcrumbs
kotlet mielony	minced-meat burger fried in breadcrumbs
kotlet schabowy	pork chop fried in breadcrumbs
krewetki	shrimps
krokiet	croquette
królik	rabbit
krupnik	thick barley soup with a variety of vegetables and small chunks of meat
kukurydza	maize
kurczak ...	... chicken
pieczony	roasted
z rożna	spit-roasted
leniwe pierogi	boiled dumplings with soft, white cheese
leszcz	bream

MENU DECODER

łosoś (wędzony)	(smoked) salmon
makaron	pasta/macaroni
makowiec	poppy seed strudel
marchewka z groszkiem	boiled carrots with green peas
marynowany/a	marinated
mielony/a	minced
mięso	meat
mizeria	sliced, fresh cucumber in sour cream
nadzienie	stuffing
naleśniki ...	crepes/pancakes ...
z dżemem	with jam
z serem	with white, soft cheese
napój	drink
nóżki w galarecie	jellied pig's knuckles
obiad firmowy	set meal
obiady domowe	home-cooked set meals
obwarzanek	pretzel; ring-shaped hard savoury biscuit
ogórek kiszony/ kwaszony	dill cucumber
oliwki	olives
omlet ...	omelette ...
z dżemem	with jam
z pieczarkami	with mushrooms
ostrygi	oysters
panierowany/a	in breadcrumbs
papryka	capsicum/paprika
parówki z musztardą	boiled frankfurters served with mustard
pasztecik	savoury pastry stuffed with minced meat
pasztet (z drobiu)	(chicken) pate
pączek/pączki	doughnut/s (sg/pl)
pieczarki (z patelni)	(fried) button mushrooms
pieczeń ...	roasted ...
cielęca	veal
wieprzowa	pork
wołowa	beef

MENU DECODER

pieprz	pepper
pierogi ...	ravioli-like dumplings made from noodle dough, stuffed with various ingredients and boiled
leniwe	with curd cheese
ruskie	with soft, white cheese and potatoes
z jagodami	with blueberries
z kapustą i grzybami	with sauerkraut and wild mushrooms
z mięsem	with minced meat
z serem	with soft, white cheese
pikantny/a	spicy/hot
piwo ...	... beer
beczkowe	draught
butelkowe	bottled
placki kartoflane/ ziemniaczane	fried potato pancakes
polędwica	sirloin
polędwica pieczona	roasted sirloin steak
pomidor	tomato
por	leek
posiłek	meal
potrawa	dish/course
potrawy jarskie	vegetarian dishes
przekąska	snack
przekąski	appetisers; hors d'oeuvres
przyprawy	spices
przystawki	side dishes; accompaniments
pstrąg	trout
pyzy	ball-shaped, steamed potato dumplings
rak	crayfish
rolmops	marinated herring
rosół	beef or chicken bouillon
rosół z makaronem	bouillon with noodles
rumsztyk	rump steak

MENU DECODER

ryba/ryby ...	fish (sg/pl) ...
w galarecie	in aspic
ryż	rice
sałatka ...	... salad
jarzynowa	potato, vegetable and mayonnaise
owocowa	fruit
z pomidorów	tomato
schab	loin of pork
schab pieczony	roast loin of pork seasoned with prunes
serdelki	sausages similar to frankfurters, but thicker
sernik	cheesecake
siekany/a	chopped
słodki/a	sweet
sos ...	... sauce/gravy
chrzanowy	horseradish
grzybowy	mushroom
pomidorowy	tomato
specjalność zakładu	speciality of the house
spis potraw	menu
stek	steak
surowy/a	raw/uncooked
surówka	vegetable salad
surówka z kiszonej kapusty	sauerkraut, sometimes served with chopped apple and onion
szaszłyk	shish kebab
szczupak	pike
sznycel	escalope/schnitzel
szprotki	sprats (small herrings)
sztuka mięsa	boiled beef served with horseradish
szarlotka	apple cake
szynka	ham
śledź	herring
śledźw oleju	herring in oil
śledźw śmietanie	herring served in sour cream

MENU DECODER

tatar	minced sirloin, served raw with onion, raw egg yolk, and often chopped dill cucumber
tort	cream cake
tuńczyk	tuna
wafle	wafers
warzywa	vegetables
wątróbka	liver
węgorz (wędzony)	(smoked) eel
wieprzowina	pork
woda	water
wołowina	beef
zając	hare
zakąski	starters; appetisers; hors d'oeuvres
zapiekanka	half bread roll with cheese and mushrooms, baked and served hot
ziemniaki	potatoes
zioła	herbs
zrazy zawijane	beef rolls stuffed with mushrooms and/or bacon, stewed and served in a sour-cream sauce
zupa ...	... soup
cebulowa	onion
fasolowa	bean
grochowa	lentil
grzybowa	mushroom
jarzynowa	vegetable
mleczna	milk-based
ogórkowa	dill cucumber
owocowa	fruit
pomidorowa	tomato
rybna	fish
szczawiowa	sorrel
ziemniaczana	potato
żeberka	ribs
żurek (z kiełbasą)	sour rye-flour soup (with smoked pork sausage)

SELF-CATERING / SAMODZIELNE PRZYRZĄDZANIE POSIŁKÓW

Food can be bought in general stores, groceries, delicatessens and supermarkets. All these stock the usual range of staples, including a selection of bread, meat, fruit and vegetables.

There are also a range of specialty shops, such as greengrocers, bakeries and butchers, as well as markets, which can be found in most towns and city suburbs. (See page 110 for shops.)

Staple Foods / Podstawowe Produkty Żywnościowe

bread	hlep	*chleb* (m)
butter	*ma*-swo	*masło* (neut)
cheese	ser	*ser* (m)
egg	*yay*-ko	*jajko* (neut)
flour	*mon*-ka	*mąka* (f)
ham	*shin*-ka	*szynka* (f)
margarine	mar-ga-*ri*-na	*margaryna* (f)
milk	*mle*-ko	*mleko* (neut)
salt	sool	*sól* (f)
sugar	*tsoo*-kyer	*cukier* (m)
yogurt	*yo*-goort	*jogurt* (m)

Fish / Ryby

bream	leshch	*leszcz* (m)
carp	karp	*karp* (m)
caviar	*ka*-vyor	*kawior* (m)
cod	dorsh	*dorsz* (m)
crayfish	rak	*rak* (m)
eel	*ven*-gosh	*węgorz* (m)
fish	*ri*-ba	*ryba* (f)
flounder	*flon*-dra	*flądra* (f)
herring	shlech	*śledź* (m)
mackerel	ma-*kre*-la	*makrela* (f)
pike	*shchoo*-pak	*szczupak* (m)
salmon	*wo*-sosh	*łosoś* (m)
sardine	sar-*din*-ka	*sardynka* (f)
sprat	*shprot*-ka	*szprotka* (f)
trout	pstronk	*pstrąg* (m)
tuna	*toon*-chik	*tuńczyk* (m)

Meat — Mięso

beef	vo-wo-*vee*-na	*wołowina* (f)
frankfurter	pa-*roof*-ka	*parówka* (f)
game	djee-*chiz*-na	*dziczyzna* (f)
ham	*shin*-ka	*szynka* (f)
kidneys	tsi-na-*der*-kee	*cynaderki* (f, pl)
lknuckle	go-*lon*-ka	*golonka* (f)
amb	ba-ra-*nee*-na	*baranina*
liver	von-*troop*-ka	*wątróbka* (f)
(minced) meat	*myen*-so (mye-*lo*-ne)	*mięso (mielone)* (neut)
pork	vyep-sho-*vee*-na	*wieprzowina* (f)
rabbit	*kroo*-leek	*królik* (m)
ribs	zhe-*ber*-ka	*żeberka* (neut, pl)
sausage	kyew-*ba*-sa	*kiełbasa* (f)
sirloin	po-lent-*vee*-tsa	*polędwica* (f)
tongue	*o*-zoor	*ozór* (m)
veal	che-len-*chee*-na	*cielęcina* (f)

Poultry — Drób

chicken	*koor*-chak	*kurczak* (m)
duck	*kach*-ka	*kaczka* (f)
goose	gensh	*gęś* (f)
pheasant	*ba*-zhant	*bażant* (m)
turkey	*een*-dik	*indyk* (m)

Seafood — Owoce Morza

lobster	*ho*-mar	*homar* (m)
mussels	*maw*-zhe	*małże* (f, pl)
oysters	os-*tri*-gee	*ostrygi* (f, pl)
shrimp	kre-*vet*-ka	*krewetka* (f)

Vegetables — Warzywa

asparagus	shpa-*ra*-gee	*szparagi* (m, pl)
beans	fa-*so*-la	*fasola* (f)
beetroot	boo-*ra*-kee	*buraki* (m, pl)
Brussels sprouts	brook-*sel*-ka	*brukselka* (f)
cabbage	ka-*poos*-ta	*kapusta* (f)
capsicum	pa-*pri*-ka	*papryka* (f)
carrot	*mar*-hef	*marchew* (f)
cauliflower	ka-*la*-fyor	*kalafior* (m)
celery	*se*-ler	*seler* (m)
corn (maize)	koo-koo-*ri*-dza	*kukurydza* (f)
cucumber	o-*goo*-rek	*ogórek* (m)
endive	tsi-*ko*-rya	*cykoria* (f)
green string beans	fa-*so*-la shpa-*ra*-go-va	*fasola szparagowa* (f)
horseradish	hshan	*chrzan* (m)
leek	por	*por* (m)
lettuce	sa-*wa*-ta	*sałata* (f)
onion	tse-*boo*-la	*cebula* (f)
peas	*gro*-shek	*groszek* (m)
potato	*zhem*-nyak	*ziemniak* (m)
	kar-*to*-fel	*kartofel* (m)
pumpkin	*di*-nya	*dynia* (f)
radish	zhot-*kyef*-ka	*rzodkiewka* (f)
spinach	*shpee*-nak	*szpinak* (m)
tomato	po-*mee*-dor	*pomidor* (m)
vegetables	va-*zhi*-va	*warzywa* (neut, pl)
	ya-*zhi*-ni	*jarzyny* (f, pl)

Fruit & Nuts — Owoce i Orzechy

almond	*meeg*-daw	*migdał* (m)
apple	*yap*-ko	*jabłko* (neut)
apricot	mo-*re*-la	*morela* (f)
banana	*ba*-nan	*banan* (m)
blackcurrant	*char*-na po-*zhech*-ka	*czarna porzeczka* (f)
blueberry	ya-*go*-da	*jagoda* (f)
cherry	*veesh*-nya/	*wiśnia* (f)/
	che-*resh*-nya	*czereśnia* (f)

coconut	*o*-zheh ko-ko-*so*-vi	*orzech kokosowy* (m)
currant	po-*zhech*-ka	*porzeczka* (f)
dried fruit and nuts	ba-*kal*-ye	*bakalie* (f, pl)
fig	*fee*-ga	*figa* (f)
gooseberry	*ag*-rest	*agrest* (m)
grape	vee-no-*gro*-no	*winogrono* (neut)
grapefruit	*greyp*-froot	*grejpfrut* (m)
hazelnut	*o*-zheh las-*ko*-vi	*orzech laskowy* (m)
lemon	tsi-*tri*-na	*cytryna* (f)
mandarin	man-da-*rin*-ka	*mandarynka* (f)
orange	po-ma-*ran*-cha	*pomarańcza* (f)
peach	bzhos-*kfee*-nya	*brzoskwinia* (f)
peanut	o-*zhe*-shek *zhem*-ni	*orzeszek ziemny* (m)
pear	*groosh*-ka	*gruszka* (f)
pineapple	a-*na*-nas	*ananas* (m)
plum	*shleef*-ka	*śliwka* (f)
raisin	ro-*dzin*-ka	*rodzynka* (f)
raspberry	ma-*lee*-na	*malina* (f)
sour cherry	*veesh*-nya	*wiśnia* (f)
strawberry	troos-*kaf*-ka	*truskawka* (f)
walnut	*o*-zheh *vwos*-kee	*orzech włoski* (m)
watermelon	*ar*-boos	*arbuz* (m)
wild stawberry	po-*zhom*-ka	*poziomka* (f)

Dairy — Nabiał

cottage cheese	*tfa*-rook	*twaróg* (m)
cheese	ser *(zhoow*-ti)	*ser (żółty)* (m)
cheese spread	ser to-*pyo*-ni	*ser topiony* (m)
cream	shmye-*tan*-ka	*śmietanka* (f)
ewe's milk cheese	*brin*-dza	*bryndza* (f)
	os-*tsi*-pek	*oscypek* (m)
	osh-*chi*-pek	*oszczypek* (m)
hard cheese	ser *zhoow*-ti	*ser żółty* (m)
sour cream	shmye-*ta*-na	*śmietana* (f)
sour milk	*zshad*-we *mle*-ko	*zsiadłe mleko* (neut)
white, medium-soft cheese	ser *bya*-wi	*ser biały* (m)

Herbs, Spices & Condiments / Zioła i Przyprawy

basil	ba-*zi*-lya	*bazylia* (f)
caraway seeds	*kmee*-nek	*kminek* (m)
cinnamon	tsi-*na*-mon	*cynamon* (m)
cloves	gozh-*djee*-kee	*goździki* (m, pl)
dill	*ko*-per/ko-*pe*-rek	*koper* (m)/*koperek* (m)
garlic	*chos*-nek	*czosnek* (m)
ginger	*eem*-beer	*imbir* (m)
herb	*zho*-wo	*zioło* (neut)
marjoram	ma-ye-*ra*-nek	*majeranek* (m)
parsley	pyet-*roosh*-ka	*pietruszka* (f)
pepper	pyepsh	*pieprz* (m)
salt	sool	*sól* (f)
thyme	ti-*mya*-nek	*tymianek* (m)

BRING ON THE BIGOS

If there's one genuine traditional Polish dish, it's *bigos*. It's made of sauerkraut, fresh chopped cabbage and a variety of meats including pork, beef, game, sausage and bacon. All this is cooked on a very low flame for several hours and put aside to be reheated a few times, a process which allegedly enhances its flavour.

The whole operation takes a couple of days but the effect can be impressive – a well cooked, several-days-old bigos is mouthwatering. Everybody has their own mysterious recipe as far as the ingredients, spices and cooking time are concerned and you will never find two identical dishes.

Because it's so time-consuming, bigos doesn't often appear on restaurant menus and the dish you encounter under this name in cheap bars and other seedy eateries is a far cry from the real thing. The best place to try bigos is a private home and if you ever happen to get such an invitation, don't miss it. Bring along a bottle of good clear vodka; bigos tastes most delicious when it's washed down.

TOASTS

To the guests!	zdro-vye *gosh*-chee!	Zdrowie gości!
To the host!	zdro-vye gos-po-*da*-zha/ gos-po-*di*-nee!	Zdrowie gospodarza/ gospodyni! (m/f)
To the ladies!	zdro-vye pan!	Zdrowie pań!
Bon apetit!	smach-*ne*-go!	Smacznego!
Cheers!	na zdro-vye!	Na zdrowie! (lit: to the health!)

DRINKS — NAPOJE

Non-Alcoholic — Bezalkoholowe

black coffee	*char*-na *ka*-va	*czarna kawa* (f)
coffee (with milk)	*ka*-va (*zmle*-kyem)	*kawa* (*z mlekiem*) (f)
herbal tea	her-*ba*-ta zho-*wo*-va	*herbata ziołowa* (f)
tea with milk	ba-*var*-ka	*bawarka* (f)
tea ...	her-*ba*-ta ...	*herbata* ... (f)
with sugar	*stsoo*-krem	*z cukrem*
without sugar	bes *tsoo*-kroo	*bez cukru*
with a slice of lemon	stsi-*tri*-nom	*z cytryną*
... juice	sok ...	*sok* ... (m)
fruit	o-vo-*tso*-vi	*owocowy*
tomato	po-mee-do-*ro*-vi	*pomidorowy*
milk	*mle*-ko	*mleko* (neut)
milkshake	*kok*-tail	*cocktail* (m)
(mineral) water	*vo*-da (mee-ne-*ral*-na)	*woda (mineralna)* (f)

NA ZDROWIE!

Wódka is Poland's national drink, and Poles claim it was invented here. You can take it for granted that there's at least one emergency bottle in every home, and that it will appear on the table as soon as a visitor arrives. Moreover, it's supposed to be emptied by the time the guest leaves.

Plenty of situations revolve around a bottle of vodka, and you're likely to have a few opportunities to share one.

In Poland, vodka's drunk neat in glasses ranging from 25 to 100mL. Regardless of size, it's drunk in one gulp, or *do dna*, 'to the bottom'. Drinkers partake in a chunk of herring in oil or a sip of mineral water just after drinking, and glasses are refilled immediately for the next drink.

Polish vodka comes in a number of colours and flavours, from very sweet to extra-dry. Clear voda should be well-chilled, while coloured vodkas can be drunk warmer or at room temperature.

bimber	*beem*-ber	home-distilled vodka
jarzębiak	ya-*zhem*-byak	vodka flavoured with rowanberry
ŵmyśliwska	mish-*leef*-ska	vodka flavoured with juniper berries
nalewka	na-*lef*-ka	home-made spirit made from vodka flavoured with herbs and berries
wiśniówka	veesh-*nyoof*-ka	cherry-flavoured vodka
wódka (f)	*voot*-ka	vodka
żubrówka	zhoo-*broof*-ka	bison vodka (flavoured with grass from the Białowieża forest on which bison feed)
żytnia	*zhit*-nya	dry vodka

Alcoholic — Alkoholowe

beer	*pee*-vo	*piwo* (neut)
brandy	*ko*-nyak	*koniak* (m)
champagne	*sham*-pan	*szampan* (m)
grape brandy	*vee*-nyak	*winiak*
honey liquer	*kroop*-neek	*krupnik*
liqueur	*lee*-kyer	*likier*
mead	myoot *peet*-ni	*miód pitny*
mulled beer	*gzha*-nyets *spee*-va	*grzaniec z piwa*
mulled wine	*gzha*-nyets *zvee*-na	*grzaniec z wina*
plum brandy	shlee-vo-*vee*-tsa	*śliwowica*
rum	room	*rum*
... wine	*vee*-no ...	*wino* ... (neut)
dry	vi-*trav*-ne	*wytrawne*
red	cher-*vo*-ne	*czerwone*
sweet	*swot*-kye	*słodkie*
white	*bya*-we	*białe*

ZA MIASTEM

IN THE COUNTRY

CAMPING — CAMPING

Camping is fairly popular in Poland. There are plenty of campsites throughout the country, in cities, towns and the countryside. Camping's also possible outside official sites, on private and public land, after asking proprietors or administrators for permission.

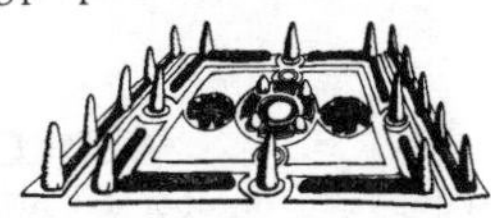

Is there a campsite nearby?
chi yest *ya*-keesh *kam*-peenk fpob-*lee*-zhoo? — *Czy jest jakiś camping w pobliżu?*

Where's the nearest campsite?
gdje yest nay-*bleesh*-shi *kam*-peenk? — *Gdzie jest najbliższy camping?*

Do you have room for a tent and a car?
chi yest *myey*-stse na *na*-myot ee sa-*mo*-hoot? — *Czy jest miejsce na namiot i samochód?*

Where can we pitch our tent?
gdje *mozh*-na *roz*-beech *na*-myot? — *Gdzie można rozbić namiot?*

Are there shower facilities?
chi som prish-*nee*-tse? — *Czy są prysznice?*

Is there hot water?
chi yest *chep*-wa *vo*-da? — *Czy jest ciepła woda?*

How much is it for a ...?	*ee*-le kosh-*too*-ye za ...?	*Ile kosztuje za ...?*
car	sa-*mo*-hoot	*samochód*
caravan	pshi-*che*-pe	*przyczepę*
night	nots	*noc*
person	o-*so*-be	*osobę*
tent	*na*-myot	*namiot*

camping	*kam*-peenk	*camping* (m)
campsite	*kam*-peenk	*camping* (m)
caravan (trailer)	pshi-*che*-pa (kam-peen-*go*-va)	*przyczepa (campingowa)* (f)
mattress	ma-*te*-rats	*materac* (m)
penknife	stsi-*zo*-rik	*scyzoryk* (m)
sleeping bag	*shpee*-voor	*śpiwór* (m)
tent	*na*-myot	*namiot* (m)
torch (flashlight)	la-*tar*-ka	*latarka* (f)

HIKING — WĘDRÓWKI PIESZ[KI]

Hiking is the most popular of outdoor activities in Poland, wit[h] hundreds of kilometres of marked trails running through the mos[t] attractive areas of the countryside, particularly in the mountain[s] along the country's southern border.

The most popular hiking routes are in the Tatra Mountains but there are many other amazing trails in the Pieniny, Bieszczad[y] and Karkonosze mountains, to mention just a few.

Where can I find out about hiking trails in the area?
gdje *znay*-de een-for-*ma*-tsye o *shla*-kah too-ris-*tich*-nih po o-ko-*lee*-tsi?
Gdzie znajdę informację o szlakach turystycznych po okolicy?

Which are the good walking trails around here?
ya-kye too som *do*-bre *shla*-kee too-ris-*tich*-ne?
Jakie tu są dobre szlaki turystyczne?

Is there a map of the trails?
chi yest *ya*-kash *ma*-pa *shla*-koof?
Czy jest jakaś mapa szlaków?

Is this trail easy/difficult?
chi ten shlak yest *wat*-fi/*trood*-ni?
Czy ten szlak jest łatwy/trudny?

Is this trail well marked?
chi ten shlak yest *do*-bzhe oz-na-ko-*va*-ni?
Czy ten szlak jest dobrze oznakowany?

How long is this trail?
yak *dwoo*-gee yest ten shlak? *Jak długi jest ten szlak?*

How many hours to ...?
ee-le *go*-djeen do ...? *Ile godzin do ...?*

Are there any campsites along the way?
chi som *ya*-kyesh kam-*peen*-geepo *dro*-dze? *Czy są jakieś campingi po drodze?*

Is there a shorter route?
chi yest *ya*-kash *kroot*-sha *tra*-sa? *Czy jest jakaś krótsza trasa?*

Which is the easiest way?
ktoo-ra *dro*-ga yest nay-wat-*fyey*-sha? *Która droga jest najłatwiejsza?*

What time does it get dark?
o *ktoo*-rey she *shchem*-nya? *O której się ściemnia?*

Where can we buy supplies?
gdje *mozh*-na *koo*-peech *pro*-vyant? *Gdzie można kupić prowiant?*

On the Path — Na Szlaku

Where have you come from?
skont pan/*pa*-nee *ee*-dje? — *Skąd pan/pani idzie?* (pol)
skont *ee*-djesh? — *Skąd idziesz?* (inf)

How far is it from here?
yak to da-*le*-ko stont? — *Jak to daleko stąd?*

Does this trail go to ...?
chi ten shlak *ee*-dje do ...? — *Czy ten szlak idzie do ...?*

Which is the trail to ...?
ktoo-ri shlak *ee*-dje do ...? — *Który szlak idzie do ...?*

I'm lost.
zgoo-*bee*-wem/wam she — *Zgubiłem/łam się* (m/f).

Where can we spend the night?
gdje *mozh*-na she za-*tshi*-mach *na* nots? — *Gdzie można się zatrzymać na noc?*

altitude	vi-*so*-koshch	*wysokość* (f)
backpack	*ple*-tsak	*plecak* (m)
binoculars	lor-*net*-ka	*lornetka* (f)
candles	*shfye*-tse	*świece* (f, pl)
to climb	*fspee*-nach she	*wspinać się*
compass	*kom*-pas	*kompas* (m)
downhill	vdoow	*w dół*
first-aid kit	ap-*tech*-ka *pyer*-fshey po-*mo*-tsi	*apteczka pierwszej pomocy* (f)
gloves	ren-ka-*veech*-kee	*rękawiczki* (f, pl)
guide	pshe-*vod*-neek	*przewodnik* (m)
to hike	ven-*dro*-vach	*wędrować*
hiking	ven-*droof*-kee *pye*-she	*wędrówki piesze* (f, pl)

LOVEBIRDS

Everyone knows that storks bring babies. In Poland, it's also believed that storks bring good luck. Each summer, the country plays host to 30,000 white stork couples, whose favourite nesting places include Masuria and Podlasie.

hiking boots	*boo*-ti tre-keen-*go*-ve	*buty trekingowe* (m, pl)
lookout	poonkt vee-do-*ko*-vi	*punkt widokowy* (m)
map	*ma*-pa	*mapa* (f)
mountain climbing	fspee-*nach*-ka *goor*-ska	*wspinaczka górska* (f)
provisions	*pro*-vyant	*prowiant* (m)
rock climbing	fspee-*nach*-ka *skal*-na	*wspinaczka skalna* (f)
rope	*lee*-na	*lina* (f)
steep	*stro*-mi/a	*stromy*
trek	trek	*trek*
uphill	pot *goo*-re	*pod górę*
view	*vee*-dok	*widok* (m)

AT THE BEACH — NA PLAŻY

Poland's Baltic seacoast has sandy beaches along almost its entire 524-km length. Some of the most beautiful and least polluted beaches are on the central coast near the town of Łeba, but there are many other attractive sandy stretches elsewhere along the seaside.

Can we swim here?
chi too *mozh*-na *pwi*-vach? — *Czy tu można pływać?*

Is it safe to swim here?
chi too yest bes-*pyech*-nye *pwi*-vach? — *Czy tu jest bezpiecznie pływać?*

beach	*pla*-zha	*plaża* (f)
diving	noor-ko-*va*-nye	*nurkowanie* (neut)
lifeguard	ra-*tov*-neek	*ratownik* (m)
rock	*ska*-wa	*skała* (f)
sand	*pya*-sek	*piasek* (m)
sea	*mo*-zhe	*morze* (neut)
sunglasses	o-koo-*la*-ri swo-*nech*-ne	*okulary słoneczne* (pl)
swimming	pwi-*va*-nye	*pływanie* (neut)
towel	*rench*-neek	*ręcznik* (m)
wave	*fa*-la	*fala* (f)

WEATHER — POGODA

Poland has a transitional climate, influenced by a continental climate from the east and a maritime climate from the west. It's characterised by four clearly differentiated seasons and changing weather, with significant differences from day to day, season to season and year to year.

SEASONS

spring	*vyos*-na	*wiosna* (f)
summer	*la*-to	*lato* (neut)
autumn	*ye*-shen	*jesień* (f)
winter	*zee*-ma	*zima* (f)

What's the weather like?
ya-ka yest po-*go*-da? — *Jaka jest pogoda?*

The weather's fine/bad.
yest *wad*-nye/ *bzhit*-ko — *Jest ładnie/brzydko.*

It's raining.
pa-da deshch — *Pada deszcz.*

Fortunately, it's not raining.
tsa-we *shchen*-shche zhe nye *pa*-da — *Całe szczęście że nie pada.*

It's snowing.
pa-da shnyek — *Pada śnieg.*

What a lovely day!
tso za tsoo-*dov*-ni djen! — *Co za cudowny dzień!*

What's the temperature?
ya-ka yest tem-pe-ra-*too*-ra? — *Jaka jest temperatura?*

What's the weather forecast for tomorrow?
ya-ka yest pro-*gno*-za po-*go*-di na *yoo*-tro? — *Jaka jest prognoza pogody na jutro?*

Today it's ...	djeesh yest ...	*Dziś jest ...*
Tomorrow it'll be ...	*yoo*-tro *ben*-dje ...	*Jutro będzie ...*
cloudy	poh-*moor*-nye	*pochmurnie*
cold	*zheem*-no	*zimno*
hot	go-*ron*-tso	*gorąco*
sunny	swo-*nech*-nye	*słonecznie*
warm	*chep*-wo	*ciepło*
windy	*vyech*-nye	*wietrznie*

climate	*klee*-mat	*klimat* (m)
cloud	*hmoo*-ra	*chmura* (f)
fog	mgwa	*mgła* (f)
forecast	pro-*gno*-za	*prognoza* (f)
frost	mroos	*mróz* (m)
hail	grat	*grad* (m)
heat	*oo*-paw	*upał* (m)
ice	loot	*lód* (m)
lightning	bwis-ka-*vee*-tsa	*błyskawica* (f)
rain	deshch	*deszcz* (m)
snow	shnyek	*śnieg* (m)
storm	*boo*-zha	*burza* (f)
sun	*swon*-tse	*słońce* (neut)
sunrise	fs-hoot *swon*-tsa	*wschód słońca* (m)
sunset	*za*-hoot *swon*-tsa	*zachód słńca* (m)
temperature	tem-pe-ra-*too*-ra	*temperatura* (f)
thunder	gzhmot	*grzmot* (m)
weather	po-*go*-da	*pogoda* (f)
wind	vyatr	*wiatr* (m)

MORZE VS MOŻE

Don't confuse *morze*, meaning 'sea', and *może*, 'perhaps'. Despite their different spellings, they sound the same, because *rz* sounds exactly like *ż*.

GEOGRAPHICAL TERMS — TERMINY GEOGRAFICZNE

bay	za-*to*-ka	*zatoka* (f)
beach	*pla*-zha	*plaża* (f)
cape	pshi-*lon*-dek	*przylądek* (m)
cave	yas-*kee*-nya	*jaskinia* (f)
cliff	oor-*vees*-ko	*urwisko* (neut)
creek	*stroo*-myen	*strumień* (m)
dune	*vid*-ma	*wydma* (f)
forest	las/ *poosh*-cha	*las* (m)/ *puszcza* (f)
gorge	*von*-voos	*wąwóz* (m)
hill	*vzgoo*-zhe	*wzgórze* (neut)
island	*vis*-pa	*wyspa* (f)
lake	ye-*zho*-ro	*jezioro* (neut)
marsh	*bag*-no	*bagno* (neut)
mountain	*goo*-ra	*góra* (f)
mountain range	*pas*-mo *goor*-skye	*pasmo górskie* (neut)
national park	park na-ro-*do*-vi	*park narodowy* (m)
pass	*pshe*-wench	*przełęcz* (f)
peak	shchit	*szczyt* (m)
peninsula	poow-*vi*-sep	*półwysep* (m)
plain	roov-*nee*-na	*równina* (f)
river	*zhe*-ka	*rzeka* (f)
road	*dro*-ga	*droga* (f)
rock	*ska*-wa	*skała* (f)
sea	*mo*-zhe	*morze* (neut)
slope	*zbo*-che	*zbocze* (neut)
spring	*zhroo*-dwo	*źródło* (neut)
stone	*ka*-myen	*kamień* (m)
stream	*stroo*-myen	*strumień* (m)
trail	shlak	*szlak* (m)
upland	vi-*zhi*-na	*wyżyna* (f)
valley	do-*lee*-na	*dolina* (f)
waterfall	vo-*dos*-pat	*wodospad* (m)

DIRECTIONS — KIERUNKI

north	*poow*-nots	*północ* (f)
south	po-*wood*-nye	*południe* (neut)
east	fs-hoot	*wschód* (m)
west	*za*-hoot	*zachód* (m)

SIGNS

KĄPIEL WZBRONIONA	NO SWIMMING
PLAŻA (NIE)STRZEŻONA	(UN)GUARDED BEACH

FAUNA — FAUNA

Largely depleted by the last ice age 10,000 years ago, and then by centuries of human activities, Poland's wildlife is not particularly abundant nor extremely diverse. However, large areas of countryside are still relatively unaffected, and form a good natural habitat for wild animals and birds.

Animal-watching, particularly bird-watching, is increasingly on offer from local tour operators. Even without taking a tour, you have a good chance of spotting birds and the occasional deer or elk while travelling around some out-of-the-way rural areas.

What's that animal/bird called?
tso to za *zvye*-zhe/ptak? — *Co to za zwierzę/ptak?*

animal	*zvye*-zhe	*zwierzę* (neut)
bird	ptak	*ptak* (m)
fish	*ri*-ba	*ryba* (f)
insect	*o*-vat	*owad* (m)
mammal	ssak	*ssak* (m)
reptile	gat	*gad* (m)

Farm & Domesticated Animals — Zwierzęta Gospodarskie i Domowe

cat	kot	*kot* (m)
chicken	*koor*-chak	*kurczak* (m)
cow	*kro*-va	*krowa* (f)
dog	pyes	*pies* (m)
donkey	*o*-show	*osioł* (m)
duck	*kach*-ka	*kaczka* (f)
goat	*ko*-za	*koza* (f)
goose	gensh	*gęś* (f)
hen	*koo*-ra	*kura* (f)
horse	kon	*koń* (m)
pig	*shfee*-nya	*świnia* (f)
rabbit	*kroo*-leek	*królik* (m)
sheep	*of*-tsa	*owca* (f)

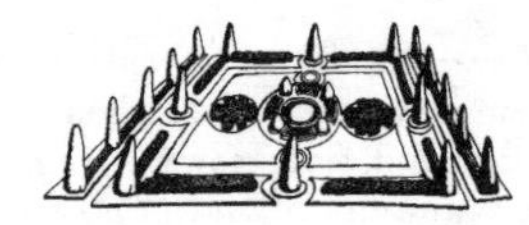

Wildlife — Dzika Zwierzyna

badger	*bor*-sook	*borsuk* (m)
beaver	boobr	*bóbr* (m)
elk	wosh	*łoś* (m)
fox	lees	*lis* (m)
frog	*zha*-ba	*żaba* (f)
hare	*za*-yonts	*zając* (m)
marmot	*shfees*-tak	*świstak* (m)
red deer/stag	*ye*-len	*jeleń* (m)
roe deer	*sar*-na	*sarna* (f)
snake	vonsh	*wąż* (m)
viper	*zhmee*-ya	*żmija* (f)
wild boar	djeek	*dzik* (m)
wolf	veelk	*wilk* (m)

Birds — Ptaki

blackbird	kos	*kos* (m)
cuckoo	koo-*koow*-ka	*kukułka* (f)
eagle	*o*-zhew	*orzeł* (m)
hawk	*yast*-shomb	*jastrząb* (m)
kingfisher	zhee-mo-*ro*-dek	*zimorodek* (m)
magpie	*sro*-ka	*sroka* (f)
nightingale	*swo*-veek	*słowik* (m)
owl	*so*-va	*sowa* (f)
pigeon	*go*-womp	*gołąb* (m)
raven	krook	*kruk* (m)
skylark	sko-*vro*-nek	*skowronek* (m)
sparrow	*vroo*-bel	*wróbel* (m)
stork	*bo*-chan	*bocian* (m)
swallow	yas-*koow*-ka	*jaskółka* (f)
woodpecker	*djen*-chow	*dzięcioł* (m)

Fish — Ryby

eel	*ven*-gosh	*węgorz* (m)
herring	shlech	*śledź* (m)
perch	*o*-kon	*okoń* (m)
pike	*shchoo*-pak	*szczupak* (m)
trout	pstronk	*pstrąg* (m)

Insects — Owady

ant	*mroof*-ka	*mrówka* (f)
bee	*pshcho*-wa	*pszczoła* (f)
bug	*ploos*-kfa	*pluskwa* (f)
butterfly	*mo*-til	*motyl* (m)
cockroach	ka-*ra*-looh	*karaluch* (m)
fly	*moo*-ha	*mucha* (f)
mosquito	*ko*-mar	*komar* (m)
spider	*pa*-yonk	*pająk* (m)
wasp	*o*-sa	*osa* (f)

FLORA — FLORA

Trees — Drzewa

beech	book	*buk* (m)
birch	*bzho*-za	*brzoza* (f)
chestnut tree	*kash*-tan	*kasztan* (m)
fir	*yo*-dwa	*jodła* (f)
larch	*mod*-zhef	*modrzew* (m)
leaf	leeshch	*liść* (m)
maple	klon	*klon* (m)
oak	domp	*dąb* (m)
pine	*sos*-na	*sosna* (f)
spruce	shfyerk	*świerk* (m)
tree	*dzhe*-vo	*drzewo* (neut)
willow	*vyezh*-ba	*wierzba* (f)

Flowers — Kwiaty

carnation	*gozh*-djeek	*goździk* (m)
flower	kfyat	*kwiat* (m)
lily	*lee*-lya	*lilia* (f)
rose	*roo*-zha	*róża* (f)
sunflower	swo-*nech*-neek	*słonecznik* (m)
tulip	too-*lee*-pan	*tulipan* (m)

Crops — Plony

barley	*yench*-myen	*jęczmień* (m)
corn	*zbo*-zhe	*zboże* (neut)
oats	*o*-vyes	*owies* (m)
rye	*zhi*-to	*żyto* (neut)
wheat	pshe-*nee*-tsa	*pszenica* (f)

FESTIWALE I ŚWIĘTA — FESTIVALS & HOLIDAYS

PUBLIC HOLIDAYS — ŚWIĘTA PAŃSTWOWE

Nowy Rok — *no*-vi rok
New Year's Day (1 January)
like in many countries of the world, 1 January is a quiet holiday, during which people recover after heavy partying all the night of New Year's Eve (*Sylwester*), with much drink, smoke and fireworks

Wielkanoc — vyel-*ka*-nots
Easter (March/April)
Easter is one of Poland's most important religious feasts. Celebrations start on Palm Sunday (*Niedziela Palmowa*) and go for the whole Holy Week (*Wielki Tydzień*) until Easter Monday (*Poniedziałek Wielkanocny*). A solemn breakfast on Easter Sunday (*Niedziela Wielkanocna*) features the consecrated food, including the painted Easter eggs (*jajka wielkanocne*).

Święto Pracy — *shfyen*-to *pra*-tsi
Labour Day (1 May)
possibly the most important non-religious holiday in communist Poland, celebrated with mass parades, it's nowadays a low-profile event

Święto Konstytucji 3-go Maja — *shfyen*-to kon-sti-*too*-tsyee tshe-*che*-go *ma*-ya
3 May Constitution Day
this holiday commemorates the constitution of 1791, passed in Warsaw on the 3 of May (and commonly referred to as such). It was the world's first fully liberal constitution after the one in the US.

Boże Ciało *bo*-zhe *cha*-wo
Corpus Christi (a Thursday in May or June)
this important religious day features church masses and processions all over the country, with the most elaborate celebrations taking place in Łowicz, near Warsaw

Wniebowzięcie vnye-bo-*vzhen*-che
Assumption (15 August)
another major religious day, it culminates at Częstochowa, Poland's spiritual capital, where mass pilgrimages from all around the country come for this holy day

Święto Zmarłych *shfyen*-to *zmar*-wih
All Souls' Day (1 November)
a day of remembrance and prayer for the souls of the dead, when people visit cemeteries to leave flowers, wreaths and lit candles on the graves of their relatives

Święto Niepodległości *shfyen*-to nye-pod-leg-*wosh*-chee
Independence Day (11 November)
this holiday is held to commemorate 11 November 1918, the day Poland regained its independence after 123 years under foreign occupation

Boże Narodzenie *bo*-zhe na-ro-*dze*-nye
Christmas (25 December)
arguably the most important religious event of the year. Unlike in English-speaking countries, the most celebrated day is Christmas Eve (*Wigilia*), featuring a solemn family supper which traditionally should consist of 12 courses.

After the meal, Santa Claus (*Święty Mikołaj*) will hand out gifts from under the Christmas tree (*choinka*). Many people will then go to church for the midnight mass (*pasterka*).

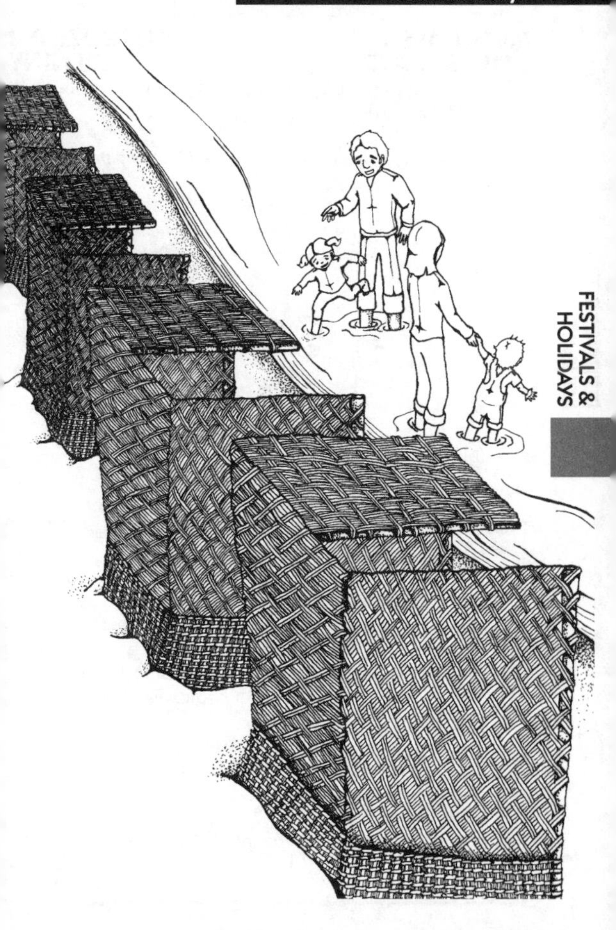

BIRTHDAYS & SAINTS' DAYS — URODZINY I IMIENINY

Unlike in most countries, saints' days in Poland are usually more celebrated than birthdays.

When's your ...?	*kye*-di som *pa*-na/ *pa*-nee ...?	*Kiedy są pana/ pani ...?* (pol)
	kye-di som *tfo*-ye ...?	*Kiedy są twoje ...?* (inf)
birthday	oo-ro-*djee*-ni	*urodziny* (pl)
saint's day	ee-mye-*nee*-ni	*imieniny* (pl)

HAPPY MIRTHDAY TO YOU!

The Polish counterpart to 'Happy birthday to you' is *Sto lat* or 'Happy 100 years to you'. As in English, it's sung to a toast and can be repeated depending on the mood of the guests. The difference is that it's suitable for various occasions, including birthdays, saints' days and weddings. It begins like this:

sto lat sto lat nyeh *zhi*-ye *zhi*-ye nam
Sto lat, sto lat, niech żyje żyje nam
yesh-che ras *yesh*-che ras
nyeh *zhi*-ye *zhi*-ye nam ...
Jeszcze raz, jeszcze raz, niech żyje żyje nam ...

WEDDINGS — ŚLUBY I WESELA

Congratulations!
gra-too-*la*-tsye! — *Gratulacje!*

CONGRATULATIONS

Polish has many ways of congratulating people. The following are some of the most popular universal expressions used for birthdays, saint's days and other occasions, in both formal and informal situations. They all roughly mean 'all the best'.

fshis-*tkye*-go nay-lep-*she*-go!	*Wszystkiego najlepszego!*
fshis-*tkye*-go do-*bre*-go!	*Wszystkiego dobrego!*
po-mishl-*nosh*-chee!	*Pomyślności!*
doo-zho *shchen*-shcha!	*Dużo szczęścia!*
doo-zho *zdro*-vya!	*Dużo zdrowia!*
po-vo-*dze*-nya!	*Powodzenia!*

To the bride and groom!
nyeh *zhi*-yom *pan*-stfo *mwo*-djee! — *Niech żyją państwo młodzi!*

engagement	za-ren-*chi*-ni	*zaręczyny* (pl)
honeymoon	*mye*-shonts myo-*do*-vi	*miesiąc miodowy* (m)
wedding (ceremony)	shloop	*ślub* (m)
wedding (reception)	ve-*se*-le	*wesele* (neut)
wedding anniversary	roch-*nee*-tsa *shloo*-boo	*rocznica ślubu* (f)
wedding cake	tort ve-*sel*-ni	*tort weselny* (m)
wedding present	*pre*-zent *shloob*-ni	*prezent ślubny* (m)

BLAST FROM THE PAST

'Skansen' is a Scandinavian word referring to an open-air ethnographic museum. Aimed at preserving the traditional folk culture and architecture, a skansen gathers together a selection of typical, mostly wooden rural buildings such as houses, barns, churches and mills, collected from the region and often reassembled to look like a natural village. The buildings are furnished and decorated in their original style, incorporating a variety of historical household equipment, tools, crafts and artefacts, giving an insight into the lives, work and customs of previous generations.

There are currently about 35 museums of this kind in Poland, scattered over most regions and featuring distinctive regional traits. They are called *muzeum budownictwa ludowego*, 'museums of folk architecture', *muzeum wsi*, 'museums of the village', or *park etnograficzny*, 'ethnographic parks', but the Scandinavian term 'skansen' applies to them all.

Most have been set up by collecting buildings from across the region, but there are also some small in situ skansens, including those in Kluki and Osiek. Skansens usually focus on general aspects of local culture, but also have specialised, such as the beekeeping skansen in Swarzędz. Poland's largest skansens include those in Sanok, Ciechanowiec, Lublin, Tokarnia, Nowy Sącz and Dziekanowice.

ZDROWIE HEALTH

Every Polish city and town has health and medical facilities, and the bigger the place the more comprehensive and developed these facilities usually are.

Most minor health problems can be solved by applying an appropriate remedy bought from an *apteka*, 'chemist/pharmacy'. They are plentiful in all sizeable urban centres, and have qualified staff, some of whom speak English and may help you with advice on buying the right medication.

If an illness continues, you should seek a specialised doctor. One way to find one is to visit a *przychodnia*, 'outpatient clinic'. They are plentiful in cities and have physicians specialising in various disorders.

In the case of a more serious health problem, you may need the *szpital*, 'hospital' or *klinika* 'clinic'. These may be either government-run or private, and can mostly be found in major cities.

Where's the nearest ...?	gdje yest nay-*bleesh*-shi/a ...?	*Gdzie jest najbliższy/a ...?*
doctor	*le*-kash	*lekarz* (m)
dentist	den-*tis*-ta	*dentysta* (m)
chemist	ap-*te*-ka	*apteka* (f)
hospital	*shpee*-tal	*szpital* (m)
outpatient clinic	pshi-*hod*-nya	*przychodnia* (f)

AT THE DOCTOR — U LEKARZA

I'm sick.
yes-tem *ho*-ri/a — *Jestem chory/a.*

My friend is sick.
mooy pshi-*ya*-chel yest *ho*-ri — *Mój przyjaciel jest chory.* (m)
mo-ya pshi-ya-*choow*-ka yest *ho*-ra — *Moja przyjaciółka jest chora.* (f)

I need a doctor who speaks English.
pot-she-*boo*-ye le-*ka*-zha *ktoo*-ri *moo*-vee po an-*gyel*-skoo — *Potrzebuję lekarza który mówi po angielsku.*

It hurts here.
too-tay mnye *bo*-lee — *Tutaj mnie boli.*

I feel better/worse.
choo-ye she *le*-pyey/*go*-zhey — *Czuję się lepiej/gorzej.*

This is my usual medicine.
to yest lek *ktoo*-ri nor-*mal*-nye *byo*-re — *To jest lek który normalnie biorę.*

I've been vaccinated.
yes-tem zash-che-*pyo*-ni/a — *Jestem zaszczepiony/a.*

I don't want a blood transfusion.
nye htse trans-*foo*-zyee — *Nie chcę transfuzji.*

Can I have a receipt for my insurance?
po-*pro*-she o ra-*hoo*-nek dla mo-*ye*-go oo-bes-pye-*che*-nya — *Poproszę o rachunek dla mojego ubezpieczenia.*

AILMENTS — DOLEGLIWOŚCI

I'm ill.	*yes*-tem *ho*-ri/a	*Jestem chory/a.* (m/f)
I feel nauseous.	mam *mdwosh*-chee	*Mam mdłości.*
I've been vomiting.	vi-myo-to-*va*-wem/wam	*Wymiotowałem/łam.* (m/f)
I can't sleep.	nye *mo*-ge spach	*Nie mogę spać.*
I feel dizzy.	mam za-*vro*-ti *gwo*-vi	*Mam zawroty głowy.*
I feel shivery.	mam *dresh*-che	*Mam dreszcze.*
I feel weak.	*choo*-ye she *swa*-bo	*Czuję się słabo.*

HEALTH

I have (a/an) ...	mam ...	*Mam ...*
allergy	oo-choo-*le*-nye	*uczulenie*
anaemia	a-*ne*-mye	*anemię*
burn	o-pa-*zhe*-nye	*oparzenie*
cancer	*ra*-ka	*raka*
cold	pshe-zhem-*bye*-nye	*przeziębienie*
constipation	zat-far-*dze*-nye	*zatwardzenie*
cough	*ka*-shel	*kaszel*
diarrhoea	bye-*goon*-ke/ roz-vol-*nye*-nye	*biegunkę/ rozwolnienie*
fever	go-*ronch*-ke	*gorączkę*
headache	bool *gwo*-vi	*ból głowy*
hepatitis	zhoow-*tach*-ke	*żółtaczkę*
indigestion	nye-*strav*-noshch	*niestrawność*
infection	za-ka-*zhe*-nye	*zakażenie*
influenza	*gri*-pe	*grypę*
injury	*ra*-ne	*ranę*
lice	fshi	*wszy*
low/high blood pressure	*nees*-kye/vi-*so*-kye cheesh-*nye*-nye	*niskie/wysokie ciśnienie*
migraine	mee-*gre*-ne	*migrenę*
pain	bool	*ból*
rash	vi-*sip*-ke	*wysypkę*
sore throat	bool *gar*-dwa	*ból gardła*
sprain	zveeh-*nyen*-che	*zwichnięcie*
stomachache	bool zho-*won*-tka	*ból żołądka*
sunburn	o-pa-*zhe*-nye swo-*nech*-ne	*oparzenie słoneczne*
sunstroke	*oo*-dar swo-*nech*-ni	*udar słoneczny*
thrush	gzhi-*bee*-tse	*grzybicę*
toothache	bool *zem*-ba	*ból zęba*
travel sickness	ho-*ro*-be lo-ko-mo-*tsiy*-nom	*chorobę lokomocyjną*
venereal disease	ho-*ro*-be ve-ne-*rich*-nom	*chorobę weneryczną*
worms	ro-*ba*-kee	*robaki*

HEALTH

THEY MAY SAY ...

tso *pa*-noo/ *pa*-nee do-*le*-ga?	
Co panu/pani dolega?	What's the matter?
chi pan/*pa*-nee ot-*choo*-va *ya*-keesh bool?	
Czy pan/pani odczuwa jakiś ból?	Do you feel any pain?
gdje *pa*-na/ *pa*-nyom *bo*-lee?	
Gdzie pana/panią boli?	Where does it hurt?
chi pan/*pa*-nee ma go-*ronch*-ke?	
Czy pan/pani ma gorączkę?	Do you have a temperature?
yak *dwoo*-go yest pan/ *pa*-nee *ho*-ri/a?	
Jak długo jest pan/ pani chory/a?	How long have you been ill?
chi *bi*-wi stim pro-*ble*-mi *fchesh*-nyey?	
Czy były z tym problemy wcześniej?	Have you had this before?
chi pan/*pa*-nee *bye*-zhe *ya*-kyesh *le*-kee?	
Czy pan/pani bierze jakieś leki?	Are you on medication?
chi pan/*pa*-nee *pa*-lee?	
Czy pan/pani pali?	Do you smoke?
chi pan/*pa*-nee *pee*-ye?	
Czy pan/pani pije?	Do you drink?
chi pan/*pa*-nee *za*-zhi-va nar-ko-*ti*-kee?	
Czy pan/pani zażywa narkotyki?	Do you take drugs?

THEY MAY SAY ...

chi ma pan/*pa*-nee *ya*-kyesh oo-choo-*le*-nye?	
Czy ma pan/pani jakieś uczulenie?	Are you allergic to anything?
chi *pa*-nee ma mye-*shonch*-ke?	
Czy pani ma miesiączkę?	Are you menstruating?
chi yest *pa*-nee *fchon*-zhi?	
Czy jest pani w ciąży?	Are you pregnant?

WOMEN'S HEALTH — ZDROWIE KOBIETY

The usual Polish terms for 'doctor' are *lekarz* (m) and *lekarka* (f), but the old-fashioned, formal *doktor* and *doktór* remain in common use. Both nouns are masculine, so if you're addressing or talking about a female doctor, you should use *pani doktor* or *pani doktór* (lit: madam doctor).

Could I have an appointment with a female doctor?	
chi *mo*-ge za-*moo*-veech vee-*zi*-te oo *pa*-nee *dok*-toor?	*Czy mogę zamówić wizytę u pani doktór?*
I'm pregnant.	
yes-tem *fchon*-zhi	*Jestem w ciąży.*
I think I'm pregnant.	
vi-*da*-ye mee she, zhe *yes*-tem *fchon*-zhi	*Wydaje mi się, że jestem w ciąży.*
I'm on the Pill.	
byo-re pee-*goow*-kee an-ti-kon-tsep-*tsiy*-ne	*Biorę pigułki antykoncepcyjne.*
I haven't had my period for ... weeks.	
nye mam mye-*shonch*-kee ot ... ti-*god*-nee	*Nie mam miesiączki od ... tygodni.*

HEALTH

abortion	psher-*va*-nye *chon*-zhi	*przerwanie ciąży* (neut)
mammogram	ma-*mo*-gram	*mamogram* (m)
menstruation	men-stroo-*a*-tsya/ mye-*shonch*-ka	*menstruacja* (f)/ *miesiączka* (f)
miscarriage	po-ro-*nye*-nye	*poronienie* (neut)
pap smear	tsi-to-*lo*-gya	*cytologia* (f)
period pain	bool mye-shonch-*ko*-vi	*ból miesiączkowy* (m)
the Pill	pee-*goow*-ka an-ti-kon-tsep-*tsiy*-na	*pigułka antykoncepcyjna* (f)
pregnancy test	test chon-*zho*-vi	*test ciążowy* (m)
premenstrual tension	na-*pyen*-che pshe-dmye-shonch-*ko*-ve	*napięcie przed-miesiączkowe* (neut)
ultrasound	ool-tra-so-no-*gra*-fya	*ultrasonografia* (f)

SPECIAL HEALTH NEEDS — PROBLEMY ZDROWOTNE

I'm diabetic.
yes-tem dya-be-*ti*-kyem/ dya-be-*tich*-kom — *Jestem diabetykiem/ diabetyczką.* (m/f)

I'm anaemic.	mam a-*ne*-mye	*Mam anemię.*
I'm asthmatic.	mam *as*-tme	*Mam astmę.*
I'm epileptic.	mam e-pee-*lep*-sye	*Mam epilepsję.*

I'm allergic to ...	mam oo-choo-*le*-nye na ...	*Mam uczulenie na ...*
antibiotics	an-ti-byo-*ti*-kee	*antybiotyki*
aspirin	as-pee-*ri*-ne	*aspirynę*
bees	*pshcho*-wi	*pszczoły*
codeine	ko-de-*ee*-ne	*kodeinę*
dairy products	pro-*dook*-ti *mlech*-ne	*produkty mleczne*
penicillin	pe-nee-tsi-*lee*-ne	*penicylinę*
pollen	*piw*-kee kfya-*to*-ve	*pyłki kwiatowe*

I have a skin allergy.
mam oo-choo-*le*-nye *skoo*-ri — *Mam uczulenie skóry.*

I've had my vaccinations.
yes-tem zash-che-*pyo*-ni/a — *Jestem zaszczepiony/a.*

I have my own syringe.
mam *vwas*-nom stshi-*kaf*-ke — *Mam własną strzykawkę.*

I'm on medication for ...
byo-re *le*-kee na ... — *Biorę leki na ...*

I need a new pair of glasses.
pot-she-*boo*-ye *no*-ve o-koo-*la*-ri — *Potrzebuję nowe okulary.*

addiction	*na*-wook	*nałóg* (m)
bite (dog)	oo-gri-*zhe*-nye	*ugryzienie* (neut)
bite (insect/ snake)	oo-kon-*she*-nye	*ukąszenie* (neut)
blood test	a-na-*lee*-za krfee	*analiza krwi* (f)
contraceptive	*shro*-dek an-ti-kon-tsep-*tsiy*-ni	*środek antykoncepcyjny* (m)
injection	*zast*-shik	*zastrzyk* (m)
injury	*ra*-na	*rana* (f)
vitamins	vee-ta-*mee*-ni	*witaminy* (f, pl)
wound	*ra*-na	*rana* (f)

DID YOU KNOW ...

There's no specific word for 'toes' in Polish. Curiously, they are known as *palce u nogi* (lit: fingers of the leg), even though there is a Polish word for 'foot' (*stopa*) and it would perhaps be more correct to call them 'fingers of the foot'.

ALTERNATIVE TREATMENTS — MEDYCYNA ALTERNATYWNA

Alternative treatments aren't well known, and are sometimes treated with suspicion. However, they're gradually gaining ground, partly because the traditional health service isn't in a particularly healthy state.

acupuncture	a-koo-poon-*ktoo*-ra	*akupunktura* (f)
aromatherapy	a-ro-mo-te-*ra*-pya	*aromoterapia* (f)
herbal medicine	zhe-*lar*-stfo	*zielarstwo* (neut)
homeopathy	ho-me-o-*pa*-tya	*homeopatia* (f)
massage	*ma*-sash	*masaż* (m)
meditation	me-di-*ta*-tsya	*medytacja* (f)
naturopath	na-too-ro-*pa*-tya	*naturopatia* (f)
reflexology	re-fle-kso-*lo*-gya	*refleksologia* (f)
yoga	*yo*-ga	*joga* (f)

REFLEX ACTIONS

Polish uses a lot of reflexive verbs (where an action is done to oneself). They're easily recognised, as they always appear with the pronoun *się*. See Grammar, page 37, for more about reflexive verbs.

PARTS OF THE BODY — CZĘŚCI CIAŁA

My ... hurts.	*bo*-lee mnye ...	*Boli mnie ...*
ankle	*kos*-tka	*kostka* (f)
appendix	*shle*-pa *keesh*-ka	*ślepa kiszka* (f)
arm	*ra*-mye	*ramię* (neut)
back	*ple*-tsi	*plecy* (pl)
bladder	*pen*-hesh	*pęcherz* (m)
blood	kref	*krew* (f)
bone	koshch	*kość* (f)
chest	pyersh	*pierś* (f)
ear	*oo*-ho	*ucho* (neut)
eye	*o*-ko	*oko* (neut)
finger	*pa*-lets	*palec* (m)
foot	*sto*-pa	*stopa* (f)
hand	*ren*-ka	*ręka* (f)
head	*gwo*-va	*głowa* (f)
heart	*ser*-tse	*serce* (neut)
kidney	*ner*-ka	*nerka* (f)
knee	ko-*la*-no	*kolano* (neut)
leg	*no*-ga	*noga* (f)
liver	von-*tro*-ba	*wątroba* (f)
lung	*pwoo*-tso	*płuco* (neut)
mouth	*oos*-ta	*usta* (pl)
muscle	*myen*-shen	*mięsień* (m)
nose	nos	*nos* (m)
rib	*zhe*-bro	*żebro* (neut)
shoulder	*ra*-mye	*ramię* (neut)
skin	*skoo*-ra	*skóra* (f)
stomach	zho-*won*-dek	*żołądek* (m)
throat	*gar*-dwo	*gardło* (neut)
tooth	zomp	*ząb* (m)
vein	*zhi*-wa	*żyła* (f)

AT THE CHEMIST — W APTECE

Where's the nearest (all-night) chemist?
gdje yest nay-*bleesh*-sha (tsa-wo-*nots*-na) ap-*te*-ka? — *Gdzie jest najbliższa (całonocna) apteka?*

Please give me something for ...
po-*pro*-she tsosh na ... — *Poproszę coś na ...*

Do I need a prescription for ...?
chi pot-she-*boo*-ye re-*tsep*-te na ...? — *Czy potrzebuję receptę na ...?*

How many times a day?
ee-le *ra*-zi *djen*-nye? — *Ile razy dziennie?*

Before or after meals?
pshet chi po ye-*dze*-nyoo? — *Przed czy po jedzeniu?*

antibiotic	an-ti-*byo*-tik	*antybiotyk* (m)
antiseptic	an-ti-*sep*-tik	*antyseptyk* (m)
aspirin	as-pee-*ri*-na	*aspiryna* (f)
bandage	*ban*-dash	*bandaż* (m)
Band-aids	plas-ter zo-pa-*troon*-kyem	*plaster z opatrunkiem* (m)
condom	pre-zer-va-*ti*-va/ *kon*-don	*prezerwatywa* (f)/ *kondon* (m)
contraceptive	*shro*-dek an-ti-kon-tsep-*tsiy*-ni	*środek antykoncepcyjny* (m)
cotton balls	va-*chee*-kee	*waciki* (m, pl)
cough medicine	lek na *ka*-shel	*lek na kaszel* (m)
gauze	*ga*-za	*gaza* (f)
laxative	*shro*-dek pshe-chish-cha-*yon*-tsi	*środek przeczyszczający* (m)
painkiller	*shro*-dek pshe-cheef-boo-*lo*-vi	*środek przeciw bólowy* (m)
sleeping pills	*prosh*-kee na-*sen*-ne	*proszki nasenne* (m, pl)

FOUNTAINS OF YOUTH

Cieplice Śląskie-Zdrój
the town of Jelenia Góra boasts one of the oldest spas in the Silesia region, with hot sulphur springs established since the 13th century

Krynica
popular mountain health resort with a variety of mineral waters

Kudowa-Zdrój
the biggest spa in the Kłodzka region, Kudowa-Zdrój offers a spa park with several mineral springs

Lądek-Zdrój
one of Poland's oldest spas, Lądek-Zdrój is located at the foot of the Góry Złote on the eastern edge of the Kłodzko Valley

Świnoujście
Westernmost town on the Polish coast which boasts both a beach resort and spa with salt springs

Szczawnica
popular mineral springs and summer resort located along the Grajcarek River

AT THE DENTIST — U DENTYSTY

I have a toothache. — *bo*-lee mnye zomp — *Boli mnie ząb.*
I have a cavity. — mam *djoo*-re — *Mam dziurę.*

I've lost a filling.
vi-*pad*-wa mee *plom*-ba — *Wypadła mi plomba.*
I've broken my tooth.
zwa-maw mee she zomp — *Złamał mi się ząb.*
My gums hurt.
djon-swa mnye *bo*-lom — *Dziąsła mnie bolą.*
I don't want it extracted.
nye htse go *vir*-vach — *Nie chcę go wyrwać.*
Please give me an anaesthetic.
pro-she o znye-choo-*le*-nye — *Proszę o znieczulenie.*

Ouch! — aw! — *Au!*

WHEN ITS 'NO GLOVE, NO LOVE'

Both 'prezerwatywa' and 'kondon' mean 'condom', but the former is more formal. If you want to buy some, you should ask the pharmacist for *prezerwatywy*, rather than *kondony*.

POTRZEBY SPECJALNE — SPECIFIC NEEDS

DISABLED TRAVELLERS — NIEPEŁNOSPRAWNI

As yet, Poland offers few facilities for people with disabilities. Wheelchair ramps are available only at a few upmarket hotels, and public transport will be a challenge for anyone with mobility problems. Hardly any office, museum or bank provides special facilities for disabled persons, and wheelchair-accessible toilets are few and far between.

Only quite recently have there been some more determined efforts to develop the infrastructure for handicapped people.

I'm disabled/handicapped.
yes-tem nye-peoo-no-*sprav*-ni/a — *Jestem niepełnosprawny/a.*

I need assistance.
pot-she-*boo*-ye po-*mo*-tsi — *Potrzebuję pomocy.*

What facilities do you have for disabled people?
ya-kye som oo-do-go-*dnye*-nya dla *o*-soop nye-peoo-no-*sprav*-nih? — *Jakie są udogodnienia dla osób niepełnosprawnych?*

Is there wheelchair access?
chi yest *dos*-temp dla *voos*-koof een-va-*lits*-keeh? — *Czy jest dostęp dla wózków inwalidzkich?*

I'm hard of hearing.
swa-bo *swi*-she — *Słabo słyszę.*

Speak more loudly, please.
pro-she *moo*-veech *gwosh*-nyey — *Proszę mówić głośniej.*

I have a hearing aid.
mam a-*pa*-rat swoo-*ho*-vi — *Mam aparat słuchowy.*

disabled person	o-*so*-ba nye-peoo-no-*sprav*-na	*osoba niepełnosprawna* (f)
guide dog	pyes pshe-*vod*-neek	*pies przewodnik* (m)
wheelchair	*voo*-zek een-va-*leets*-kee	*wózek inwalidzki* (m)

GAY TRAVELLERS GEJE

The Polish gay and lesbian scene is still very much underground and pretty limited. The overwhelmingly Catholic society tends to both deny and suppress homosexuality, even though it's not illegal.

To be openly gay in Poland can often limit vocational and social opportunities, and may cause family ostracism. Consequently, few gays, and still fewer lesbians, want to voice their attitudes in a family or workplace forum, opting instead for pursuing their lifestyles with discretion.

Don't expect a flourishing gay life and thriving gay hangouts, nor much information and publications about the community. Use common sense and be discreet when bringing up the issue.

Is there a gay bar/club around here?
chi yest too *ya*-keesh bar/ kloop ge-*yof*-skee? — *Czy jest tu jakiś bar/klub gejowski?*

Is there a gay telephone emergency hotline?
chi yest *ya*-keesh ge-*yof*-skee te-*le*-fon za-oo-*fa*-nya? — *Czy jest jakiś gejowski telefon zaufania?*

TRAVELLING WITH THE FAMILY — PODRÓŻ Z RODZINĄ

I'm travelling with my family.
po-droo-*zhoo*-ye zro-*djee*-nom — *Podróżuję z rodziną.*

Are there any facilities for children/babies?
chi som *ya*-kyesh oo-do-go-*dnye*-nya dla dje-chee/nye-*mov*-lont? — *Czy są jakieś udogodnienia dla dzieci/niemowląt?*

Where can I find a (English-speaking) babysitter?
gdje *mozh*-na *zna*-leshch (an-glo-yen-*zich*-nom) o-pye-*koon*-ke do *djets*-ka? — *Gdzie można znaleźć (anglojęzyczną) opiekunkę do dziecka?*

Can you put an extra bed in the room?
po-*pro*-she o do-dat-*ko*-we *woosh*-ko fpo-*ko*-yoo. — *Poproszę o dodatkowe łóżko w pokoju.*

I need a car with a child seat.
pot-she-*boo*-ye sa-*mo*-hoot sfo-te-*lee*-kyem dla *djets*-ka — *Potrzebuję samochód z fotelikiem dla dziecka.*

Is there children's entertainment here?
chi som too *ya*-kyesh roz-*rif*-kee dla *dje*-chee? — *Czy są tu jakieś rozrywki dla dzieci?*

Is there a concession for children?
chi yest *zneesh*-ka dla *dje*-chee? — *Czy jest zniżka dla dzieci?*

Are children allowed to enter?
chi *dje*-chee *mo*-gom veyshch? — *Czy dzieci mogą wejść?*

Do you have a children's menu?
chi som *ya*-kyesh *da*-nya dla *dje*-chee? — *Czy są jakieś dania dla dzieci?*

Could you make it a child's portion?
chi *mo*-ge *pro*-sheech o *por*-tsye dla *djets*-ka? — *Czy mogę prosić o porcję dla dziecka?*

LOOKING FOR A JOB — SZUKANIE PRACY

Poland isn't exactly the best place to look for a casual job. Wages are low, unemployment high, and to work legally you need a working visa which involves complex and lengthy paperwork.

Qualified English teachers have perhaps the best chance of getting a job on the spot – try the English-teaching institutions and private language schools, which are now popping up like mushrooms.

If you're seriously thinking of a long-term legal working contract in Poland, it's best to start making enquiries well ahead of your arrival. The Internet is an increasingly helpful and efficient means of getting into Polish business circles.

I'm looking for a job.
shoo-kam *pra*-tsi — *Szukam pracy.*

Where's the best place to look for a job?
gdje nay-*le*-pyey *shoo*-kach *pra*-tsi? — *Gdzie najlepiej szukać pracy?*

I have qualifications.
mam kfa-lee-fee-*ka*-tsye — *Mam kwalifikacje.*

I have experience in ...	mam dosh-fyat-*che*-nye v ...	*Mam doświadczenie w ...*
acting	ak-*tor*-stfye	*aktorstwie*
childcare	o-*pye*-tse nad *djech*-mee	*opiece nad dziećmi*
cleaning	spshon-*ta*-nyoo	*sprzątaniu*
construction work	*pra*-tsi na boo-*do*-vye	*pracy na budowie*
computer work	*pra*-tsi na kom-poo-*te*-zhe	*pracy na komputerze*
design	pro-yek-to-*va*-nyoo	*projektowaniu*
fruit picking	zbye-*ra*-nyoo o-*vo*-tsoof	*zbieraniu owoców*
photography	fo-to-*gra*-fee	*fotografii*
office work	*pra*-tsi byoo-*ro*-vey	*pracy biurowej*
teaching	na-oo-*cha*-nyoo	*nauczaniu*

What kind of work is it?
tso to za pra-tsa? — *Co to za praca?*

How much will I get (per hour)?
ee-le dos-ta-ne (za go-djee-ne)? — *Ile dostanę (za godzinę)?*

I can start tomorrow/next week.
mo-ge za-chonch yoo-tro/ fpshish-wim ti-god-nyoo — *Mogę zacząć jutro/w przyszłym tygodniu.*

casual work	*pra*-tsa do-*rif*-cha	*praca dorywcza* (f)
employee	pra-*tsov*-neek	*pracownik* (m)
	pra-tsov-*neech*-ka	*pracowniczka* (f)
employer	pra-tso-*daf*-tsa	*pracodawca* (m)
	pra-tso-*daf-chi*-nee	*pracodawczyni* (f)
full-time job	*pra*-tsa na *peoo*-ni *e*-tat	*praca na pełny etat* (f)
part-time job	*pra*-tsa na nye-*peoo*-ni *e*-tat	*praca na niepełny etat* (f)
insurance	oo-bes-pye-*che*-nye	*ubezpieczenie* (neut)
job/work	*pra*-tsa	*praca* (f)
profession	*za*-voot	*zawód* (m)
work permit	poz-vo-*le*-nye na *pra*-tse	*pozwolenie na pracę* (neut)

ON BUSINESS — NA DELEGACJI

I'm here on business.
yes-tem too swoozh-bo-vo — *Jestem tu służbowo.*

I'm attending a conference.
byo-re oo-djaw fkon-fe-ren-tsyee — *Biorę udział w konferencji.*

I came for a trade fair.
pshi-ye-ha-wem/wam na tar-gee han-dlo-ve — *Przyjechałem/łam na targi handlowe.*

I'm on a course.
yes-tem na koor-she — *Jestem na kursie.*

I have an appointment with ...
mam spot-ka-nye s ... — *Mam spotkanie z ...*

Here's my business card.
o-to mo-ya vee-zi-toof-ka — *Oto moja wizytówka.*

I need an interpreter.
pot-she-*boo*-ye twoo-*ma*-cha — *Potrzebuję tłumacza.*
I need to use a computer.
moo-she sko-*zhis*-tach skom-poo-*te*-ra — *Muszę skorzystać z komputera.*
I need to send a fax/an email.
moo-she *vi*-swach faks/*ee*-meil — *Muszę wysłać faks/email.*

client	*klee*-yent	*klient* (m)
	klee-yen-tka	*klientka* (f)
contract	*kon*-trakt	*kontrakt* (m)
exhibition	vis-*ta*-va	*wystawa* (f)
loss	*stra*-ta	*strata* (f)
mobile phone	te-*le*-fon ko-moor-*ko*-vi	*telefon komórkowy* (m)
profit	zisk	*zysk* (m)
proposal	o-*fer*-ta	*oferta* (f)
sales	o-*bro*-ti	*obroty* (m, pl)

ON TOUR — WYJAZDY GRUPOWE

We're travelling in a group.
po-*droo*-zhoo-*ye*-mi *vgroo*-pye — *Podróżujemy w grupie.*
Please speak with our manager.
pro-she roz-*ma*-vyach *zna*-shim kye-rov-*nee*-kyem — *Proszę rozmawiać z naszym kierownikiem.*
I'm with a band.
yes-tem zzes-*po*-wem moo-*zich*-nim — *Jestem z zespołem muzycznym.*
We're on a concert tour.
yes-*tesh*-mi na *tra*-she kon-tser-*to*-vey — *Jesteśmy na trasie koncertowej.*
We're here for (two days).
ben-*dje*-mi too (dva dnee) — *Będziemy tu (dwa dni).*
We're playing on (Sunday).
ben-*dje*-mi grach (vnye-*dje*-le) — *Będziemy grać w (niedzielę).*

PILGRIMAGE & RELIGION — RELIGIA

Is there a church nearby?
chi yest *kosh*-choow fpo-*blee*-zhoo? — *Czy jest kościół w pobliżu?*

When's it open?
kye-di yest ot-*far*-ti? — *Kiedy jest otwarty?*

When are the masses held?
kye-di som mshe? — *Kiedy są msze?*

Is there a mass held in English?
chi yest msha po an-*gyel*-skoo? — *Czy jest msza po angielsku?*

altar	*ow*-tash	*ołtarz* (m)
baptism/christening	hshest	*chrzest* (m)
bible	*bee*-blya	*biblia* (f)
cathedral	ka-*te*-dra	*katedra* (f)
cemetery	*tsmen*-tash	*cmentarz* (m)
chapel	ka-*plee*-tsa	*kaplica* (f)
church	*kosh*-choow	*kościół* (m)
communion	ko-*moo*-nya	*komunia* (f)
confession	*spo*-vyech	*spowiedź* (f)
funeral	*pog*-zhep	*pogrzeb* (m)
god	book	*bóg* (m)
grave	groop	*grób* (m)
mass	msha	*msza* (f)
monastery	*klash*-tor	*klasztor* (m)
monk	mneeh	*mnich* (m)
mosque	*me*-chet	*meczet* (m)
nun	za-kon-*nee*-tsa	*zakonnica* (f)
Pope	*pa*-pyesh	*Papież* (m)
prayer	mo-*dleet*-fa	*modlitwa* (f)
priest	kshonts	*ksiądz* (m)
religious procession	pro-*tse*-sya	*procesja* (f)
sabbath	*sha*-bas	*szabas* (m)
saint	*shfyen*-ti/a	*święty/a* (m/f)
synagogue	si-na-*go*-ga	*synagoga* (f)
temple	shfyon-*ti*-nya	*świątynia* (f)

(See also Religion, page 52.)

TRACING ROOTS & HISTORY — SZUKANIE KORZENI RODZINNYCH

(I think) my family came from this area.
(vi-*da*-ye mee she zhe) *mo*-ya ro-*djee*-na po-*ho*-djee *ste*-go re-*gyo*-noo
(Wydaje mi się że) moja rodzina pochodzi z tego regionu.

My ancestors lived around here.
mo-ee pshot-*ko*-vye gdjesh too myesh-*ka*-lee
Moi przodkowie gdzieś tu mieszkali.

Their family name was ...
eeh naz-*vees*-ko ro-*do*-ve *bi*-wo ...
Ich nazwisko rodowe było ...

Is there anyone here who remembers this name?
chi yest too ktosh kto pa-*myen*-ta to naz-*vees*-ko?
Czy jest tu ktoś kto pamięta to nazwisko?

My (father/grandfather) fought here in WWII.
mooy (*oy*-chets/ *dja*-dek) *val*-chiw too *fcha*-she *droo*-gyey *voy*-ni
Mój (ojciec/dziadek) walczył tu w czasie drugiej wojny.

I think he died/perished here.
vi-*da*-ye mee she zhe on too *oo*-marw/ *zgee*-now
Wydaje mi się że on tu umarł/zginął.

Where's the local cemetery?
gdje yest myey-*stso*-vi *tsmen*-tash?
Gdzie jest miejscowy cmentarz?

CZAS I DATY TIME & DATES

TELLING THE TIME KTÓRA GODZINA

A 24-hour clock is used in Poland for official purposes, particularly in print form such as transportation schedules, opening hours, cinema programs. In everyday life, especially in verbal language, Poles commonly use the 2 x 12-hour clock and, if necessary, add 'in the morning', 'in the afternoon' or 'at night'.

Telling the time in Polish is a little different than in English. Unlike in English, where hours are expressed in cardinal numbers (such as 'two'), in Polish, they're indicated in ordinal numbers (such as 'second').

two o'clock *druga godzina* (lit: second hour)

The word *godzina*, 'hour', is usually omitted if the meaning's clear from context.

Instead of the English 'half past', Polish language uses 'half to'.

half past two *wpół do trzeciej* (lit: half to the third)

Minutes in Polish are expressed in cardinal numbers, as in English.

ten past two *dziesięć po drugiej* (lit: ten past the second)
ten to two *za dziesięć druga* (lit: ten to the second)

What time is it?
ktoo-ra (yest) go-*djee*-na? *Która (jest) godzina?*

(It's) one o'clock.
(yest) *pyer*-fsha *(Jest) pierwsza.*

(It's) ten o'clock.
(yest) dje-*shon*-ta *(Jest) dziesiąta.*

Half past one.
fpoow do *droo*-gyey *Wpół do drugiej.*

Half past three.
fpoow do *chfar*-tey *Wpół do czwartej.*

Five past one.
pyench po *pyer*-fshey *Pięć po pierwszej.*

in the morning	*ra*-no	*rano*
in the afternoon	po po-*wood*-nyoo	*po południu*
in the evening	vye-*cho*-rem	*wieczorem*
at night	*vno*-tsi	*w nocy*

DAYS — DNI TYGODNIA

Monday	po-nye-*dja*-wek	*poniedziałek* (m)
Tuesday	*fto*-rek	*wtorek* (m)
Wednesday	*shro*-da	*środa* (f)
Thursday	*chfar*-tek	*czwartek* (m)
Friday	*pyon*-tek	*piątek* (m)
Saturday	so-*bo*-ta	*sobota* (f)
Sunday	nye-*dje*-la	*niedziela* (f)

MONTHS — MIESIĄCE

January	*sti*-chen	*styczeń* (m)
February	*loo*-ti	*luty* (m)
March	*ma*-zhets	*marzec* (m)
April	*kfye*-chen	*kwiecień* (m)
May	may	*maj* (m)
June	*cher*-vyets	*czerwiec* (m)
July	*lee*-pyets	*lipiec* (m)
August	*sher*-pyen	*sierpień* (m)
September	*vzhe*-shen	*wrzesień* (m)
October	pazh-*djer*-neek	*październik* (m)
November	lees-*to*-pat	*listopad* (m)
December	*groo*-djen	*grudzień* (m)

SEASONS — PORY ROKU

spring	*vyos*-na	*wiosna* (f)
summer	*la*-to	*lato* (neut)
autumn	*ye*-shen	*jesień* (f)
winter	*zee*-ma	*zima* (f)

DATES — DATY

Ordinal numbers are used for days of the month when expressing dates. They're usually written in figures with the relevant word-ending added after a hyphen. Note that, unlike English, Polish doesn't use initial capital letters for months or days of the week.

What date it is today?
ktoo-*re*-go yest *djee*-shay? — *Którego jest dzisiaj?*
It's the 18th of February.
yest o-shem-nas-*te*-go loo-*te*-go — *Jest 18-go lutego.*
Today it's the 2nd of May.
djeesh yest droo-*gye*-go *ma*-ya — *Dziś jest 2-go maja.*
What day of the week it is today?
ya-kee djeesh djen ti-*god*-nya? — *Jaki dziś dzień tygodnia?*
Today it's Tuesday.
djeesh yest *fto*-rek — *Dziś jest wtorek.*

day	djen	*dzień* (m)
week	*ti*-djen	*tydzień* (m)
month	*mye*-shonts	*miesiąc* (m)
year	rok	*rok* (m)

PRESENT — TERAŹNIEJSZOŚĆ

now	*te*-ras	*teraz*
today	djeesh/*djee*-shay	*dziś/dzisiaj*
this morning	djeesh *ra*-no	*dziś rano*
this afternoon	djeesh po po-*wood*-nyoo	*dziś po południu*
tonight	djeesh vye-*cho*-rem	*dziś wieczorem*
this week	ftim ti-*god*-nyoo	*w tym tygodniu*
this month	ftim mye-*shon*-tsoo	*w tym miesiącu*
this year	ftim *ro*-koo	*w tym roku*

DZIŚ & DZISIAJ

Dziś and *dzisiaj* both mean 'today', and can be used interchangeably in all situations.

PAST — PRZESZŁOŚĆ

yesterday	*fcho*-ray	*wczoraj*
day before yesterday	pshet-*fcho*-ray	*przedwczoraj*
yesterday ...	*fcho*-ray ...	*wczoraj ...*
morning	*ra*-no	*rano*
afternoon	po po-*wood*-nyoo	*po południu*
last night	*fcho*-ray vye-*cho*-rem	*wczoraj wieczorem*

last ...	*vzesh*-wim ...	*w zeszłym ...*
week	ti-*god*-nyoo	*tygodniu*
month	mye-*shon*-tsoo	*miesiącu*
year	*ro*-koo	*roku*
... ago	... *te*-moo	*... temu*
half an hour	poow go-*djee*-ni	*pół godziny*
(three) days	(tshi) dnee	*(trzy) dni*
(five) years	(pyench) lat	*(pięć) lat*
a long time	*dav*-no	*dawno*
a moment ago	pshet *hfee*-lom	*przed chwilą*
since (May)	ot (*ma*-ya)	*od maja*

FUTURE — PRZYSZŁOŚĆ

tomorrow	*yoo*-tro	*jutro*
day after tomorrow	po-*yoo*-tshe	*pojutrze*
tomorrow ...	*yoo*-tro ...	*jutro ...*
morning	*ra*-no	*rano*
afternoon	po po-*wood*-nyoo	*po południu*
evening	vye-*cho*-rem	*wieczorem*
next ...	*fpshish*-wim ...	*w przyszłym ...*
week	ti-*god*-nyoo	*tygodniu*
month	mye-*shon*-tsoo	*miesiącu*
year	*ro*-koo	*roku*
in (five) minutes	za (pyench) *mee*-noot	*za (pięć) minut*
in (four) days	za (*chte*-ri) dni	*za (cztery) dni*
within an hour	*fchon*-goo go-*djee*-ni	*w ciągu godziny*
until (December)	do (*grood*-nya)	*do (grudnia)*

BISON BONUSES

The European bison (*Bison bonasus*), known in Polish as *ţubr*, is Europe's largest native mammal.

Bison were once found all over the continent, but by 1916, only 150 survived in the wild – in Biaćowieţa Forest. Three years later they'd totally been wiped out. However, around 50 animals were kept in zoos throughout the world.

In 1929, several animals were brought from zoos to Biaćowieţa in an attempt to breed them and reintroduce them to the wild. Today around 250 bison live in freedom in the Biaćowieţa Forest and another 350 live in a dozen other places around Poland. Many bison from Biaćowieţa have been distributed among European zoos and forests, and today their total population is around 2500.

DURING THE DAY — W CIĄGU DNIA

afternoon	po-po-*wood*-nye	*popołudnie* (neut)
dawn	shfeet	*świt* (m)
day	djen	*dzień* (m)
early	*fchesh*-nye	*wcześnie*
hour	go-*djee*-na	*godzina* (f)
midnight	*poow*-nots	*północ* (f)
minute	mee-*noo*-ta	*minuta* (f)
morning	*ra*-no	*rano* (neut)
night	nots	*noc* (f)
noon	po-*wood*-nye	*południe* (neut)
second	se-*koon*-da	*sekunda* (f)
sunrise	fs-hoot *swon*-tsa	*wschód słońca* (m)
sunset	*za*-hoot *swon*-tsa	*zachód słońca* (m)

LICZBY I ILOŚCI

NUMBERS & AMOUNTS

CARDINAL NUMBERS LICZEBNIKI GŁÓWNE

0	*ze*-ro	*zero*
1	*ye*-den	*jeden*
2	dva	*dwa*
3	tshi	*trzy*
4	*chte*-ri	*cztery*
5	pyench	*pięć*
6	sheshch	*sześć*
7	*she*-dem	*siedem*
8	*o*-shem	*osiem*
9	*dje*-vyench	*dziewięć*
10	*dje*-shench	*dziesięć*
11	ye-de-*nash*-che	*jedenaście*
12	dva-*nash*-che	*dwanaście*
13	tshi-*nash*-che	*trzynaście*
14	chter-*nash*-che	*czternaście*
15	pyent-*nash*-che	*piętnaście*
16	shes-*nash*-che	*szesnaście*
17	she-dem-*nash*-che	*siedemnaście*
18	o-shem-*nash*-che	*osiemnaście*
19	dje-vyet-*nash*-che	*dziewiętnaście*
20	dva-*djesh*-cha	*dwadzieścia*
21	dva-*djesh*-cha *ye*-den	*dwadzieścia jeden*
22	dva-*djesh*-cha dva	*dwadzieścia dwa*
30	tshi-*djesh*-chee	*trzydzieści*
31	tshi-*djesh*-chee *ye*-den	*trzydzieści jeden*
32	tshi-*djesh*-chee dva	*trzydzieści dwa*
40	chter-*djesh*-chee	*czterdzieści*
41	chter-*djesh*-chee *ye*-den	*czterdzieści jeden*
50	pyen-*dje*-shont	*pięćdziesiąt*
51	pyen-*dje*-shont *ye*-den	*pięćdziesiąt jeden*

60	shesh-*dje*-shont	*sześćdziesiąt*
70	she-dem-*dje*-shont	*siedemdziesiąt*
80	o-shem-*dje*-shont	*osiemdziesiąt*
90	dje-vyen-*dje*-shont	*dziewięćdziesiąt*
100	sto	*sto*
101	sto *ye*-den	*sto jeden*
110	sto *dje*-shench	*sto dziesięć*
200	*dvyesh*-che	*dwieście*
300	*tshis*-ta	*trzysta*
400	chte-*ris*-ta	*czterysta*
500	*pyen*-tset	*pięćset*
600	*shesh*-set	*sześćset*
700	she-*dem*-set	*siedemset*
800	o-*shem*-set	*osiemset*
900	dje-*vyen*-tset	*dziewięćset*
1000	*ti*-shonts	*tysiąc*
1100	*ti*-shonts sto	*tysiąc sto*
2000	dva ti-*shon*-tse	*dwa tysiące*
5000	pyench ti-*shen*-tsi	*pięć tysięcy*
10,000	*dje*-shench ti-*shen*-tsi	*dziesięć tysięcy*
100,000	sto ti-*shen*-tsi	*sto tysięcy*
a million	*mee*-lyon	*milion*

48	chter-*djesh*-chee *o*-shem	*czterdzieści osiem*
335	*tshis*-ta tshi-*djesh*-chee pyench	*trzysta trzydzieści pięć*
1280	*ti*-shonts *dvyesh*-che o-shem-*dje*-shont	*tysiąc dwieście osiemdziesiąt*
14,500	chter-*nash*-che ti-*shen*-tsi *pyen*-tset	*czternaście tysięcy pięćse*

ABBREVIATIONS

al	*aleja*	avenue
dr	*doktor*	doctor
godz	*godzina*	hour
gr	*grosz*	Polish currency
inż	*inżynier*	engineer
itp	*i tym podobne*	etcetera
LOT	*linia lotnicza*	LOT Polish Airlines
mgr	*magister*	MA, MSc
min	*minuta*	minute
ONZ	*Organizacja Narodów Zjeknoczonych*	United Nations

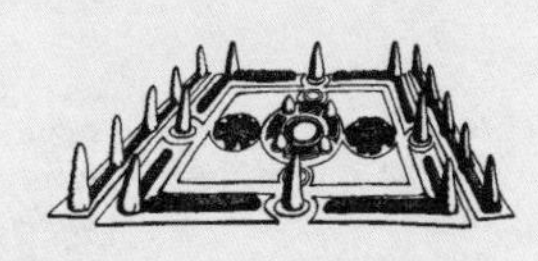

PKP	*Polskie Koleje Państwowe*	Polish State Railways
PKS	*Państwowa Komunikacja Samochodowa*	Polish State Bus Company
PTSM	*Polskie Towarzystwo Schronisk Młodzieżowych*	Polish Youth Hostel Association
PTTK	*Polskie Towarzystwo Turystyczno-Krajoznawcze*	Polish Tourist Association
PZM	*Polski Związek Motorowy*	Polish Motoring Association
ul	*ulica*	street
zł	*złoty*	Polish currency

ORDINAL NUMBERS / LICZEBNIKI PORZĄDKOWE

Ordinal numbers agree in gender and case with the noun they refer to, in much the same way as adjectives.

1st	*pyer*-fshi/a	*pierwszy/a*	6th	*shoos*-ti/a	*szósty/a*
2nd	*droo*-gee/a	*drugi/a*	7th	*shood*-mi/a	*siódmy/a*
3rd	*tshe*-chee/a	*trzeci/a*	8th	*oos*-mi/a	*ósmy/a*
4th	*chfar*-ti/a	*czwarty/a*	9th	dje-*vyon*-ti/a	*dziewiąty/a*
5th	*pyon*-ti/a	*piąty/a*	10th	dje-*shon*-ti/a	*dziesiąty/a*

FRACTIONS / UŁAMKI

a quarter	*yed*-na *chfar*-ta	*jedna czwarta*
a third	*yed*-na *tshe*-cha	*jedna trzecia*
a half	*yed*-na *droo*-ga/poow	*jedna druga/pół*
three-quarters	tshi *chfar*-te	*trzy czwarte*

AMOUNTS / ILOŚCI

dozen	*too*-zheen	*tuzin*
few	*keel*-ka	*kilka*
less	mnyey	*mniej*
a little (amount)	nye-*doo*-zho	*niedużo*
many/much	*doo*-zho	*dużo*
more	*vyen*-tsey	*więcej*
once	ras	*raz*
pair	*pa*-ra	*para*
percent	*pro*-tsent	*procent*
some	*tro*-he	*trochę*
too little	za *ma*-wo	*za mało*
too much/many	za *doo*-zho	*za dużo*
twice	dva *ra*-zi	*dwa razy*

NAGŁE PRZYPADKI
EMERGENCIES

Help!	ra-*toon*-koo!;	*Ratunku!;*
	po-*mo*-tsi!;	*Pomocy!;*
	na *po*-mots!	*Na pomoc!*
Stop!	stach!	*Stać!*
Go away!	*pro*-she *o*-deyshch!	*Proszę odejść!* (pol)
	o-deych!	*Odejdź!* (inf)
Thief!	*zwo*-djey!	*Złodziej!*
Fire!	*po*-zhar!;	*Pożar!;*
	pa-lee she!	*Pali się!*
Watch out!	*pro*-she oo-*va*-zhach!	*Proszę uważać!* (pol)
	oo-*va*-zhay!	*Uważaj!* (inf)

It's an emergency.
to yest *na*-gwi pshi-*pa*-dek — *To jest nagły przypadek.*

Could you help me please?
pro-she mee *po*-moots? — *Proszę mi pomóc.*

Could I please use the telephone?
chi *mo*-ge sko-*zhis*-tach ste-le-*fo*-nu? — *Czy mogę skorzystać z telefonu?*

I'm lost.
zgoo-*bee*-wem/wam she — *Zgubiłem/łam się.* (m/f)

Where are the toilets?
gdje som to-a-*le*-ti? — *Gdzie są toalety?*

POLICE — POLICJA

As almost everywhere around the world, it's best to stay a safe distance from the police, unless you need them. If you happen to get involved with the police, keep calm and be polite, but not overly friendly. Don't get angry or hostile – it will only work against you.

Please call the police!
pro-she *vez*-vach po-*lee*-tsye! — *Proszę wezwać policję!*

Where's the police station?
gdje yest pos-te-*roo*-nek po-*lee*-tsyee? — *Gdzie jest posterunek policji?*

I want to report a/an ...	htse *zgwo*-sheech ...	*Chcę zgłosić ...*
accident	vi-*pa*-dek	*wypadek*
attack	*na*-pat	*napad*
loss	*zgoo*-be	*zgubę*
theft	*kra*-djesh	*kradzież*

I've lost ...	zgoo-*bee*-wem/wam ...	*Zgubiłem/łam* (m/f) ...
My ... has/have been stolen.	skra-*djo*-no mee ...	*Skradziono mi ...*
backpack	*ple*-tsak	*plecak*
bicycle	*ro*-ver	*rower*
camera	a-*pa*-rat (fo-to-gra-*feech*-ni)	*aparat (fotograficzny)*
car	sa-*mo*-hoot	*samochód*
credit card	*kar*-te kre-di-*to*-vom	*kartę kredytową*
money	pye-*nyon*-dze	*pieniądze*
papers	do-koo-*men*-ti	*dokumenty*
passport	*pash*-port	*paszport*
travellers cheques	*che*-kee po-*droozh*-ne	*czeki podróżne*
wallet	*por*-tfel	*portfel*

I've been assaulted.
na-pad-*nyen*-to na mnye — *Napadnięto na mnie.*

I've been robbed.
o-bra-bo-*va*-no mnye — *Obrabowano mnie.*

I've been raped.
zgvaw-*tso*-no mnye — *Zgwałcono mnie.*

My car has been broken into.
vwa-*ma*-no she do mo-*ye*-go sa-mo-*ho*-doo — *Włamano się do mojego samochodu.*

My possessions are insured.
mo-ye *zhe*-chi son oo-bes-pye-*cho*-ne — *Moje rzeczy są ubezpieczone.*

I'm a tourist.
yes-tem too-*ris*-tom/ too-*rist*-kom — *Jestem turystą/turystką.* (m/f)

I'm sorry, I don't speak Polish.
pshi-kro mee *a*-le nye *moo*-vye po *pol*-skoo — *Przykro mi ale nie mówię po polsku.*

Does anyone here speak English?
chi ktosh too *moo*-vee po an-*gyel*-skoo? — *Czy ktoś tu mówi po angielsku?*

I (don't) understand.
nye ro-*zoo*-myem — *(Nie) rozumiem.*

I need an interpreter.
pot-she-*boo*-ye twoo-*ma*-cha — *Potrzebuję tłumacza.*

I'm innocent.
yes-tem nye-*veen*-ni/a — *Jestem niewinny/a.* (m/f)

I didn't do it.
nye zro-*bee*-wem/wam *te*-go — *Nie zrobiłem/łam tego.* (m/f)

I didn't realise I was doing anything wrong.
nye son-*djee*-wem/wam zhe *ro*-bye tsosh *zwe*-go — *Nie sądziłem/łam że robię coś złego.* (m/f)

I want to contact my embassy.
htse she skon-tak-*to*-vach *zmo*-yom am-ba-*sa*-dom — *Chcę się skontaktować z moją ambasadą.*

Can I call my consulate?
chi *mo*-ge za-*dzvo*-neech do mo-*ye*-go kon-soo-*la*-too? — *Czy mogę zadzwonić do mojego konsulatu?*

I know my rights.
  znam *mo*-ye *pra*-va — *Znam moje prawa.*

I want to see a lawyer.
  htse she zo-*ba*-chich sprav-*nee*-kyem — *Chcę się zobaczyć z prawnikiem.*

Can I have a lawyer who speaks English?
  po-*pro*-she o prav-*nee*-ka *ktoo*-ri *moo*-vee po an-*gyel*-skoo? — *Poproszę o prawnika który mówi po angielsku.*

What's the charge?
  o tso yest os-kar-*zhe*-nye? — *O co jest oskarżenie?*

assault	*na*-pat	*napad*
disturbing the peace	za-*kwoo*-tse-nye po-*zhon*-tkoo	*zakłócenie porządku*
possession of drugs	po-sha-*da*-nye nar-ko-*ti*-koof	*posiadanie narkotyków*
illegal entry	nye-le-*gal*-ni vyast	*nielegalny wjazd*
entering without a visa	brak *vee*-zi	*brak wizy*
staying without a valid visa	*po*-bit bes *vazh*-ney *vee*-zi	*pobyt bez ważnej wizy*
rape	gvawt	*gwałt*
theft	*kra*-djesh	*kradzież*
traffic violation	na-roo-*she*-nye pshe-*pee*-soof dro-*go*-vih	*naruszenie przepisów drogowych*
working without a permit	*pra*-tsa bes poz-vo-*le*-nya	*praca bez pozwolenia*

Useful Words — Przydatne Słowa

charge	os-kar-*zhe*-nye	*oskarżenie* (neut)
complaint	*skar*-ga	*skarga* (f)
consulate	kon-*soo*-lat	*konsulat* (m)
embassy	am-ba-*sa*-da	*ambasada* (f)

EMERGENCIES

fine (payment)	*ka*-ra	*kara* (f)
guilty	*veen*-ni/a	*winny/a* (m/f)
lawyer	*prav*-neek	*prawnik* (m)
	prav-*neech*-ka	*prawniczka* (f)
not guilty	nye-*veen*-ni/a	*niewinny/a* (m/f)
police officer	po-*lee*-tsyant	*policjant* (m)
	po-*lee-tsyan*-tka	*policjantka* (f)
police station	ko-mee-*sa*-ryat;	*komisariat* (m);
	pos-te-*roo*-nek po-*lee*-tsyee	*posterunek policji* (m)
prison	vyen-*zhe*-nye	*więzienie* (neut)
thief	*zwo*-djey	*złodziej* (m)
theft	*kra*-djesh	*kradzież* (f)
traffic fine	*man*-dat	*mandat* (m)
trial	*pro*-tses	*proces* (m)

THE POLICE MAY SAY ...

po-*pro*-she o ...	*Poproszę o ...*	Please show me your ...
do-koo-*men*-ti	*dokumenty*	identity papers
pash-port	*paszport*	passport
pra-vo *yaz*-di	*prawo jazdy*	drivers licence

yest pan/*pa*-nee za-tshi-*ma*-ni/a
Jest pan/pani zatrzymany/a. (m/f) — You've been arrested.

moo-shee pan/*pa*-nee pooyshch *zna*-mee na pos-te-*roo*-nek
Musi pan/pani pójść z nami na posterunek. (m/f) — You must come with us to the police station.

pwa-chi pan/*pa*-nee *man*-dat
Płaci pan/pani mandat. (m/f) — You're getting a traffic fine.

HEALTH — ZDROWIE

Call a/an ...!	*pro*-she *vez*-vach ...!	*Proszę wezwać ...!*
ambulance	ka-*ret*-ke	*karetkę*
doctor	le-*ka*-zha	*lekarza*

I'm ill.
yes-tem *ho*-ri/a — *Jestem chory/a.*

My friend is ill.
mooy pshi-*ya*-chel yest *ho*-ri — *Mój przyjaciel jest chory.* (m)
mo-ya pshi-ya-*choow*-ka yest *ho*-ra — *Moja przyjaciółka jest chora.* (f)

I have medical insurance.
mam oo-bes-pye-*che*-nye me-*dich*-ne — *Mam ubezpieczenie medyczne.*

Most nouns in Polish are masculine, feminine or neuter.

compass	*kom*-pas	*kompas* (m)
beach	*pla*-zha	*plaża* (f)
field	*po*-le	*pole* (neut)

Some nouns, such as those referring to people, can be either masculine or feminine. In most cases, masculine and feminine endings are separated by a slash:

adult	do-*ros*-wi/a	*dorosły/a* (m/f)

When the masculine and feminine endings are more complicated, both forms of a word are given in full:

teacher	na-oo-chi-*che*-lem/ na-oo-chi-*chel*-kom	*nauczycielem/ nauczycielką* (m/f)

Adjectives agree with the noun they describe. Only the masculine form of an adjective is given in this dictionary. Since there are straightforward rules for forming endings in other genders (see Grammar, page 25), you shouldn't have any problem determining the feminine and neuter forms. Remember that you'll still be understood if you use the masculine form.

The imperfective form is given for most verbs, unless the perfective form is more common. If both forms are included, the impefective is given first.

A

able (to be); can	moots	*móc*

Can (may) I take a photo?
chi *mo*-ge *zro*-beech *zdyen*-che?
Czy mogę zrobić zdjęcie?

Can you show me on the map?
chi *mo*-zhe mee pan/*pa*-nee po-*ka*-zach na *ma*-pye?
Czy może mi pan/pani pokazać na mapie?

abortion	pshe-ri-*va*-nye *chon*-zhi	*przerywanie ciąży*
about (someone/thing)	o	*o*
(approximately)	o-*ko*-wo	*około*
above	nat	*nad*
abroad	za gra-*nee*-tsom	*za granicą*
to accept	pshiy-*mo*-vach	*przyjmować*
accident	vi-*pa*-dek	*wypadek* (m)
accommodation	*nots*-lek	*nocleg* (m)

across the street
po *droo*-gyey *stro*-nye oo-*lee*-tsi
po drugiej stronie ulicy

addiction	*na*-wook	*nałóg* (m)
address	*a*-dres	*adres* (m)
to admire	po-*djee*-vyach	*podziwiać*
admission	fstemp	*wstęp* (m)
to admit	pshi-*zna*-vach	*przyznawać*

adult	do-*ros*-wi/a	*dorosły/a* (m/f)
advance (payment)	za-*leech*-ka	*zaliczka* (f)
advantage	*ko*-zhishch	*korzyść* (f)
advice	po-*ra*-da	*porada* (f)
aeroplane	sa-*mo*-lot	*samolot* (m)

to be afraid of

o-*ba*-vyach she
obawiać się

after	po	*po*
afternoon	po-po-*wood*-nye	*popołudnie* (neut)

in the afternoon

po po-*wood*-nyoo
po południu

this afternoon

djeesh po po-*wood*-nyoo
dziś po południu

again	*zno*-voo	*znowu*
against	pshe-*cheef*-ko	*przeciwko*
age	vyek	*wiek* (m)
to agree	*zga*-dzach she	*zgadzać się*

I don't agree.

nye *zga*-dzam she
Nie zgadzam się.

Agreed.

zgo-da
Zgoda.

agriculture	rol-*neets*-tfo	*rolnictwo* (neut)
ahead	*na*-pshoot	*naprzód*
aid (help)	*po*-mots	*pomoc* (f)
AIDS	ayds	*AIDS*
air	po-*vyet*-she	*powietrze* (neut)
air-con-ditioned	klee-ma-ti-zo-*va*-ni	*klimatyzowany*
airmail	*poch*-ta lot-*nee*-cha	*poczta lotnicza* (f)
airport	lot-*nees*-ko	*lotnisko* (neut)
airport tax	o-*pwa*-ta lot-nees-*ko*-va	*opłata lotniskowa* (f)
alarm clock	*boo*-djeek	*budzik* (m)
all	*fshis*-tko	*wszystko*
allergy	oo-choo-*le*-nye	*uczulenie* (neut)
to allow	po-*zva*-lach	*pozwalać*

It's (not) allowed.

(nye) *vol*-no
(Nie) wolno.

almost	*pra*-vye	*prawie*
alone	sam	*sam* (m)
	sa-ma	*sama* (f)
already	yoosh	*już*
also	tesh • *tak*-zhe	*też* • *także*
altitude	vi-*so*-koshch	*wysokość* (f)
always	*zaf*-she	*zawsze*
amateur	a-*ma*-tor	*amator* (m)
amazing	tsoo-*dov*-ni	*cudowny*
ambassador	am-ba-*sa*-dor	*ambasador* (m)
ambulance	ka-*ret*-ka po-go-*to*-vya	*karetka pogotowia* (f)
among	fshroot • *myen*-dzi	*wśród* • *między*
amount	*ee*-loshch	*ilość* (f)
ancient	sta-ro-*zhit*-ni	*starożytny*
and	ee	*i*
angry	zwi	*zły*
animal	*zvye*-zhe	*zwierzę* (neut)
another		
(different)	*een*-ni	*inny*
(one more)	*yesh*-che *ye*-den	*jeszcze jeden*
answer	ot-*po*-vyech	*odpowiedź* (f)
to answer	ot-po-*vya*-dach	*odpowiadać*
ant	*mroof*-ka	*mrówka* (f)
antibiotic	an-ti-*byo*-tik	*antybiotyk* (m)
antique	*an*-tik	*antyk* (m)
antique shop	an-ti-*kfa*-ryat	*antykwariat* (m)

English	Pronunciation	Polish
antiseptic	an-ti-sep-*tich*-ni	*antyseptyczny*
any	*ya*-keesh	*jakiś*
anybody	ktosh • kto-*kol*-vyek	*ktoś* • *ktokolwiek*
anything	tsosh • tso-*kol*-vyek	*coś* • *cokolwiek*
apartment	myesh-*ka*-nye	*mieszkanie* (neut)
appointment		
(general)	spot-*ka*-nye	*spotkanie* (neut)
(with doctor)	vee-*zi*-ta	*wizyta* (f)
approximate	pshi-blee-*zho*-ni	*przybliżony*
approximately	o-*ko*-wo	*około*
April	*kfye*-chen	*kwiecień* (m)
architecture	ar-hee-tek-*too*-ra	*architektura* (f)
area	*op*-shar	*obszar* (m)
area code (phone)	*noo*-mer kye-roon-*ko*-vi	*numer kierunkowy* (m)
arm	*ra*-mye	*ramię* (neut)
to arrive	pshi-*ye*-hach	*przyjechać*
arrivals		
(plane)	pshi-*lo*-ti	*przyloty* (m, pl)
(train, bus)	pshi-*yas*-di	*przyjazdy* (m, pl)
art	*shtoo*-ka	*sztuka* (f)
art gallery	ga-*le*-rya *shtoo*-kee	*galeria sztuki* (f)
artist	ar-*tis*-ta/ ar-*tist*-ka	*artysta/ artystka* (m/f)
artwork	*dje*-wo *shtoo*-kee	*dzieło sztuki* (neut)
ashtray	po-pyel-*neech*-ka	*popielniczka* (f)
to ask		
(for something)	*pro*-sheech	*prosić*
(a question)	*pi*-tach	*pytać*
aspirin	as-pee-*ri*-na	*aspiryna* (f)
asthma	*ast*-ma	*astma* (f)
atmosphere	at-mos-*fe*-ra	*atmosfera* (f)
August	*sher*-pyen	*sierpień* (m)
aunt	*chot*-ka	*ciotka* (f)
automatic teller machine (ATM)	ban-*ko*-mat	*bankomat* (m)
autumn	*ye*-shen	*jesień* (f)
avalanche	la-*vee*-na	*lawina* (f)
avenue	a-*le*-ya	*aleja* (f)
average	pshe-*chent*-ni	*przeciętny*
awful	o-*krop*-ni	*okropny*

B

English	Pronunciation	Polish
baby	nye-*mov*-le	*niemowlę* (neut)
baby food	od-*zhif*-ka dla nye-*mov*-lont	*odżywka dla niemowląt* (f)
baby powder	za-*sip*-ka dla nye-*mov*-lont	*zasypka dla niemowląt* (f)
back		
(body)	*ple*-tsi	*plecy* (pl)
(side)	tiw	*tył* (m)
at the back (behind)	za/*sti*-woo	*za/z tyłu*
backpack	*ple*-tsak	*plecak* (m)
bad	zwi	*zły*
bag	*tor*-ba	*torba* (f)
baggage	*ba*-gash	*bagaż* (m)
baggage claim	*ot*-byoor ba-*ga*-zhoo	*odbiór bagażu* (m)
bakery	pye-*kar*-nya	*piekarnia* (f)
balcony	*bal*-kon	*balkon* (m)
ball	*peew*-ka	*piłka* (f)
ballet	*ba*-let	*balet* (m)
band (music)	*zes*-poow • *groo*-pa	*zespół* (m) • *grupa* (f)
bandage	*ban*-dash	*bandaż* (m)
bank	bank	*bank* (m)
banknote	*ban*-knot	*banknot* (m)
bar	bar	*bar* (m)
basket	*ko*-shik	*koszyk* (m)
bath	*kom*-pyel	*kąpiel* (f)

bathing suit	*kos*-tyoom kom-pye-*lo*-vi	*kostium kąpielowy* (m)
bathroom	wa-*zhen*-ka	*łazienka* (f)
battery	ba-*te*-rya	*bateria* (f)
to be	bich	*być*
beach	*pla*-zha	*plaża* (f)
beautiful	*pyen*-kni	*piękny*
because	po-*nye*-vash	*ponieważ*
because of	spo-*vo*-doo	*z powodu*
to become	stach she	*stać się*
bed	*woosh*-ko	*łóżko* (neut)
bedlinen	*posh*-chel	*pościel* (f)
bedroom	si-*pyal*-nya	*sypialnia* (f)
bedsheet	pshe-shche-*ra*-dwo	*prześcieradło* (neut)
before (time/space)	pshet	*przed*
beggar	*zhe*-brak/ zhe-brach-ka	*żebrak/ żebraczka* (m/f)
to begin	za-*chi*-nach	*zaczynać*
behind	za	*za*
below	pot • po-*nee*-zhey	*pod* • *poniżej*
beside	*o*-bok	*obok*
best	nay-*lep*-shi	*najlepszy*
better	*lep*-shi	*lepszy*
between	*myen*-dzi	*między*
bible	*bee*-blya	*biblia* (f)
bicycle	*ro*-ver	*rower* (m)
racing bike	*ro*-ver vish-chee-*go*-vi	*rower wyścigowy* (m)
big	*doo*-zhi	*duży*
bike	*ro*-ver	*rower* (m)
bill	ra-*hoo*-nek	*rachunek* (m)

The bill please.
po-pro-she o ra-hoo-nek
Poproszę o rachunek.

binoculars	lor-*net*-ka	*lornetka* (f)
biography	byo-*gra*-fya	*biografia* (f)
bird	ptak	*ptak* (m)
birth certificate	met-*ri*-ka oo-ro-*dze*-nya	*metryka urodzenia* (f)
birthday	oo-ro-*djee*-ni	*urodziny* (pl)
bite (dog)	oo-gri-*zhe*-nye	*ugryzienie* (neut)
bite (insect)	oo-kon-*she*-nye	*ukąszenie* (neut)
black	*char*-ni	*czarny*
B&W film	feelm *char*-no-*bya*-wi	*film czarno-biały*
blanket	kots	*koc* (m)
to bleed	*krfa*-veech	*krwawić*
blind	nye-vee-*do*-mi	*niewidomy*
blood	kref	*krew* (f)
blood group	*groo*-pa krfee	*grupa krwi* (f)
blood pressure	cheesh-*nye*-nye krfee	*ciśnienie krwi* (neut)
blood test	a-na-*lee*-za krfee	*analiza krwi* (f)
blue	nye-*byes*-kee	*niebieski*
boarding pass	*kar*-ta po-kwa-*do*-va	*karta pokładowa* (f)
boat	wooch	*łódź* (f)
body	*cha*-wo	*ciało* (neut)

Bon appetit!
smach-*ne*-go!
Smacznego!

Bon voyage!
shchen-*shlee*-vey po-*droo*-zhi!
Szczęśliwej podróży!

bone	koshch	*kość* (f)
book	*kshon*-shka	*książka* (f)
to book (make a booking)	re-zer-*vo*-vach	*rezerwować*
bookshop	kshen-*gar*-nya	*księgarnia* (f)
boots	*boo*-ti	*buty* (m, pl)
border	gra-*nee*-tsa	*granica* (f)
bored	znoo-*dzo*-ni	*znudzony*
boring	*nood*-ni	*nudny*
to borrow	po-*zhi*-chach	*pożyczać*
both	*o*-bay/ *o*-bye/ o-*bo*-ye	*obaj* (m)/ *obie* (f)/ *oboje* (neut)
bottle	boo-*tel*-ka	*butelka* (f)

English	Pronunciation	Polish
bottle opener	ot-*fye*-rach do boo-*te*-lek	*otwieracz do butelek* (m)
bottom	dno	*dno* (neut)

at the bottom
na dnye
na dnie

English	Pronunciation	Polish
box	poo-*deoo*-ko	*pudełko* (neut)
boxing	boks	*boks* (m)
boy	*hwo*-pyets	*chłopiec* (m)
boyfriend	na-zhe-*cho*-ni	*narzeczony* (m)
bra	byoos-*to*-nosh	*biustonosz* (m)
branch (of tree)	*ga*-wonsh	*gałąź* (f)
branch (of institution)	*ot*-djaw	*oddział* (m)
brave	ot-*vazh*-ni	*odważny*
bread	hlep	*chleb* (m)
to break	*wa*-mach	*łamać*

to break down (vehicle/machine)
zep-sooch she
zepsuć się

English	Pronunciation	Polish
breakdown	a-*va*-rya	*awaria* (f)
break-in	vwa-*ma*-nye	*włamanie* (neut)
breakfast	shnya-*da*-nye	*śniadanie* (neut)
to breathe	ot-*di*-hach	*oddychać*
bribe	wa-*poof*-ka	*łapówka* (f)
to bribe	dach wa-*poof*-ke	*dać łapówkę*
bridge	most	*most* (m)
brilliant	*shwyet*-ni	*świetny*
to bring	pshi-*no*-sheech • *pshi*-nyeshch	*przynosić* • *przynieść*
brochure	bro-*shoo*-ra	*broszura* (f)
broken	za-wa-*ma*-ni	*załamany*
brother	brat	*brat* (m)
brown	bron-*zo*-vi	*brązowy*
brush	*shchot*-ka	*szczotka* (f)
bucket	*vya*-dro	*wiadro* (neut)
to build	boo-*do*-vach	*budować*
building	boo-*di*-nek	*budynek* (m)
bulb (light)	zha-*roof*-ka	*żarówka* (f)
bus	aw-*to*-boos	*autobus* (m)
bus station	*dvo*-zhets aw-to-boo-*so*-vi	*dworzec autobusowy* (m)
bus stop	pshis-*ta*-nek aw-to-boo-*so*-vi	*przystanek autobusowy* (m)
business	*beez*-nes	*biznes* (m)
business person	beez-*nes*-men/ beez-nes-*men*-ka	*biznesmen/ biznesmenka* (m/f)
busy (person)	za-*yen*-ti	*zajęty*
busy (street)	rooh-*lee*-vi	*ruchliwy*
but	*a*-le • lech	*ale* • *lecz*
butcher (shop)	sklep *myen*-sni	*sklep mięsny* (m)
butter	*ma*-swo	*masło* (neut)
butterfly	*mo*-til	*motyl* (m)
button	*goo*-zheek	*guzik* (m)
to buy	koo-*po*-vach • *koo*-peech	*kupować* • *kupić*

I'd like to buy ...
htse *koo*-peech ...
Chcę kupić ...

Where can I buy a ticket?
gdje *mo*-ge *koo*-peech *bee*-let?
Gdzie mogę kupić bilet?

C

English	Pronunciation	Polish
cab	tak-*soof*-ka	*taksówka* (f)
cafe	ka-*vyar*-nya	*kawiarnia* (f)
calendar	ka-*len*-dash	*kalendarz* (m)
to call	*vo*-wach	*wołać*
to call (to phone)	*dzvo*-neech	*dzwonić*
camera	a-*pa*-rat fo-to-gra-*feech*-ni	*aparat fotograficzny* (m)
camera shop	fo-to-*op*-ti-ka	*fotooptyka* (f)
campsite	*kam*-peenk	*camping* (m)

Can we camp here?
chi *mozh*-na too *ros*-beech *na*-myot?
Czy można tu rozbić namiot?

C

can (to be able)	moots	*móc*

We can do it.
mo-*zhe*-mi to *zro*-beech
Możemy to zrobić.

I can't do it.
nye *mo*-ge *te*-go *zro*-beech
Nie mogę tego zrobić.

can (tin)	*poosh*-ka	*puszka* (f)
can opener	ot-*fye*-rach do *kon*-serf	*otwieracz do konserw* (m)
to cancel	ot-*vo*-wach	*odwołać*
candle	*shfye*-tsa	*świeca* (f)
car	sa-*mo*-hoot	*samochód* (m)
caravan (trailer)	pshi-*che*-pa	*przyczepa* (f)
card	*kar*-ta	*karta* (f)
cards (playing)	*kar*-ti do gri	*karty do gry* (pl)
careful	os-*trozh*-ni	*ostrożny*

Careful!
os-*trozh*-nye!
Ostrożnie!

carpet	*di*-van	*dywan* (m)
carpark	*par*-keenk	*parking* (m)
car rental	vi-*na*-yem sa-mo-*ho*-doof	*wynajem samochodów* (m)
to carry	*no*-sheech	*nosić*
cash	go-*toof*-ka	*gotówka* (f)
cashier	*ka*-syer/ ka-*syer*-ka	*kasjer/ kasjerka* (m/f)
cassette	ka-*se*-ta	*kaseta* (f)
castle	*za*-mek	*zamek* (m)
cat	kot	*kot* (m)
to catch	*wa*-pach	*łapać*
cathedral	ka-*te*-dra	*katedra* (f)
Catholic (adj)	ka-to-*leets*-kee	*katolicki*
a Catholic	ka-*to*-leek/ ka-to-*leech*-ka	*katolik/ katoliczka* (m/f)
cave	yas-*kee*-nya	*jaskinia* (f)
CD	*pwi*-ta kom-pak-*to*-va	*płyta kompaktowa* (f)
cellar	peev-*nee*-tsa	*piwnica* (f)
cellular phone	te-*le*-fon ko-moor-*ko*-vi	*telefon komórkowy* (m)
cemetery	*tsmen*-tash	*cmentarz* (m)
centimetre	tsen-*ti*-metr	*centymetr* (m)
central	tsen-*tral*-ni	*centralny*
centre (of town)	*tsen*-troom	*centrum* (neut)
centre (institution)	osh-*ro*-dek	*ośrodek* (m)
certainly	o-chi-*veesh*-che	*oczywiście*
chair	*kshe*-swo	*krzesło* (neut)
champagne	*sham*-pan	*szampan* (m)
to change	*zmye*-nyach	*zmieniać*
to change (money)	vi-*mye*-nyach	*wymieniać*
change (coins)	*drob*-ne • *resh*-ta	*drobne* (pl) • *reszta* (f)
chapel	ka-*plee*-tsa	*kaplica* (f)
charge (fee)	o-*pwa*-ta	*opłata* (f)
cheap	*ta*-nee	*tani*

cheap hotel
ta-nee *ho*-tel
tani hotel (m)

cheat	o-*shoos*-tfo	*oszustwo* (neut)
to check	*sprav*-dzach	*sprawdzać*
checkpoint	poonkt kon-*tro*-lee	*punkt kontroli* (m)
cheese	ser	*ser* (m)
chemist	ap-*te*-ka	*apteka* (f)
cheque	chek	*czek* (m)
chess	*sha*-hi	*szachy* (m, pl)
chessboard	sha-hov-*nee*-tsa	*szachownica* (f)
chest (body part)	pyersh	*pierś* (f)
chewing gum	*goo*-ma do *zhoo*-cha	*guma do żucia* (f)
chicken	*koor*-chak	*kurczak* (m)
child	*djets*-ko	*dziecko* (neut)
child-minding	o-*pye*-ka do *djets*-ka	*opieka do dziecka* (f)

DICTIONARY

children	*dje*-chee	*dzieci* (pl)
chips	*frit*-kee	*frytki* (f, pl)
chocolate	che-ko-*la*-da	*czekolada* (f)
to choose	vi-*bye*-rach • *vi*-brach	*wybierać* • *wybrać*
Christian name	*ee*-mye	*imię* (neut)
Christmas	*bo*-zhe na-ro-*dze*-nye	*Boże Narodzenie* (neut)
Christmas Eve	vee-*gee*-lya	*Wigilia* (f)
church	*kosh*-choow	*kościół* (m)
cigarette	pa-*pye*-ros	*papieros* (m)
cigarette lighter	za-pal-*neech*-ka	*zapalniczka* (f)
cinema	*kee*-no	*kino* (neut)
circus	tsirk	*cyrk* (m)
citizenship	o-bi-va-*tel*-stfo	*obywatelstwo* (neut)
city	*mya*-sto	*miasto* (neut)
city centre	*tsen*-troom	*centrum* (neut)
class	*kla*-sa	*klasa* (f)
clean	*chis*-ti	*czysty*
clean hotel	*chis*-ti *ho*-tel	*czysty hotel* (m)
cleaning	spshon-*ta*-nye	*sprzątanie* (neut)
client	*klee*-yent klee-*yen*-tka	*klient* (m) *klientka* (f)
cliff	oor-*vees*-ko	*urwisko* (neut)
to climb	*fspee*-nach she	*wspinać się*
climbing (the sport)	fspee-*nach*-ka	*wspinaczka* (f)
cloakroom	*shat*-nya	*szatnia* (f)
clock	*ze*-gar	*zegar* (m)
to close	za-*mi*-kach • *zam*-knonch	*zamykać* • *zamknąć*
closed	zam-*knyen*-ti	*zamknięty*
clothing	oo-*bra*-nye • *o*-djesh	*ubranie* (neut) • *odzież* (f)
clothing store	sklep o-dje-*zho*-vi	*sklep odzieżowy* (m)
cloud	*hmoo*-ra	*chmura* (f)
cloudy	poh-*moor*-ni	*pochmurny*
coach (bus)	aw-*to*-boos • aw-*to*-kar	*autobus* (m) • *autokar* (m)
coast	vi-*bzhe*-zhe	*wybrzeże* (neut)
coat	pwashch	*płaszcz* (m)
cocaine	ko-ka-*ee*-na	*kokaina* (f)
coffee	*ka*-va	*kawa* (f)
coin	mo-*ne*-ta	*moneta* (f)
cold		
(n)	pshe-zhem-*bye*-nye	*przeziębienie* (neut)
(adj)	*zheem*-ni	*zimny*

It's cold.
yest *zheem*-no
Jest zimno.

I have a cold.
yes-tem pshe-zhem-*byo*-ni
Jestem przeziębiony.

cold water	*zheem*-na *vo*-da	*zimna woda* (f)
colleague	ko-*le*-ga/ ko-le-*zhan*-ka	*kolega/ koleżanka* (m/f)
collect	*zbye*-rach	*zbierać*
colour	*ko*-lor	*kolor* (m)
comb	*gzhe*-byen	*grzebień* (m)
to come	pshi-*ho*-djeech • pshiyshch	*przychodzić* • *przyjść*
comedy	ko-*me*-dya	*komedia* (f)
comfortable	vi-*god*-ni	*wygodny*
common	*fspool*-ni • pof-*sheh*-ni	*wspólny* • *powszechny*
communion	ko-*moo*-nya	*komunia* (f)
communism	ko-*moo*-neezm	*komunizm* (m)
compact disc	*pwi*-ta kom-pak-*to*-va	*płyta kompaktowa* (f)
company	pshet-shem-*byor*-stfo • *feer*-ma	*przedsiębiorstwo* (neut) • *firma* (f)
compass	*kom*-pas	*kompas* (m)
computer games	gri kom-poo-te-*ro*-ve	*gry komputerowe* (f, pl)
concert	*kon*-tsert	*koncert* (m)
confession (religious)	*spo*-vyech	*spowiedź* (f)

to confirm (a booking)	pot-*fyer*-djeech	*potwierdzić*

Congratulations!
gra-too-*la*-tsye!
Gratulacje!

connection	po-won-*che*-nye	*połączenie* (neut)
constipation	zat-far-*dze*-nye	*zatwardzenie* (f)

to be constipated
myech zat-far-*dze*-nye
mieć zatwardzenie

construction work	*pra*-tsa na boo-*do*-vye	*praca na budowie* (f)
consulate	kon-*soo*-lat	*konsulat* (m)
contact lenses	shkwa kon-tak-*to*-ve	*szkła kontaktowe* (neut, pl)
contemporary	fspoow-*ches*-ni	*współczesny*
contraception	za-po-bye-*ga*-nye *chon*-zhi	*zapobieganie ciąży* (neut)
contraceptive	*shro*-dek an-ti-kon-tsep-*tsiy*-ni	*środek antykoncepcyjny* (m)
contract	*kon*-trakt	*kontrakt* (m)
convent	*klash*-tor	*klasztor* (m)
to cook	go-*to*-vach	*gotować*
cool	*hwod*-ni	*chłodny*
corner		
(of street)	rook	*róg* (m)
(of room)	kont	*kąt* (m)
corruption	ko-*roop*-tsya	*korupcja* (f)
cost	kosht	*koszt* (m)
to cost	kosh-*to*-vach	*kosztować*

How much does it cost?
ee-le to kosh-*too*-ye?
Ile to kosztuje?

cotton	ba-*veoo*-na	*bawełna* (f)
couchette	koo-*shet*-ka	*kuszetka* (f)
cough	*ka*-shel	*kaszel* (m)
to count	*lee*-chich	*liczyć*
country	kray	*kraj* (m)
couple (two people)	*pa*-ra	*para* (f)

a couple of
pa-re
parę

coupon	*koo*-pon	*kupon* (m)
course	*da*-nye	*danie* (neut)

Of course.
o-chi-*veesh*-che
Oczywiście.

court		
(legal)	sont	*sąd* (m)
(tennis)	kort	*kort* (m)
cousin	*koo*-zin/koo-*zin*-ka	*kuzyn/kuzynka* (m/f)
cow	*kro*-va	*krowa* (f)
craft	zhe-*myo*-swo	*rzemiosło* (neut)
crazy	zva-ryo-*va*-ni	*zwariowany*
credit card	*kar*-ta kre-di-*to*-va	*karta kredytowa* (f)
cross (religious)	kshish	*krzyż* (m)
crowded	za-two-*cho*-ni	*zatłoczony*
crown	ko-*ro*-na	*korona* (f)
to cry	*pwa*-kach	*płakać*
cup	fee-lee-*zhan*-ka	*filiżanka* (f)
cupboard	*sha*-fa • *kre*-dens	*szafa* (f) • *kredens* (m)
currency	va-*loo*-ta	*waluta* (f)
current	pront	*prąd* (m)
customs	tswo	*cło* (neut)
cut (wound)	*ra*-na • ska-le-*che*-nye	*rana* (f) • *skaleczenie* (neut)
to cut	chonch • *kro*-eech	*ciąć* • *kroić*
cycling		
(sport)	ko-*lar*-stfo	*kolarstwo* (neut)
(recreation)	*jaz*-da na ro-*ve*-zhe	*jazda na rowerze* (neut)
cyclist	ro-ve-*zhis*-ta/ro-ve-*zhist*-ka	*rowerzysta/rowerzystka* (m/f)

D

English	Pronunciation	Polish
dad	*ta*-ta	*tata* (m)
daily	tso-*djen*-nye	*codziennie*
daily newspaper	*djen*-neek	*dziennik* (m)
dairy products	*na*-byaw	*nabiał* (m)
to dance	*tan*-chich	*tańczyć*
dance	*ta*-nyets	*taniec* (m)
dangerous	nye-bes-*pyech*-ni	*niebezpieczny*
dark	*chem*-ni	*ciemny*
date		
(appointment)	spot-*ka*-nye • *ran*-tka	*spotkanie* (neut) • *randka* (f)
(time)	*da*-ta	*data* (f)
date of birth	*da*-ta oo-ro-*dze*-nya	*data urodzenia* (f)
daughter	*tsoor*-ka	*córka* (f)
dawn	shfeet	*świt* (m)
day	djen	*dzień* (m)

day after tomorrow
po-*yoot*-she
pojutrze

day before yesterday
pshet-*fcho*-ray
przedwczoraj

every day
tso-*djen*-nye
codziennie

English	Pronunciation	Polish
dead		
(person)	*zmar*-wi	*zmarły*
(animal)	*zdeh*-wi	*zdechły*
deaf	*gwoo*-hi	*głuchy*
death	shmerch	*śmierć* (f)
December	*groo*-djen	*grudzień* (m)
to decide	de-tsi-*do*-vach	*decydować*
decision	de-*tsi*-zya	*decyzja* (f)
deck		
(of cards)	*ta*-lya	*talia* (f)
(of ship)	*po*-kwat	*pokład* (m)
deep	gwem-*bo*-kee	*głęboki*
deer	*ye*-len	*jeleń* (m)
deforestation	de-fo-res-*ta*-tsya	*deforestacja* (f)
degree	*sto*-pyen	*stopień* (m)
delay	o-poozh-*nye*-nye	*opóźnienie* (neut)
delicatessen	de-lee-ka-*te*-si	*delikatesy* (pl)
delivery	dos-*ta*-va	*dostawa* (f)
democracy	de-mo-*kra*-tsya	*demokracja* (f)
demonstration	de-mon-*stra*-tsya	*demonstracja* (f)
dentist	den-*tis*-ta/ den-*tist*-ka	*dentysta/ dentystka* (m/f)
to deny	ot-*moo*-veech	*odmówić*
deodorant	de-so-*do*-rant	*dezodorant* (m)
to depart (leave)	ot-*yesh*-djach	*odjeżdżać*
department store	dom to-va-*ro*-vi	*dom towarowy* (m)
departures		
(bus, train)	ot-*yas*-di	*odjazdy* (m, pl)
(plane)	ot-*lo*-ti	*odloty* (m, pl)
desert	poos-*ti*-nya	*pustynia* (f)
design		
(project)	*pro*-yekt	*project* (m)
(intention)	*za*-myar	*zamiar* (m)
destination	tsel po-*droo*-zhi	*cel podróży* (m)
to destroy	*neesh*-chich • *zneesh*-chich	*niszczyć* • *zniszczyć*
detail	*shche*-goow	*szczegół* (m)
development	*roz*-vooy	*rozwój* (m)
diabetes	tsook-*shi*-tsa	*cukrzyca* (f)
diarrhoea	bye-*goon*-ka • roz-vol-*nye*-nye	*biegunka* (f) • *rozwolnienie* (neut)
diary		
(record)	pa-*myent*-neek	*pamiętnik* (m)
(book)	no-*tat*-neek	*notatnik* (m)

D

dictionary	*swov*-neek	*słownik* (m)
to die	oo-*mye*-rach	*umierać*
difference	roozh-*nee*-tsa	*różnica* (f)
different	*een*-ni	*inny*
difficult	*trood*-ni	*trudny*
dining car	*va*-gon res-ta-oo-ra-*tsiy*-ni	*wagon restauracyjny* (m)
dining room	ya-*dal*-nya	*jadalnia* (f)
dinner	*o*-byat	*obiad* (m)
direct	bes-posh-*red*-nee	*bezpośredni*
direction	kye-*roo*-nek	*kierunek* (m)
director		
(company)	di-*rek*-tor/ di-rek-*tor*-ka	*dyrektor/ dyrektorka* (m/f)
(film)	re-*zhi*-ser/ re-zhi-*ser*-ka	*reżyser/ reżyserka* (m/f)
dirty	*brood*-ni	*brudny*
disabled	nye-peoo-no-*sprav*-ni	*niepełnosprawny*
disadvantage	nye-*ko*-zhishch	*niekorzyść* (f)
to disappear	*znee*-kach	*znikać*
discount	*zneesh*-ka	*zniżka* (f)
to discover	ot-*kri*-vach	*odkrywać*
discrimination	dis-kri-mee-*na*-tsya	*dyskryminacja* (f)
disease	ho-*ro*-ba	*choroba* (f)
dish	*da*-nye	*danie* (neut)
distance	*dis*-tans	*dystans* (m)
diving	noor-ko-*va*-nye	*nurkowanie* (neut)
to do	*ro*-beech • *zro*-beech	*robić* • *zrobić*

What are you doing? (m/f)
tso pan/pa-nee ro-bee?
Co pan/pani robi?

I didn't do it.
nye sro-bee-wem te-go
Nie zrobiłem tego.

doctor	*dok*-toor • *le*-kash/ le-*kar*-ka	*doktór* (m) • *lekarz/ lekarka* (m/f)
document	do-*koo*-ment	*dokument* (m)
dog	pyes	*pies* (m)
dole	za-*shee*-wek	*zasiłek* (m)
doll	*lal*-ka	*lalka* (f)
door	dzhvee	*drzwi* (pl)
dope (drugs)	nar-ko-*ti*-kee	*narkotyki* (m, pl)
double	pod-*vooy*-ni	*podwójny*
double bed	*woosh*-ko maw-*zhen*-skye	*łożko małżeńskie* (neut)
double room	*po*-kooy dvoo-o-so-*bo*-vi	*pokój dwuosobowy* (m)
down	na doow	*na dół*
downtown	*tsen*-troom	*centrum* (neut)
dozen	*too*-zheen	*tuzin* (m)
drama	*dra*-mat	*dramat* (m)
dramatic	dra-ma-*tich*-ni	*dramatyczny*
dream	sen	*sen* (m)
to dream	shneech • *ma*-zhich	*śnić* • *marzyć*
dress	oo-*bra*-nye • soo-*kyen*-ka	*ubranie* (neut) • *sukienka* (f)
to dress	oo-*bye*-rach she	*ubierać się*
drink	*na*-pooy	*napój* (m)
to drink	peech • *vi*-peech	*pić* • *wypić*
drinking water	*vo*-da *peet*-na	*woda pitna* (f)
to drive	kye-*ro*-vach	*kierować*
driver	kye-*rof*-tsa	*kierowca* (m)
driving licence	*pra*-vo *yaz*-di	*prawo jazdy* (neut)
drug		
(medicine)	lek	*lek* (m)
(narcotic)	nar-*ko*-tik	*narkotyk* (m)
drug addict	nar-*ko*-man/ nar-ko-*man*-ka	*narkoman/ narkomanka* (m/f)
drug dealer	*han*-dlash nar-ko-*ti*-koof	*handlarz narkotyków* (m)

DICTIONARY

drum	*bem*-ben	*bęben* (m)
drunk (inebriated)	pee-*ya*-ni	*pijany*
drunk driving	*yas*-da po pee-ya-*ne*-moo	*jazda po pijanemu* (f)
to dry (clothes)	*soo*-shich	*suszyć*
drycleaner	*pral*-nya he-*meech*-na	*pralnia chemiczna* (f)
duck	*kach*-ka	*kaczka* (f)
dummy (baby's)	*smo*-chek	*smoczek* (m)
during	*pot*-chas	*podczas*
dusk	zmyeshh	*zmierzch* (m)
dust	koosh	*kurz* (m)
dustbin	po-*yem*-neek na *shmye*-chee	*pojemnik na śmieci* (m)
dusty	za-koo-*zho*-ni	*zakurzony*
duty-free zone	*stre*-fa vol-no-*tswo*-va	*strefa wolnocłowa* (f)

E

each	*kazh*-di	*każdy*
ear	*oo*-ho	*ucho* (neut)
early	*fchesh*-nye	*wcześnie*
to earn	za-*ra*-byach	*zarabiać*
earrings	do-*ho*-di • za-*rop*-kee	*dochody* (m) • *zarobki* (m)
Earth	*zhe*-mya	*ziemia* (f)
earth (soil)	*gle*-ba	*gleba* (f)
earthquake	tshen-*she*-nye *zhe*-mee	*trzęsienie ziemi* (neut)
east	fs-hoot	*wschód* (m)
Easter	vyel-*ka*-nots	*Wielkanoc* (f)
easy	*wat*-fi	*łatwy*
to eat	yeshch	*jeść*
economy	e-ko-*no*-mya • gos-po-*dar*-ka	*ekonomia* (f) • *gospodarka* (f)
editor	re-*dak*-tor/ re-dak-*tor*-ka	*redaktor/ redaktorka* (m/f)
education	osh-*fya*-ta	*oświata* (f)
egg	*yay*-ko	*jajko* (neut)
elections	vi-*bo*-ri	*wybory* (m, pl)
electric	e-lek-*trich*-ni	*elektryczny*
electricity	e-lek-*trich*-noshch	*elektryczność* (f)
elevator (lift)	*veen*-da	*winda* (f)
embarassed	za-kwo-po-*ta*-ni	*zakłopotany*
embarassment	za-kwo-po-*ta*-nye	*zakłopotanie* (neut)
embassy	am-ba-*sa*-da	*ambasada* (f)
emergency	*na*-gwi pshi-*pa*-dek	*nagły przypadek* (m)
emergency exit	*viy*-shche a-va-*riy*-ne • *viy*-shche bes-pye-*chen*-stfa	*wyjście awaryjne* (neut) • *wyjście bezpieczeństwa* (neut)
employee	pra-*tsov*-neek/ pra-tsov-*neech*-ka	*pracownik/ pracowniczka* (m/f)
employer	pra-tso-*daf*-tsa/ pra-tso-daf-*chi*-nee	*pracodawca/ pracodawczyni* (m/f)
employment	za-trood-*nye*-nye	*zatrudnienie* (neut)
empty	*poos*-ti	*pusty*
end	*ko*-nyets	*koniec* (m)
to end	*kon*-chich	*kończyć*
energy	e-*ner*-gya	*energia* (f)
engaged		
(toilet)	za-*yen*-ti	*zajęty*
(hitched)	za-ren-*cho*-ni	*zaręczony*
engine		
(machine)	ma-*shi*-na	*maszyna* (f)
(of car)	*sheel*-neek	*silnik* (m)
engineer	een-*zhi*-nyer	*inżynier* (m)
English	an-*gyel*-skee	*angielski*
to enjoy (yourself)	*che*-shich she	*cieszyć się*
enjoyable	pshi-*yem*-ni	*przyjemny*
enough	*do*-sich	*dosyć*

F

> Enough!
> doshch!
> *Dość!*

to enter	*fho*-djeech • veyshch	*wchodzić* • *wejść*
entertainment	roz-*rif*-ka	*rozrywka* (f)
entrance	*vey*-shche	*wejście* (neut)
envelope	ko-*per*-ta	*koperta* (f)
environment	shro-do-*vees*-ko	*środowisko* (neut)
epileptic	e-pee-*lep*-tik/ e-pee-lep-*tich*-ka	*epileptyk/ epileptyczka* (m/f)
equal	*roov*-ni	*równy*
equality	*roov*-noshch	*równość* (f)
equipment	spshent	*sprzęt* (m)
error	bwont • po-*miw*-ka	*błąd* (m) • *pomyłka* (f)
essential	nyes-*bend*-ni • pot-sta-*vo*-vi	*niezbędny* • *podstawowy*
European	ew-ro-*pey*-skee	*europejski*
European Union	*oo*-nya ew-ro-*pey*-ska	*Unia Europejska* (f)
euthanasia	ew-ta-*na*-zya	*eutanazja* (f)
even		
(adv)	*na*-vet	*nawet*
(number)	pa-*zhis*-ti	*parzysty*
evening	*vye*-choor	*wieczór* (m)
every	*kazh*-di	*każdy*
every day	tso-*djen*-nye	*codziennie*
everyone	*fshis*-tsi	*wszyscy*
everything	*fshis*-tko	*wszystko*
everywhere	*fshen*-dje	*wszędzie*
exam	e-*gza*-meen	*egzamin* (m)
example	*pshi*-kwat	*przykład* (m)

> For example, ...
> na *pshi*-kwat ...
> *Na przykład, ...*

excellent	dos-ko-*na*-wi	*doskonały*
except	*o*-prooch	*oprócz*
excess baggage	nat-*va*-ga ba-*ga*-zhoo	*nadwaga bagażu* (f)
exchange	vi-*mya*-na	*wymiana* (f)
to exchange	vi-*mye*-nyach	*wymieniać*
exchange rate	koors vi-*mya*-ni	*kurs wymiany* (m)
excluding	svi-*yont*-kyem	*z wyjątkiem*

> Excuse me.
> pshe-*pra*-sham
> *Przepraszam.*

exhibition	vis-*ta*-va	*wystawa* (f)
exit	*viy*-shche	*wyjście* (neut)
to expect	spo-*dje*-vach she	*spodziewać się*
expensive	*dro*-gee	*drogi*
experience	dosh-fyat-*che*-nye	*doświadczenie* (neut)
experienced	dosh-fyat-*cho*-ni	*doświadczony*
to explain	vi-*yash*-neech	*wyjaśnić*
express mail	leest eks-pre-*so*-vi	*list ekspresowy* (m)
express train	*po*-chonk eks-pre-*so*-vi	*pociąg ekspresowy* (m)
extension (phone)	vev-*nench*-ni	*wewnętrzny*
extension lead	pshe-*dwoo*-zhach	*przedłużacz* (m)
extra (adj)	do-dat-*ko*-vi	*dodatkowy*
eye	*o*-ko	*oko* (neut)

F

face	tfash	*twarz* (f)
factory	fa-*bri*-ka	*fabryka* (f)
factory worker	ro-*bot*-neek/ ro-bot-*nee*-tsa	*robotnik/ robotnica* (m/f)
fair		
(trade)	*tar*-gee	*targi* (m, pl)
(bazaar)	*yar*-mark	*jarmark* (m)
fall	*ye*-shen	*jesień* (f)
to fall	oo-*pa*-dach	*upadać*
false (fake)	faw-*shi*-vi	*fałszywy*
family	ro-*djee*-na	*rodzina* (f)
famous	*swav*-ni	*sławny*

DICTIONARY

English	Pronunciation	Polish
fan		
(electrical)	ven-ti-*la*-tor	*wentylator* (m)
(of a team)	*kee*-beets	*kibic* (m)
fan belt	*pa*-sek klee-*no*-vi	*pasek klinowy* (m)
fantastic	fan-tas-*tich*-ni	*fantastyczny*
far	da-*le*-kee	*daleki*
fare	ta-*ri*-fa	*taryfa* (f)
farm	gos-po-*dar*-stfo *rol*-ne	*gospodarstwo rolne* (neut)
farmer	*rol*-neek	*rolnik* (m)
fashionable	*mod*-ni	*modny*
fast (quick)	*ship*-kee	*szybki*
fast train	*po*-chonk pos-*pyesh*-ni	*pociąg pospieszny* (m)
fat (person)	*groo*-bi	*gruby*
fat (meat)	*twoos*-ti	*tłusty*
father	*oy*-chets	*ojciec* (m)
father-in-law	teshch	*teść* (m)
fault		
(someone's)	*vee*-na	*wina* (f)
(something's)	*va*-da	*wada* (f)
faulty	vad-*lee*-vi	*wadliwy*
favourite	oo-loo-*byo*-ni	*ulubiony*
fear	strah • o-*ba*-va	*strach* (m) • *obawa* (f)
to fear	bach she	*bać się*
feature film	feelm fa-boo-*lar*-ni	*film fabularny* (m)
February	*loo*-ti	*luty* (m)
fee	o-*pwa*-ta	*opłata* (f)
to feel	chooch (she)	*czuć (się)*

I feel fine.
choo-ye she *do*-bzhe
Czuję się dobrze.

How are you feeling?
yak she *choo*-yesh?
Jak się czujesz?

I feel like ...
mam o-*ho*-te ...
Mam ochotę ...

English	Pronunciation	Polish
feeling	oo-*choo*-che	*uczucie* (neut)
female (animal)	sa-*mee*-tsa	*samica* (f)
fence	pwot	*płot* (m)
ferry	prom	*prom* (m)
festival	fes-*tee*-val	*festiwal* (m)
fever	go-*ronch*-ka	*gorączka* (f)
a few	*keel*-koo/ *keel*-ka	*kilku* (m)/ *kilka* (f, neut)
fiancé	na-zhe-*cho*-ni	*narzeczony* (m)
fiancée	na-zhe-*cho*-na	*narzeczona* (f)
fiction	*feek*-tsya	*fikcja* (f)
field	*po*-le	*pole* (neut)
fight	*val*-ka	*walka* (f)
to fight	*val*-chich	*walczyć*
to fill in	vi-*peoo*-neech	*wypełnić*
to fill up	na-*peoo*-neech	*napełnić*
film (cinema /camera)	feelm	*film* (m)
film processing	vi-vo-*wa*-nye *feel*-moo	*wywołanie filmu* (neut)
film speed	*choo*-woshch *feel*-moo	*czułość filmu* (f)
filthy	*brood*-ni	*brudny*
to find	*zna*-leshch	*znaleźć*

to find out
do-*vye*-djech she
dowiedzieć się

English	Pronunciation	Polish
fine		
(nice)	*wad*-ni	*ładny*
(penalty)	*ka*-ra	*kara* (f)
(traffic penalty)	*man*-dat	*mandat* (m)
finger	*pa*-lets	*palec* (m)
fir (tree)	*yo*-dwa	*jodła* (f)
fire		
(flames)	*o*-gyen	*ogień* (m)
(campfire)	og-*nees*-ko	*ognisko* (neut)
(emergency)	*po*-zhar	*pożar* (m)

Fire!
po-zhar! • *pa*-lee she!
Pożar! • Pali się!

F

English	Pronunciation	Polish
fire alarm	*a*-larm pshe-cheef-po-zha-*ro*-vi	*alarm przeciwpożarowy* (m)
fire brigade	strash po-*zhar*-na	*straż pożarna* (neut)
fire extinguisher	gash-*nee*-tsa	*gaśnica* (f)
fire fighter	*stra*-zhak	*strażak* (m)
first	*pyer*-fshi	*pierwszy*
first aid	*pyer*-fsha *po*-mots	*pierwsza pomoc* (f)
first-aid kit	ap-*tech*-ka *pyer*-fshey po-*mo*-tsi	*apteczka pierwszej pomocy* (f)
first class	*pyer*-fsha *kla*-sa	*pierwsza klasa* (f)
first name	*ee*-mye	*imię* (neut)
fish	*ri*-ba	*ryba* (f)
to fish	*wo*-veech *ri*-bi	*łowić ryby*
fishing (hobby)	vent-*kar*-stfo	*wędkarstwo* (neut)
fishmonger	sklep *rib*-ni	*sklep rybny* (m)
to fit	pa-*so*-vach	*pasować*
to fix		
(arrange)	za-*wat*-feech	*załatwić*
(repair)	na-*pra*-veech	*naprawić*
flag	ban-*de*-ra	*bandera* (f)
flat		
(adj)	*pwas*-kee	*płaski*
(apartment)	myesh-*ka*-nye	*mieszkanie* (neut)
flea	phwa	*pchła* (f)
flash (camera)	flesh	*flesz* (m)
flashlight (torch)	la-*tar*-ka	*latarka* (f)
flavour	smak	*smak* (m)
flight	lot	*lot* (m)
flood	*po*-vooch	*powódź* (f)
floor		
(of room)	po-*dwo*-ga	*podłoga* (f)
(storey)	*pyen*-tro	*piętro* (neut)
florist	kfya-*char*-nya	*kwiaciarnia* (f)
flour	*mon*-ka	*mąka* (f)
flower	kfyat	*kwiat* (m)
flu	*gri*-pa	*grypa* (f)
fluent	*bye*-gwi	*biegły*
fly	*moo*-ha	*mucha* (f)
to fly	*la*-tach • po-*le*-chech	*latać* • *polecieć*
fog	mgwa	*mgła* (f)
folk	loo-*do*-vi	*ludowy*
folk art	*shtoo*-ka loo-*do*-va	*sztuka ludowa* (f)
folklore	*fol*-klor	*folklor* (m)
to follow	eeshch za	*iść za*
food	*zhiv*-noshch • ye-*dze*-nye	*żywność* (f) • *jedzenie* (neut)
food poisoning	za-*troo*-che po-kar-*mo*-ve	*zatrucie pokarmowe* (neut)
grocery store	sklep spo-*zhif*-chi	*sklep spożywczy* (m)
foot	*sto*-pa	*stopa* (f)
football (soccer)	*peew*-ka *nozh*-na	*piłka nożna* (f)
footpath	*shchesh*-ka	*ścieżka* (f)
for	dla	*dla*
foreign		
(alien)	za-gra-*neech*-ni	*zagraniczny*
(unfamiliar)	*op*-tsi	*obcy*
foreigner	tsoo-dzo-*zhe*-myets/ tsoo-dzo-*zhem*-ka	*cudzoziemiec/ cudzoziemka* (m/f)
forest	las	*las* (m)
forever	na *zaf*-she	*na zawsze*
to forget	za-po-*mee*-nach • za-*pom*-nyech	*zapominać* • *zapomnieć*

I've forgotten my passport.
za-pom-*nya*-wem pash-*por*-too
Zapomniałem paszportu.

Don't forget an umbrella.
nye za-*pom*-neey pa-ra-*so*-la
Nie zapomnij parasola.

DICTIONARY

English	Pronunciation	Polish
to forgive	pshe-*ba*-chich	*przebaczyć*
form (paperwork)	for-*moo*-lash	*formularz* (m)
fortnight	dva ti-*go*-dnye	*dwa tygodnie*
fortunately	na *shchen*-shche	*na szczęście*
fortune teller	vroozh-*bee*-ta/ *vroosh*-ka	*wróżbita/ wróżka* (m/f)
foundation	foon-*da*-tsya	*fundacja* (f)
fountain	fon-*tan*-na	*fontanna* (f)
fracture	zwa-*ma*-nye	*złamanie* (neut)
frame	*ra*-ma	*rama* (f)
free		
(unbound)	*vol*-ni	*wolny*
(gratis)	bes-*pwat*-ni	*bezpłatny*
freeway	aw-to-*stra*-da	*autostrada* (f)
to freeze	za-*mra*-zhach	*zamrażać*
freezer	za-mra-*zhar*-ka	*zamrażarka* (f)
frequent	*chen*-sti	*częsty*
fresh	*shfye*-zhi	*świeży*
Friday	*pyon*-tek	*piątek* (m)
fridge	lo-*doof*-ka	*lodówka* (f)
fried	sma-*zho*-ni	*smażony*
friend	pshi-*ya*-chel/ pshi-ya-*choow*-ka	*przyjaciel/ przyjaciółka* (m/f)
friendly	zhich-*lee*-vi	*życzliwy*
front	pshoot	*przód* (m)
frost	mroos	*mróz* (m)
frozen foods	mro-*zhon*-kee	*mrożonki* (f, pl)
fruit	*o*-vots • o-*vo*-tse	*owoc* (m) • *owoce* (pl)
fruit juice	sok o-vo-*tso*-vi	*sok owocowy* (m)
full	*pew*-ni	*pełny*
fun	za-*ba*-va	*zabawa* (f)

for fun
dla *zhar*-too
dla żartu

to have fun
ba-veech she
bawić się

to make fun of
zhar-*to*-vach s
żartować z

English	Pronunciation	Polish
funeral	*pog*-zhep	*pogrzeb* (m)
furniture	*me*-ble	*meble* (m, pl)
fuse	bes-*pyech*-neek	*bezpiecznik* (m)
future	*pshish*-woshch	*przyszłość* (f)

G

English	Pronunciation	Polish
game	gra	*gra* (f)
games	za-*vo*-di	*zawody* (pl)
Olympic Games	o-leem-*pya*-da	*olimpiada* (f)
garage		
(parking)	*ga*-rash	*garaż* (m)
(mechanic)	*var*-shtat sa-mo-ho-*do*-vi	*warsztat samochodowy* (m)
garbage	*shmye*-chee	*śmieci* (pl)
gardening	o-grod-*neets*-tfo	*ogrodnictwo* (neut)
garden	*o*-groot	*ogród* (m)
gate	*bra*-ma	*brama* (f)
gay	gey	*gej* (m)
general (adj)	o-*gool*-ni	*ogólny*
German (adj)	nye-*myets*-kee	*niemiecki*
Germany	*nyem*-tsi	*Niemcy* (pl)
to get		
(serve)	*po*-dach	*podać*
(obtain)	*dos*-tach	*dostać*

to get to
dos-tach she
dostać się

to get up (from bed)
fstach
wstać

English	Pronunciation	Polish
gift	*pre*-zent	*prezent* (m)
girl	djef-*chi*-na	*dziewczyna* (f)
girlfriend	na-zhe-*cho*-na	*narzeczona* (f)
to give	*da*-vach • dach	*dawać* • *dać*

Please give me ...
pro-sze mee dach ...
Proszę mi dać ...

glass		
(material)	shkwo	*szkło* (neut)
(for water)	*shklan*-ka	*szklanka* (f)
(for wine)	kye-*lee*-shek	*kieliszek* (m)
to go	eeshch • pooyshch • *ye*-hach • po-*ye*-hach	*iść* • *pójść* • *jechać* • *pojechać*

Let's go.
hoch-mi
Chodźmy.

We'd like to go to ...
htse-mi pooyshch do ...
Chcemy pójść do ...

Go straight ahead.
pro-she eeshch *pros*-to
Proszę iść prosto.

Does this train go to ...?
chi ten *po*-chonk *ye*-dje do ...?
Czy ten pociąg jedzie do ...?

goal		
(aim)	tsel	*tsel* (m)
(in soccer)	gol	*gol* (m)
goalkeeper	*bram*-kash	*bramkarz* (m)
goat	*ko*-za	*koza* (f)
God	book	*Bóg* (m)
gold	*zwo*-to	*złoto* (neut)
good	*do*-bri	*dobry*

Goodbye.
do vee-*dze*-nya
Do widzenia.

Good evening.
do-bri *vye*-choor
Dobry wieczór.

Good luck!
po-vo-*dze*-nya!
Powodzenia!

Good morning.
djen *do*-bri
Dzień dobry.

Goodnight.
do-*bra*-nots
Dobranoc.

goose	gensh	*gęś* (f)
government	zhont	*rząd* (m)
gram	gram	*gram* (m)
grammar	gra-*ma*-ti-ka	*gramatyka* (f)
granddaughter	*vnooch*-ka	*wnuczka* (f)
grandfather	*dja*-dek	*dziadek* (m)
grandmother	*bap*-ka	*babka* (f)
grandson	vnook	*wnuk* (m)
grape	vee-no-*gro*-no	*winogrono* (m)
graphic art	*gra*-fee-ka	*grafika* (f)
grass	*tra*-va	*trawa* (f)
grateful	*vdjench*-ni	*wdzięczny*
grave	groop	*grób* (m)
gravestone	na-*gro*-bek	*nagrobek* (m)
great	fspa-*nya*-wi	*wspaniały*
Great Britain	*vyel*-ka bri-*ta*-nya	*Wielka Brytania* (f)
green	zhe-*lo*-ni	*zielony*
greengrocer	sklep o-vo-*tso*-vo va-*zhiv*-ni	*sklep owocowo-warzywny* (m)
grey	*sha*-ri	*szary*
grocery store	sklep spo-*zhif*-chi	*sklep spożywczy* (m)
ground floor	*par*-ter	*parter* (m)
group	*groo*-pa	*grupa* (f)
to grow	*ros*-nonch	*rosnąć*
guest	goshch	*gość* (m)
guesthouse	pen-*syo*-nat	*pensjonat* (m)
guide (person)	pshe-*vod*-neek/ pshe-vod-*neech*-ka	*przewodnik/ przewodniczka* (m/f)
guidebook	pshe-*vod*-neek	*przewodnik* (m)
guided tour	vi-*chech*-ka spshe-vod-*nee*-kyem	*wycieczka z przewodnikiem* (f)
guidedog	pyes pshe-*vod*-neek	*pies przewodnik* (m)

English	Pronunciation	Polish
guilty	veen-ni	winny
guitar	gee-ta-ra	gitara (f)
gum (chewing)	goo-ma do zhoo-cha	guma do żucia (f)
gymnastics	geem-nas-ti-ka	gimnastyka (f)

H

English	Pronunciation	Polish
hair	vwos • vwo-si	włos (m) • włosy (pl)
hairbrush	shchot-ka do vwo-soof	szczotka do włosów (f)
haircut	stshi-zhe-nye	strzyżenie (neut)
hairdressing salon	fri-zyer	fryzjer (m)
half	poow • po-wo-va	pół • połowa
ham	shin-ka	szynka (f)
hammer	mwo-tek	młotek (m)
hammock	ha-mak	hamak (m)
hand	ren-ka	ręka (f)
handbag	to-rep-ka	torebka (f)
handicrafts	ren-ko-dje-wo	rękodzieło (neut)
handmade	rench-nye sro-byo-ne	ręcznie zrobione
hand luggage	ba-gash pod-rench-ni	bagaż podręczny (m)
handsome	pshis-toy-ni	przystojny
hangover	kats	kac (m)
happy	shchen-shlee-vi	szczęśliwy
harbour	port	port (m)
hard		
(not soft)	tfar-di	twardy
(difficult)	trood-ni	trudny
to hate	nye-na-vee-djech	nienawidzieć
to have	myech	mieć

Do you have ...?
chi pan/pa-nee ma ...?
Czy pan/pani ma ...?

I have ...
mam ...
Mam ...

English	Pronunciation	Polish
hayfever	ka-tar shen-ni	katar sienny (m)
he	on	on
head	gwo-va	głowa (f)
headache	bool gwo-vi	ból głowy (m)
headphones	swoo-haf-kee	słuchawki (f)
health	zdro-vye	zdrowie (neut)
healthy	zdro-vi	zdrowy
to hear	swi-shech	słyszeć
hearing aid	a-pa-rat swoo-ho-vi	aparat słuchowy (m)
heart	ser-tse	serce (neut)
heat	oo-paw	upał (m)
heater	gzhey-neek	grzejnik (m)
heating	o-gzhe-va-nye	ogrzewanie (neut)
heavy	chen-shkee	ciężki

Hello. (making a call)
ha-lo
Halo.

Hello. (answering a call)
swoo-ham
Słucham.

English	Pronunciation	Polish
helmet	kask	kask (m)
help	po-mots	pomoc (f)

Help!
ra-toon-koo! • po-mo-tsi!
Ratunku! • Pomocy!

English	Pronunciation	Polish
to help	po-ma-gach • po-moots	pomagać • pomóc
helpful	po-mots-ni	pomocny
herb	zho-wo	zioło (neut)
here	too/too-tay	tu/tutaj
heroin	he-ro-ee-na	heroina (f)
high	vi-so-kee	wysoki
high school	shko-wa vish-sha	szkoła wyższa (f)
highway	sho-sa	szosa (f)
to hike	ven-dro-vach	wędrować
hiking	ven-droof-kee pye-she	wędrówki piesze
hill	vzgoo-zhe	wzgórze (neut)

to hire	vi-nay-*mo*-vach	*wynajmować*
for hire	do vi-na-*yen*-cha	*do wynajęcia*
hitchhiking	aw-*to*-stop	*autostop* (m)
holiday	*shfyen*-to	*święto* (m)
holidays	va-*ka*-tsye • *oor*-lop	*wakacje* (pl) • *urlop* (m)
holy	*shfen*-ti	*święty*
home	dom	*dom* (m)
homeless	bes-*dom*-ni	*bezdomny*
honest	ooch-*chee*-vi	*uczciwy*
honey	myoot	*miód* (m)
honeymoon	*mye*-shonts myo-*do*-vi	*miesiąc miodowy* (m)
hope	na-*dje*-ya	*nadzieja* (f)
horrible	o-*krop*-ni	*okropny*
horse	kon	*koń* (m)
horse riding	*yas*-da *kon*-na	*jazda konna* (f)
hospital	*shpee*-tal	*szpital* (m)
hospitality	gosh-*cheen*-noshch	*gościnność* (f)
hot	go-*ron*-tsi	*gorący*

It's hot.
yest go-*ron*-tso
Jest gorąco.

I'm hot.
yest mee go-*ron*-tso
Jest mi gorąco.

hot water	*chep*-wa *vo*-da	*ciepła woda* (f)
house	dom	*dom* (m)
how	yak	*jak*

How do I get to ...?
yak she *dos*-tach do ...?
Jak się dostać do ...?

How do you say ...?
yak po-*vye*-djech ...?
Jak powiedzieć ...?

human being	*chwo*-vyek	*człowiek* (m)
hundred	sto	*sto*
hungry	*gwod*-ni	*głodny*
to hurry	*spye*-shich she	*spieszyć się*
to hurt	*bo*-lech	*boleć*
husband	monsh	*mąż* (m)

I

I	ya	*ja*
ice	loot	*lód* (m)
ice cream	*lo*-di	*lody* (m, pl)
idea	*po*-misw	*pomysł* (m)
identification card	do-*koo*-ment tosh-sa-*mosh*-chee	*dokument tożsamości* (m)
idiot	ee-*dyo*-ta / ee-*dyot*-ka	*idiota/ idiotka* (m/f)
if	*yesh*-lee	*jeśli*
ill	*ho*-ri	*chory*
illness	ho-*ro*-ba	*choroba* (f)
immediately	na-*tih*-myast	*natychmiast*
important	*vazh*-ni	*ważny*

It's (not) important.
to (nye)-*vazh*-ne
To (nie)ważne.

impossible	nye-mozh-*lee*-vi	*niemożliwy*
to improve	oo-*lep*-shach	*ulepszać*
to include	*vwon*-chach	*włączać*
income tax	po-*da*-tek do-ho-*do*-vi	*podatek dochodowy* (m)
inconvenient	nye-vi-*god*-ni	*niewygodny*
independence	nye-pod-*leg*-woshch	*niepodległość* (f)
indicator (for car)	kye-roon-*kof*-skas	*kierunkowskaz* (m)
indigestion	nye-*strav*-noshch	*niestrawność* (f)
industrial	pshe-mi-*swo*-vi	*przemysłowy*
industry	*pshe*-misw	*przemysł* (m)
inequality	nye-*roov*-noshch	*nierówność* (f)
information	een-for-*ma*-tsya	*informacja* (f)
injection	*zas*-tshik	*zastrzyk* (m)

njured	*ran*-ni	*ranny*
njury	*ra*-na	*rana* (f)
nsect	*o*-vat	*owad* (m)
nside	*vev*-nonch	*wewnątrz*
o insist	na-*le*-gach	*nalegać*
nstead of	*za*-myast	*zamiast*
nsurance	oo-bes-pye-*che*-nye	*ubezpieczenie* (neut)
nteresting	een-te-re-soo-*yon*-tsi	*interesujący*
ntermission	*psher*-va	*przerwa* (f)
inter-national	myen-dzi-na-ro-*do*-vi	*międzynarodowy*
nterpreter	*twoo*-mach/ two-*mach*-ka	*tłumacz/ tłumaczka* (m/f)
intersection	skshi-zho-*va*-nye	*skrzyżowanie* (neut)
nterview	*vi*-vyat	*wywiad* (m)
invitation	za-*pro*-she-nye	*zaproszenie* (neut)
o invite	za-*pra*-shach • za-*pro*-sheech	*zapraszać* • *zaprosić*
iron (for ironing)	zhe-*las*-ko	*żelazko* (neut)
island	*vis*-pa	*wyspa* (f)
tch	sfen-*dze*-nye	*swędzenie* (neut)
itinerary	*tra*-sa po-*droo*-zhi	*trasa podróży* (f)

J

jacket	*koor*-tka	*kurtka* (f)
jail	vyen-*zhe*-nye	*więzienie* (neut)
January	*sti*-chen	*styczeń* (m)
jar	*swo*-eek	*słoik* (m)
jealous	zaz-*dros*-ni	*zazdrosny*
jeans	*djeen*-si	*dżinsy* (pl)
Jew	zhit/ zhi-*doof*-ka	*żyd/ żydówka* (m/f)
jewellery	bee-zhoo-*te*-rya	*biżuteria* (f)
jewellery store	yoo-*bee*-ler	*jubiler* (m)
Jewish	zhi-*dof*-skee	*żydowski*
job	*pra*-tsa	*praca* (f)
joke	zhart • *dof*-cheep	*żart* (m) • *dowcip* (m)
to joke	zhar-*to*-vach	*żartować*
journalist	djen-*nee*-kash/ djen-nee-*kar*-ka	*dziennikarz/ dziennikarka* (m/f)
journey	*po*-droosh	*podróż* (f)
judge	*sen*-dja	*sędzia* (m)
to judge	*son*-djeech	*sądzić*
juice	sok	*sok* (m)
June	*cher*-vyets	*czerwiec* (m)
July	*lee*-pyets	*lipiec* (m)
to jump	*ska*-kach • *sko*-chich	*skakać* • *skoczyć*
jumper	*sfe*-ter	*sweter* (m)
justice	spra-vyed-*lee*-voshch	*sprawiedliwość* (f)

K

to keep	*tshi*-mach • za-*tshi*-mach	*trzymać* • *zatrzymać*
kettle	*chay*-neek	*czajnik* (m)
key	klooch	*klucz* (m)
to kill	*za*-beech	*zabić*
kilometre	kee-*lo*-metr	*kilometr* (m)
kind		
(good)	*do*-bri	*dobry*
(type)	*ro*-dzay	*rodzaj* (m)
kindergarten	pshet-*shko*-le	*przedszkole* (neut)
king	krool	*król* (m)
kiss	po-tsa-*woo*-nek	*pocałunek* (m)
to kiss	tsa-*wo*-vach	*całować*
kitchen	*kooh*-nya	*kuchnia* (f)
knee	ko-*la*-no	*kolano* (neut)
knife	noosh	*nóż* (m)
to know		
(someone)	znach	*znać*
(something)	*vye*-djech	*wiedzieć*

I don't know him.
nye znam go
Nie znam go.

I know how to say it.
vyem yak to po-*vye*-djech
Wiem jak to powiedzieć.

L

lake	ye-*zho*-ro	*jezioro* (neut)
lamp	*lam*-pa	*lampa* (f)
land	lont	*ląd* (m)
language	*yen*-zik	*język* (m)
language course	koors yen-zi-*ko*-vi	*kurs językowy* (m)
large	*doo*-zhi	*duży*
last	os-*tat*-nee	*ostatni*

last night
fcho-ray vye-*cho*-rem
wczoraj wieczorem

last week
vzesh-wim ti-*god*-nyoo
w zeszłym tygodniu

last year
vzesh-wim *ro*-koo
w zeszłym roku

late	*poozh*-no	*późno*
later	*poozh*-nyey	*później*
laugh	shmyeh	*śmiech* (m)
to laugh	shmyach she	*śmiać się*
launderette	*pral*-nya sa-mo-op-swoo-*go*-va	*pralnia samoobsługowa* (f)
laundry	*pral*-nya	*pralnia* (f)
law	*pra*-vo	*prawo* (neut)
lawn	*trav*-neek	*trawnik* (m)
lawyer	*prav*-neek/ prav-*neech*-ka	*prawnik/ prawniczka* (m/f)
laxative	*shro*-dek pshe-chish-cha-*yon*-tsi	*środek przeczyszczający* (m)
lazy	le-*nee*-vi	*leniwy*
to lead	pro-*va*-djeech	*prowadzić*
leaded (petrol/gas)	(ben-*zi*-na) o-wo-*vyo*-va	*(benzyna) ołowiowa* (f)
leaf	leeshch	*liść* (m)
leaflet	bro-*shoo*-ra	*broszura* (f)
to learn	*oo*-chich she	*uczyć się*
leather	*skoo*-ra	*skóra* (f)
leather-goods	ar-ti-*koo*-wi skoo-*zha*-ne	*artykuły skórzane* (m)
to leave (depart)	vi-*yesh*-djach	*wyjeżdżać*
to leave (behind)	zos-*ta*-vyach	*zostawiać*

I'm leaving tomorrow.
vi-*yesh*-djam *yoo*-tro
Wyjeżdżam jutro.

Can I leave the backpack here?
chi *mo*-ge too zos-*ta*-veech *ple*-tsak?
Czy mogę tu zostawić plecak?

left (not right)	*le*-vi	*lewy*
left luggage office	pshe-ho-*val*-nya ba-*ga*-zhoo	*przechowalnia bagażu* (f)
left-wing (politics)	le-vee-*tso*-vi	*lewicowy*
leg	*no*-ga	*noga* (f)
legal	*prav*-ni	*prawny*
legislation	pra-vo-*das*-tfo	*prawodawstwo* (neut)
to lend	po-*zhi*-chach	*pożyczać*
lens (camera)	o-*byek*-tif	*obiektyw* (m)
Lent	*vyel*-kee post	*Wielki Post* (m)
lesbian	les-*beey*-ka	*lesbijka* (f)
less	mnyey	*mniej*
lesson	*lek*-tsya	*lekcja* (f)
to let (allow)	poz-*va*-lach	*pozwalać*
letter	leest	*list* (m)
letter-box	*skshin*-ka poch-*to*-va	*skrzynka pocztowa* (f)
library	bee-blyo-*te*-ka	*biblioteka* (f)
lice	fshi	*wszy* (f, pl)
to lie	*kwa*-mach	*kłamać*
life	*zhi*-che	*życie* (neut)
lifeguard	ra-*tov*-neek	*ratownik* (m)

English	Pronunciation	Polish
life jacket	ka-mee-zel-ka ra-toon-ko-va	kamizelka ratunkowa (f)
lift (elevator)	veen-da	winda (f)
light		
(n)	shfya-two	światło (neut)
(weight)	lek-kee	lekki
(color)	yas-ni	jasny
light bulb	zha-roof-ka	żarówka (f)
light meter	shfya-two-myesh	światłomierz (m)
lighter	za-pal-neech-ka	zapalniczka (f)
to like	loo-beech	lubić
line	lee-nya	linia (f)
lips	oos-ta	usta (pl)
lipstick	shmeen-ka	szminka (f)
to listen	swoo-hach	słuchać
little (small)	ma-wi	mały
a little (amount)	tro-he	trochę
to live		
(life)	zhich	żyć
(somewhere)	myesh-kach	mieszkać
liver	von-tro-ba	wątroba (f)
loaf	bo-he-nek	bochenek (m)
local	myey-stso-vi	miejscowy
location	po-wo-zhe-nye	położenie (neut)
lock	za-mek	zamek (m)
to lock	za-mi-kach na klooch	zamykać na klucz
lonely	sa-mot-ni	samotny
long	dwoo-gee	długi
long ago	dav-no te-moo	dawno temu
long-distance call	roz-mo-va myen-dzi-myas-to-va	rozmowa między-miastowa (f)
to look at	pat-shech	patrzeć
to look after	o-pye-ko-vach she	opiekować się
to look for	shoo-kach	szukać
loose change	drob-ne	drobne
lorry	sa-mo-hoot chen-zha-ro-vi	samochód ciężarowy (m)
to lose	goo-beech • zgoo-beech	gubić • zgubić
loss	stra-ta • zgoo-ba	strata (f) • zguba (f)
a lot	doo-zho	dużo
loud	gwosh-ni	głośny
love	mee-woshch	miłość (f)
to love	ko-hach	kochać
lovely	shleech-ni	śliczny
low	nees-kee	niski
luck		
(chance)	los	los (m)
(good fortune)	shchen-shche	szczęście (neut)
lucky	shchen-shlee-vi	szczęśliwy
luggage	ba-gash	bagaż (m)
lump	goos	guz (m)
lungs	pwoo-tsa	płuca (neut)
luxurious	look-soo-so-vi	luksusowy
luxury	look-soos	luksus (m)

M

English	Pronunciation	Polish
machine	ma-shi-na	maszyna (f)
mad (crazy)	zva-ryo-va-ni • sha-lo-ni	zwariowany • szalony
made (of)	zro-byo-ni (s)	zrobiony (z)
magazine	ma-ga-zin	magazyn (m)
mail	poch-ta	poczta (f)
mailbox	skshin-ka poch-to-va	skrzynka pocztowa (f)
main	gwoov-ni	główny
main course	droo-gye da-nye	drugie danie (neut)
majority	vyenk-shoshch	większość (f)
make (brand name)	mar-ka	marka (f)

to make	*ro*-beech • *zro*-beech	*robić* • *zrobić*
make-up	ma-*kee*-yash	*makijaż* (m)
man	mensh-*chiz*-na	*mężczyzna* (m)
manager	di-*rek*-tor/ di-rek-*tor*-ka	*dyrektor/ dyrektorka* (m/f)
manual worker	ro-*bot*-neek/ ro-bot-*nee*-tsa	*robotnik/ robotnica* (m/f)
many	*doo*-zho	*dużo*
map	*ma*-pa	*mapa* (f)

Please show me on the map.
pro-sze mee po-*ka*-zach na *ma*-pye
Proszę mi pokazać na mapie.

March	*ma*-zhets	*marzec* (m)
marital status	stan tsi-*veel*-ni	*stan cywilny* (m)
market	tark • *ba*-zar	*targ* (m) • *bazar* (m)
marriage	maw-*zhen*-stfo	*małżeństwo* (neut)
marvellous	tsoo-*dov*-ni	*cudowny*
mass (Catholic)	msha	*msza* (f)
massage	*ma*-sash	*masaż* (m)
match (sport)	mech	*mecz* (m)
matches	za-*paw*-kee	*zapałki* (f, pl)
matter	*spra*-va	*sprawa* (f)

It doesn't matter.
neets nye *shko*-djee • nye ma zna-*che*-nya
Nic nie szkodzi. • Nie ma znaczenia.

What's the matter?
o tso *ho*-djee?
O co chodzi?

mattress	ma-*te*-rats	*materac* (m)
May	may	*maj* (m)
maybe	bich *mo*-zhe	*być może*
mayor	*boor*-meeshch	*burmistrz* (m)
meal	po-*shee*-wek	*posiłek* (m)
to mean	*zna*-chich	*znaczyć*
meat	*myen*-so	*mięso* (neut)
mechanic	me-*ha*-neek	*mechanik* (m)
medicine (the science)	me-di-*tsi*-na	*medycyna* (f)
(drug)	lek • le-*kar*-stfo	*lek* (m) • *lekarstwo* (neut)
medium	*shred*-ni	*średni*
to meet	spo-*ti*-kach • *spot*-kach	*spotykać* • *spotkać*
meeting	ze-*bra*-nye	*zebranie* (neut)
menstruation	men-stroo-*a*-tsya	*menstruacja* (f)
to mention	fspo-*mee*-nach	*wspominać*
menu	ya-*dwos*-pees • *kar*-ta dan	*jadłospis* (m) • *karta dań* (f)
message	vya-*do*-moshch	*wiadomość* (f)
metre	metr	*metr* (m)
midday	po-*wood*-nye	*południe* (neut)
middle	*shro*-dek	*środek* (m)
midnight	*poow*-nots	*północ* (f)
migraine	mee-*gre*-na	*migrena* (f)
military service	*swoozh*-ba voy-*sko*-va	*służba wojskowa* (f)
mild	wa-*god*-ni	*łagodny*
milk	*mle*-ko	*mleko* (neut)
millimetre	mee-*lee*-metr	*milimetr* (m)
million	*mee*-lyon	*milion* (m)
mind	*ro*-zoom	*rozum* (m)
mineral water	*vo*-da mee-ne-*ral*-na	*woda mineralna* (f)
minute	mee-*noo*-ta	*minuta* (f)

Just a minute.
hfee-*lech*-ke
Chwileczkę.

in (five) minutes
za (pyench) *mee*-noot
za (pięć) minut

mirror	*loos*-tro	*lustro* (neut)
mis-carriage	po-ro-*nye*-nye	*poronienie* (neut)
to miss		
(feel absence)	ot-*choo*-vach brak	*odczuwać brak*
(be late)	*spoozh*-neech she	*spóźnić się*
mist	mgwa	*mgła* (f)
mistake	po-*miw*-ka	*pomyłka* (f)
to mix	*mye*-shach	*mieszać*
mobile phone	te-*le*-fon ko-moor-*ko*-vi	*telefon komórkowy* (m)
modern	no-vo-*ches*-ni	*nowoczesny*
moisturiser	krem na-veel-zha-*yon*-tsi	*krem nawilżający* (m)
monastery	*klash*-tor	*klasztor* (m)
Monday	po-nye-*dja*-wek	*poniedziałek* (m)
money	pye-*nyon*-dze	*pieniądze* (m, pl)
monk	mneeh	*mnich* (m)
month	*mye*-shonts	*miesiąc* (m)

this month
ftim mye-*shon*-tsoo
w tym miesiącu

monument	*pom*-neek	*pomnik* (m)
moon	*kshen*-zhits	*księżyc* (m)
more	*vyen*-tsey	*więcej*
morning	*ra*-no	*rano* (neut)
mosque	*me*-chet	*meczet* (m)
mosquito	*ko*-mar	*komar* (m)
mother	*mat*-ka	*matka* (f)
mother-in-law	tesh-*cho*-va	*teściowa* (f)
motorboat	mo-to-*roof*-ka	*motorówka* (f)
motorcycle	mo-*to*-tsikl	*motocykl* (m)
motorway	aw-to-*stra*-da	*autostrada* (f)
mountain	*goo*-ra	*góra* (f)
mountain bike	*ro*-ver *goor*-skee	*rower górski* (m)
mountain range	*pas*-mo *goor*-skye	*pasmo górskie* (neut)
mountain refuge	sro-*nees*-ko *goor*-skye	*schronisko górskie* (neut)
mountain-eering	fspee-*nach*-ka *goor*-ska	*wspinaczka górska* (f)
mouse	mish	*mysz* (f)
moustache	*von*-si	*wąsy* (m, pl)
mouth	*oos*-ta	*usta* (pl)
to move	*roo*-shach	*ruszać*
movement	rooh	*ruch* (m)
movie	feelm	*film*
much	*doo*-zho	*dużo*
mud	*bwo*-to	*błoto* (neut)
mug	*koo*-bek	*kubek* (m)
Mum	*ma*-ma	*mama* (f)
muscle	*myen*-shen	*mięsień* (m)
museum	*moo*-ze-oom	*muzeum* (neut)
mushroom	gzhib	*grzyb* (m)
music	*moo*-zi-ka	*muzyka* (f)
musician	*moo*-zik	*muzyk* (m)
mute	*nye*-mi	*niemy*

N

name		
(first)	*ee*-mye	*imię* (neut)
(family)	naz-*vees*-ko	*nazwisko* (neut)
nappy	pye-*loosh*-ka	*pieluszka* (f)
narrow	*von*-skee	*wąski*
national park	park na-ro-*do*-vi	*park narodowy* (m)
nationality	na-ro-*do*-voshch	*narodowość* (f)
nature	na-*too*-ra	*natura* (f)
natural	na-too-*ral*-ni	*naturalny*
nausea	*mdwosh*-chee	*mdłości* (pl)
near	*blees*-kee	*bliski*
nearby	fpo-*blee*-zhoo	*w pobliżu*
necessary	ko-*nyech*-ni	*konieczny*
neck	*shi*-ya	*szyja* (f)
necklace	na-*shiy*-neek	*naszyjnik* (m)
to need	pot-she-*bo*-vach	*potrzebować*
needle		
(sewing)	*ee*-gwa	*igła* (f)
(syringe)	stshi-*kaf*-ka	*strzykawka* (f)

neither	*zha*-den	*żaden*
net	*shat*-ka	*siatka* (f)
never	*neeg*-di	*nigdy*
new	*no*-vi	*nowy*
news	vya-do-*mosh*-chee	*wiadomości* (f, pl)
newspaper	ga-*ze*-ta	*gazeta* (f)
newspaper kiosk	kyosk sga-ze-*ta*-mee	*kiosk z gazetami* (m)
New Year's Day	*no*-vi rok	*Nowy Rok* (m)
New Year's Eve	sil-*ves*-ter	*Sylwester* (m)
New Zealand	*no*-va ze-*lan*-dya	*Nowa Zelandia* (f)
next		
(in space)	nas-*temp*-ni	*następny*
(in time)	*pshish*-wi	*przyszły*

next to
o-bok
obok

next week
fpshish-wim ti-*god*-nyoo
w przyszłym tygodniu

next year
fpshish-wim *ro*-koo
w przyszłym roku

nice		
(person)	*mee*-wi	*miły*
(thing)	*wad*-ni	*ładny*
night	nots	*noc* (f)

No.
nye
Nie.

nobody	neekt	*nikt*
noise	*ha*-was	*hałas (m)*
noisy	ha-wash-*lee*-vi	*hałaśliwy*
none	*zha*-den	*żaden*
noon	po-*wood*-nye	*południe* (neut)
north	*poow*-nots	*północ* (f)
nose	nos	*nos* (m)
notebook	no-*tat*-neek	*notatnik* (m)
nothing	neets	*nic*
not yet	*yesh*-che nye	*jeszcze nie*
novel (book)	*po*-vyeshch	*powieść* (f)
November	lees-*to*-pat	*listopad* (m)
now	*te*-ras	*teraz*
nuclear energy	e-*ner*-gya noo-kle-*ar*-na	*energia nuklearna* (f)
nun	za-kon-*nee*-tsa	*zakonnica* (f)
nurse	pye-*leng*-nyash/ pye-leng-*nyar*-ka	*pielęgniarz/ pielęgniarka* (m/f)

O

obvious	o-chi-*vees*-ti	*oczywisty*
occupation	*za*-voot	*zawód* (m)
occupied (seat, toilet)	za-*yen*-ti	*zajęty*
October	pazh-*djer*-neek	*październik* (m)
odd		
(strange)	*djeev*-ni	*dziwny*
(number)	nye-pa-*zhis*-ti	*nieparzysty*
office	*byoo*-ro	*biuro* (neut)
office work	*pra*-tsa byoo-*ro*-va	*praca biurowa* (f)
often	*chen*-sto	*często*
oil		
(cooking)	*o*-ley	*olej* (m)
(crude)	*ro*-pa naf-*to*-va	*ropa naftowa* (f)

OK.
do-bzhe
Dobrze.

old	*sta*-ri	*stary*
old town	*sta*-re *mya*-sto	*stare miasto* (neut)
old town square	*ri*-nek	*rynek* (m)
olive oil	o-*lee*-va	*oliwa* (f)
olives	o-*leef*-kee	*oliwki* (f, pl)
Olympic Games	o-leem-*pya*-da	*olimpiada* (f)

English	Pronunciation	Polish
on	na	*na*
once	ras	*raz*
one-way ticket	*bee*-let *fyed*-nom *stro*-ne	*bilet w jedną stronę* (m)
only	*til*-ko	*tylko*
open	ot-*far*-ti	*otwarty*
to open	ot-*fye*-rach • ot-*fo*-zhich	*otwierać* • *otworzyć*
opening	ot-*far*-che	*otwarcie* (neut)
opening hours	go-*djee*-ni ot-*far*-cha	*godziny otwarcia*
opera (play/house)	*o*-pe-ra	*opera* (f)
operation	o-pe-*ra*-tsya	*operacja* (f)
opinion	o-*pee*-nya	*opinia* (f)
opposite		
(adj)	pshe-*cheev*-ni	*przeciwny*
(adv)	na-pshe-*cheef*-ko	*naprzeciwko*
or	*al*-bo/loop	*albo/lub*
oral (drug)	do-*oost*-ni	*doustny*
orange	po-ma-*ran*-cha	*pomarańcza* (f)
orchestra	or-*kyes*-tra	*orkiestra* (f)
order		
(system)	po-*zhon*-dek	*porządek* (m)
(request)	za-moo-*vye*-nye	*zamówienie* (neut)
to order (in restaurant)	za-*moo*-veech	*zamówić*
ordinary	zvi-*chay*-ni	*zwyczajny*
to organise	or-ga-nee-*zo*-vach	*organizować*
other	*een*-ni	*inny*
outside		
(adj)	zev-*nench*-ni	*zewnętrzny*
(outdoors)	na *zev*-nonch	*na zewnątrz*
owner	vwash-*chee*-chel/ vwash-chee-*chel*-ka	*właściciel/ właścicielka* (m/f)
oxygen	tlen	*tlen* (m)

P

English	Pronunciation	Polish
pacifier	*smo*-chek	*smoczek* (m)
to pack	pa-*ko*-vach	*pakować*
package/packet	*pach*-ka	*paczka* (f)
padlock	*kwoot*-ka	*kłódka* (f)
page	*stro*-na	*strona* (f)
pain	bool	*ból* (m)
painful	bo-*les*-ni	*bolesny*
painkillers	*shrot*-kee pshe-cheef-boo-*lo*-ve	*środki przeciwbólowe* (m)
paint	*far*-ba	*farba* (f)
to paint	ma-*lo*-vach	*malować*
painter	*ma*-lash/ ma-*lar*-ka	*malarz/ malarka* (m/f)
painting		
(the art)	ma-*lar*-stfo	*malarstwo* (neut)
(picture)	*o*-bras	*obraz* (m)
pair (a couple)	*pa*-ra	*para*
palace	*pa*-wats	*pałac* (m)
pan	*gar*-nek	*garnek* (m)
paper	*pa*-pyer	*papier* (m)
parcel	*pach*-ka	*paczka* (f)
parents	ro-*djee*-tse	*rodzice* (m)
park	park	*park* (m)
to park	par-*ko*-vach	*parkować*
parking lot	*par*-keenk	*parking* (m)
parliament	par-*la*-ment	*parlament* (m)
part	chenshch	*część* (f)
party		
(fiesta)	za-*ba*-va • pshi-*yen*-che	*zabawa* (f) • *przyjęcie* (neut)
(politics)	*par*-tya	*partia* (f)
(group)	*groo*-pa	*grupa* (f)
pass (in mountains)	*pshe*-wench	*przełęcz* (f)
passenger	pa-*sa*-zher/ pa-sa-*zher*-ka	*pasażer/ pasażerka* (m/f)
passport	*pash*-port	*paszport* (m)
passport number	*noo*-mer pash-*por*-too	*numer paszportu* (m)

P

DICTIONARY

English	Pronunciation	Polish
past		
(adj)	*dav*-ni • *pshesh*-wi	*dawny* • *przeszły*
(history)	*pshesh*-woshch	*przeszłość* (f)
path	*shchesh*-ka	*ścieżka* (f)
patient		
(n)	*pa*-tsyent/ pa-*tsyen*-tka	*pacjent/ pacjentka* (m/f)
(adj)	cher-*plee*-vi	*cierpliwy*
pavement	*hod*-neek	*chodnik* (m)
to pay	*pwa*-cheech • za-*pwa*-cheech	*płacić* • *zapłacić*
payment	za-*pwa*-ta	*zapłata* (f)
peace	*po*-kooy	*pokój* (m)
peak	shchit	*szczyt* (m)
pedestrian (adj/n)	*pye*-shi	*pieszy*
pedestrian crossing	*pshey*-shche dla *pye*-shih	*przejście dla pieszych* (neut)
pen	*pyoo*-ro	*pióro* (neut)
pen (ball-point)	dwoo-*go*-pees	*długopis* (m)
pencil	o-*woo*-vek	*ołówek* (m)
penknife	stsi-*zo*-rik	*scyzoryk* (m)
pensioner	ren-*chees*-ta/ ren-*cheest*-ka	*rencista/ rencistka* (m/f)
people	*loo*-dje	*ludzie* (pl)
pepper	pyepsh	*pieprz* (m)
percent	*pro*-tsent	*procent* (m)
perfor-mance	pshet-sta-*vye*-nye	*przedsta-wienie* (neut)
perhaps	*mo*-zhe	*może*
period		
(time)	*o*-kres	*okres* (m)
(menstru-ation)	mye-*shon*-chka	*miesiączka* (f)
permanent	*sta*-wi	*stały*
permission	poz-vo-*le*-nye	*pozwolenie* (neut)
to permit	poz-*va*-lach	*pozwalać*
person	o-*so*-ba	*osoba* (f)
personality	o-so-*bo*-voshch	*osobowość* (f)
petrol	ben-*zi*-na	*benzyna* (f)
petrol station	*sta*-tsya ben-zi-*no*-va	*stacja benzy-nowa* (f)

English	Pronunciation	Polish
pharmacy	ap-*te*-ka	*apteka* (f)
phone	te-*le*-fon	*telefon* (m)
to phone	te-le-fo-*no*-vach	*telefonować*
phonebook	*kshon*-shka te-le-fo-*neech*-na	*książka tele-foniczna* (f)
phone box	*boot*-ka te-le-fo-*neech*-na	*budka tele-foniczna* (f)
phonecard	*kar*-ta te-le-fo-*neech*-na	*karta tele-foniczna* (f)
phone number	*noo*-mer te-le-*fo*-noo	*numer telefonu* (m)
photo	*zdyen*-che	*zdjęcie* (neut)

> Can I take photos here?
> chi *mo*-ge too *ro*-beech *zdyen*-cha?
> *Czy mogę tu robić zdjęcia?*

English	Pronunciation	Polish
photo-grapher	fo-*to*-graf	*fotograf* (m)
phrasebook	roz-*moof*-kee	*rozmówki* (f)
piano	pya-*nee*-no	*pianino* (neut)
grand piano	for-*te*-pyan	*fortepian* (m)
pickpocket	*zwo*-djey kye-shon-*ko*-vi	*złodziej kie-szonkowy* (m)
picture		
(painting)	*o*-bras	*obraz* (m)
(photo)	*zdyen*-che	*zdjęcie* (neut)
pie	za-pye-*kan*-ka	*zapiekanka* (f)
piece	ka-*va*-wek	*kawałek* (m)
pig	*shfee*-nya	*świnia* (f)
pill	pee-*goow*-ka	*pastylka* (f)
the Pill	pee-*goow*-ka an-ti-kon-tsep-*tsiy*-na	*pigułka antykoncep-cyjna* (f)
pilgrim	*pyel*-gzhim	*pielgrzym* (m)
pilgrimage	pyel-*gzhim*-ka	*pielgrzymka* (f)
pillow	po-*doosh*-ka	*poduszka* (f)
pillowcase	po-*vwoch*-ka	*powłoczka* (f)
pine (tree)	*sos*-na	*sosna* (f)
pink	roo-*zho*-vi	*różowy*
pipe		
(water)	*roo*-ra	*rura* (f)
(smoking)	*fay*-ka	*fajka* (f)
place	*myey*-stse	*miejsce* (neut)

English	Pronunciation	Polish
place of birth	*myey*-stse oo-ro-*dze*-nya	*miejsce urodzenia* (neut)
plain (flat area)	roov-*nee*-na	*równina* (f)
plane	sa-*mo*-lot	*samolot* (m)
planet	pla-*ne*-ta	*planeta* (f)
plant	rosh-*lee*-na	*roślina* (f)
plate	*ta*-lesh	*talerz* (m)
platform (train)	*pe*-ron	*peron* (m)
play (theatre)	*shtoo*-ka	*sztuka* (f)
to play (music, games)	grach	*grać*
playground	plats *za*-baf	*plac zabaw* (m)
playing cards	*kar*-ti do gri	*karty do gry* (pl)
pleasant	pshi-*yem*-ni	*przyjemny*

Please.
pro-she
Proszę.

English	Pronunciation	Polish
pleasure	pshi-*yem*-noshch	*przyjemność* (f)
plug (electric)	*ftich*-ka	*wtyczka* (f)
pocket	*kye*-shen	*kieszeń* (f)
poetry	po-*e*-zya	*poezja* (f)
point	poonkt	*punkt* (m)
Poland	*pol*-ska	*Polska* (f)
Pole	*po*-lak/*pol*-ka	*Polak Polka* (m/f)
Poles	po-*la*-tsi	*Polacy* (pl)
police	po-*lee*-tsya	*policja* (f)
police officer	po-lee-tsyant/po-lee-*tsyan*-tka	*policjant/policjantka* (m/f)
police station	ko-mee-*sa*-ryat • pos-te-*roo*-nek po-*lee*-tsyee	*komisariat* (m) • *posterunek policji* (m)
Polish	*pol*-skee	*polski*
polite	oo-*pshey*-mi	*uprzejmy*
politics	po-*lee*-ti-ka	*polityka* (f)
pollution	ska-*zhe*-nye • za-nye-chish-*che*-nye	*skażenie* (neut) • *zanieczyszczenie* (neut)
pool (swimming)	*ba*-sen pwi-*val*-nya	*basen* (m) • *pływalnia* (f)
poor (not rich)	*byed*-ni	*biedny*
Pope	*pa*-pyesh	*Papież* (m)
popular	po-poo-*lar*-ni	*popularny*
population	*lood*-noshch	*ludność* (f)
port	port	*port* (m)
possible	mozh-*lee*-vi	*możliwy*

It's (not) possible.
to (nye)-mozh-*lee*-ve
To (nie)możliwe.

English	Pronunciation	Polish
postage	o-*pwa*-ta poch-*to*-va	*opłata pocztowa* (f)
postcard	poch-*toof*-ka	*pocztówka* (f)
postcode	kot poch-*to*-vi	*kod pocztowy* (m)
poster	*pla*-kat	*plakat* (m)
post office	*poch*-ta	*poczta* (f)
main post office	*poch*-ta *gwoov*-na	*poczta główna* (f)
power		
(authority)	*vwa*-dza	*władza* (f)
(electricity)	e-lek-*trich*-noshch	*elektryczność* (f)
prayer	mod-*leet*-fa	*modlitwa* (f)
to prefer	*vo*-lech	*woleć*
pregnant	*fchon*-zhi	*w ciąży*
prescription	re-*tsep*-ta	*recepta* (f)
to prepare	pshi-go-*to*-vach	*przygotować*
present (gift)	*pre*-zent	*prezent* (m)
president	pre-*zi*-dent	*prezydent* (m)
pressure	cheesh-*nye*-nye	*ciśnienie* (neut)
pretty	*wad*-ni	*ładny*
to prevent	za-po-*bye*-gach	*zapobiegać*
price	*tse*-na	*cena* (f)
pride	*doo*-ma	*duma* (f)
priest	kshonts	*ksiądz* (m)

P

DICTIONARY

prime minister	*pre*-myer	*premier* (m)
print (artwork)	gra-*fee*-ka	*grafika* (f)
prison	vyen-*zhe*-nye	*więzienie* (neut)
private	pri-*vat*-ni	*prywatny*
private bathroom	*vwas*-na wa-*zhen*-ka	*własna łazienka* (f)
privatisation	pri-va-ti-*za*-tsya	*prywatyzacja* (f)
probably	prav-do-po-*dob*-nye	*prawdopodobnie*
problem	*pro*-blem	*problem* (m)
profession	*za*-voot	*zawód* (m)
profit	zisk	*zysk* (m)
program	*pro*-gram	*program* (m)
to promise	pshi-*zhe*-kach	*przyrzekać*
property	*vwas*-noshch	*własność* (f)
proposal	pro-po-*zi*-tsya	*propozycja* (f)
to protect	*hro*-neech	*chronić*
protected species	ga-*toon*-kee pot oh-*ro*-nom	*gatunki pod ochroną*
protest	*pro*-test	*protest* (m)
to protest	pro-tes-*to*-vach	*protestować*
public holiday	*shfyen*-to pan-*stfo*-ve	*święto państwowe* (neut)
public telephone	aw-*to*-mat te-le-fo-*neech*-ni	*automat telefoniczny* (m)
public toilet	to-a-*le*-ta poo-*bleech*-na	*toaleta publiczna* (f)
to pull	*chong*-nonch	*ciągnąć*
pump	*pom*-pa	*pompa* (f)
puncture (in tyre)	pshe-*bee*-che fo-*po*-nye	*przebicie w oponie*
to punish	*ka*-rach • oo-*ka*-rach	*karać • ukarać*
puppy	*shche*-nye	*szczenię* (neut)
pure	*chis*-ti	*czysty*
purple	fyo-le-*to*-vi	*fioletowy*
to push	phach	*pchać*
to put	kwashch • po-*wo*-zhich	*kłaść • położyć*

Q

qualifications	kfa-lee-fee-*ka*-tsye	*kwalifikacje* (f, pl)
quality	*ya*-koshch	*jakość* (f)
quarantine	kfa-ran-*tan*-na	*kwarantanna* (f)
quarrel	*kwoot*-nya	*kłótnia* (f)
quarter	chfyerch	*ćwierć* (f)
queen	kroo-*lo*-va	*królowa* (f)
question		
(issue)	*spra*-va	*sprawa* (f)
(query)	pi-*ta*-nye	*pytanie* (neut)
to question	*pi*-tach • za-*pi*-tach	*pytać • zapytać*
queue	ko-*ley*-ka	*kolejka* (f)
quick	*ship*-kee	*szybki*
quiet (adj)	spo-*koy*-ni	*spokojny*

R

rabbit	*kroo*-leek	*królik* (m)
race		
(ancestry)	*ra*-sa	*rasa* (f)
(sport)	*vish*-cheek	*wyścig* (m)
racism	*ra*-sheezm	*rasizm* (m)
racquet (tennis)	ra-*kye*-ta	*rakieta* (f)
radiator		
(in car)	hwod-*nee*-tsa	*chłodnica* (f)
(in room)	ka-lo-*ri*-fer	*kaloryfer* (m)
railway	*ko*-ley	*kolej* (f)
railway station	*dvo*-zhets ko-le-*yo*-vi • *sta*-tsya ko-le-*yo*-va	dworzec *kolejowy* (m) • *stacja kolejowa* (f)
rain	deshch	*deszcz* (m)

It's raining.
pa-da deshch
Pada deszcz.

rape	gvawt	*gwałt* (m)
rare (uncommon)	*zhat*-kee	*rzadki*

English	Pronunciation	Polish
rash	vi-*sip*-ka	*wysypka* (f)
rat	shchoor	*szczur* (m)
rather	*ra*-chey	*raczej*
razor	ma-*shin*-ka do go-*le*-nya	*maszynka do golenia* (f)
razor blade	zhi-*let*-ka	*żyletka* (f)
to read	*chi*-tach • pshe-*chi*-tach	*czytać* • *przeczytać*
ready	go-*to*-vi	*gotowy*
real (genuine)	prav-*djee*-vi	*prawdziwy*
really	na-*prav*-de	*naprawdę*
reason (cause)	*po*-voot	*powód* (m)
reasonable	ros-*sond*-ni	*rozsądny*
receipt		
(for left-luggage/laundry)	pok-fee-to-*va*-nye	*pokwitowanie* (neut)
(for goods)	ra-*hoo*-nek	*rachunek* (m)
to receive	*dos*-tach	*dostać*
recent	nye-*dav*-ni	*niedawny*
recently	os-*tat*-nyo	*ostatnio*
reception desk	re-*tsep*-tsya	*recepcja* (f)
to recognise		
(acknowledge)	*ooz*-nach	*uznać*
(identify)	ros-*poz*-nach	*rozpoznać*
to recommend	po-*le*-tsach	*polecać*
record	*pwi*-ta	*płyta* (f)
red	cher-*vo*-ni	*czerwony*
reflection		
(mirror)	ot-*bee*-che	*odbicie* (neut)
(thinking)	re-*flek*-sya	*refleksja* (f)
refrigerator	lo-*doof*-ka	*lodówka* (f)
refugee	oo-*hoch*-tsa	*uchodźca* (m)
refund	zvrot pye-*nyen*-dzi	*zwrot pieniędzy* (m)
to refuse	ot-*moo*-veech	*odmówić*
regional	re-gyo-*nal*-ni	*regionalny*
registered mail	*poch*-ta po-le-*tso*-na	*poczta polecona* (f)
to regret	zha-*wo*-vach	*żałować*
relationship	*zvyon*-zek	*związek* (m)
to relax	ot-po-*chi*-vach	*odpoczywać*
religion	re-*lee*-gya	*religia* (f)
religious	re-lee-*geey*-ni	*religijny*
to remember	pa-*myen*-tach	*pamiętać*
remote (distant)	ot-*le*-gwi	*odległy*
remote control	*zdal*-ne ste-ro-*va*-nye	*zdalne sterowanie* (neut)
rent (payment)	chinsh	*czynsz* (m)
for rent	do vi-na-*yen*-cha	*do wynajęcia*
to rent	vi-nay-*mo*-vach	*wynajmować*
(car) rental	vi-*na*-yem (sa-mo-*ho*-doof)	*wynajem (samochodów)* (m)
to repair	na-*pra*-veech	*naprawić*
to repeat	pof-*too*-zhich	*powtórzyć*
republic	re-poo-*blee*-ka	*republika* (f)
reservation (booking)	re-zer-*va*-tsya	*rezerwacja* (f)
to reserve (make a booking)	za-re-zer-*vo*-vach	*zarezerwować*
respect	sha-*tsoo*-nek	*szacunek* (m)
rest		
(relaxation)	ot-po-*chi*-nek	*odpoczynek* (m)
(what's left)	*resh*-ta	*reszta* (f)
to rest	ot-po-*chi*-vach • ot-*po*-chonch	*odpoczywać* • *odpocząć*
restaurant	res-ta-oo-*ra*-tsya	*restauracja* (f)
retired (adj)	e-me-ri-to-*va*-ni • nae-me-ri-*too*-zhe	*emerytowany* • *naemeryturze*
return	*po*-vroot	*powrót* (m)
to return	*vra*-tsach • *vroo*-cheech	*wracać* • *wrócić*
return ticket	*bee*-let po-*vrot*-ni	*bilet powrotny* (m)

English	Pronunciation	Polish
review	*pshe*-glont	*przegląd* (m)
rhythm	ritm	*rytm* (m)
rich (wealthy)	bo-*ga*-ti	*bogaty*
to ride (a horse/ bicycle)	*yezh*-djeech	*jeździć*
right		
(not left)	*pra*-vi	*prawy*
(correct)	pra-vee-*dwo*-vi	*prawidłowy*
to be right	myech *ra*-tsye	*mieć rację*

You're right.
ma pan/*pa*-nee *ra*-tsye
Ma pan/pani rację.

English	Pronunciation	Polish
rights (civil/ human)	*pra*-va	*prawa* (neut)
right-wing (politics)	pra-vee-*tso*-vi	*prawicowy*
ring (on finger)	pyer-*shcho*-nek	*pierścionek* (m)
to ring (phone)	za-*dzvo*-neech	*zadzwonić*

I'll give you a ring.
zadz-*vo*-nye do *pa*-na/*pa*-nee
Zadzwonię do pana/pani.

English	Pronunciation	Polish
risk	ri-*zi*-ko	*ryzyko* (neut)
risky	ri-zi-*kov*-ni	*ryzykowny*
river	*zhe*-ka	*rzeka* (f)
road	*dro*-ga • *sho*-sa	*droga* (f) • *szosa* (f)
road map	*ma*-pa dro-*go*-va	*mapa drogowa* (f)
road sign	znak dro-*go*-vi	*znak drogowy* (m)
to rob	ra-*bo*-vach	*rabować*

I've been robbed.
o-bra-bo-*va*-no mnye
Obrabowano mnie.

English	Pronunciation	Polish
rock	*ska*-wa	*skała* (f)
rock climbing	*fspee*-nach-ka *skal*-na	*wspinaczka skalna* (f)
rock music	*moo*-zi-ka ro-*ko*-va	*muzyka rockowa* (f)
roll of film	*rol*-ka *feel*-moo	*rolka filmu* (f)
romance	*ro*-mans	*romans* (m)
room	*po*-kooy	*pokój* (m)

single room
po-kooy yed-no-o-so-*bo*-vi
pokój jednoosobowy (m)

double room
po-kooy dvoo-o-so-*bo*-vi
pokój dwuosobowy (m)

English	Pronunciation	Polish
room number	*noo*-mer po-*ko*-yoo	*numer pokoju* (m)
rope	*lee*-na	*lina* (f)
round	o-*kron*-gwi	*okrągły*
roundabout	*ron*-do	*rondo* (neut)
route	*tra*-sa	*trasa* (f)
rubber	*goo*-ma	*guma* (f)
rubbish (waste)	*shmye*-chee	*śmieci* (m, pl)
rubbish bin	po-*yem*-neek na *shmye*-chee	*pojemnik na śmieci* (m)
rug	*di*-van	*dywan* (m)
ruins	roo-*ee*-ni	*ruiny* (f, pl)
to run	*bye*-gach	*biegać*
rush hour	go-*djee*-na *shchi*-too	*godzina szczytu* (f)

S

English	Pronunciation	Polish
sad	*smoot*-ni	*smutny*
safe (adj)	bes-*pyech*-ni	*bezpieczny*
sailing	zhe-*glar*-stfo	*żeglarstwo* (neut)
sailing boat	zha-*gloof*-ka	*żaglówka* (f)
saint	*shfyen*-ti/ta	*święty/ta* (m/f)
salad	sa-*wat*-ka	*sałatka* (f)
salary	*pen*-sya	*pensja* (f)
sale	*spshe*-dash	*sprzedaż* (f)
for sale	na *spshe*-dash	*na sprzedaż*
sales de--partment	djaw spshe-*da*-zhi	*dział sprze-daży* (m)
salt	sool	*sól* (f)
sand	*pya*-sek	*piasek* (m)
sandwich	ka-*nap*-ka	*kanapka* (f)

English	Pronunciation	Polish
sanitary napkins	pot-*pas*-kee hee-gye-*neech*-ne	*podpaski higieniczne* (f, pl)
Saturday	so-*bo*-ta	*sobota* (f)
to save		
(rescue)	ra-*to*-vach • oo-ra-*to*-vach	*ratować* • *uratować*
(money)	osh-*chen*-dzach	*oszczędzać*
to say	*moo*-veech • po-*vye*-djech	*mówić* • *powiedzieć*
to scale (climb)	*fspee*-nach she	*wspinać się*
schedule	*ros*-kwat *yaz*-di	*rozkład jazdy* (m)
school	*shko*-wa	*szkoła* (f)
science	na-*oo*-ka	*nauka* (f)
scientist	na-oo-*ko*-vyets	*naukowiec* (m)
scissors	no-*zhich*-kee	*nożyczki* (pl)
screen	*e*-kran	*ekran* (m)
screwdriver	shroo-*bo*-krent	*śrubokręt* (m)
script (film)	stse-*na*-ryoosh	*scenariusz* (m)
sculpture	*zhezh*-ba	*rzeźba* (f)
sea	*mo*-zhe	*morze* (neut)
seasickness	ho-*ro*-ba *mor*-ska	*choroba morska* (f)
seaside (adj)	nad-*mor*-skee	*nadmorski*
seat	she-*dze*-nye	*siedzenie* (neut)
seatbelts	*pa*-si bes-pye-*chen*-stfa	*pasy bezpieczeństwa* (m)
second		
(time)	se-*koon*-da	*sekunda* (f)
(adj)	*droo*-gee	*drugi*
second class	*droo*-ga *kla*-sa	*druga klasa* (f)
second-hand	oo-zhi-*va*-ni	*używany*
secretary	se-kre-*tar*-ka	*sekretarka* (f)
to see	*vee*-djech • zo-*ba*-chich	*widzieć* • *zobaczyć*

We'll see.
zo-ba-*chi*-mi
Zobaczymy.

See you tomorrow.
do zo-ba-*che*-nya *yoo*-tro
Do zobaczenia jutro.

English	Pronunciation	Polish
self service	sa-mo-op-*swoo*-ga	*samoobsługa* (f)
to sell	spshe-*da*-vach • *spshe*-dach	*sprzedawać* • *sprzedać*
to send	*vi*-swach	*wysłać*
sender	na-*daf*-tsa	*nadawca* (m)
sentence		
(words)	*zda*-nye	*zdanie* (neut)
(prison)	*vi*-rok	*wyrok* (m)
separate (adj)	o-*sob*-ni	*osobny*
September	*vzhe*-shen	*wrzesień* (m)
serious	po-*vazh*-ni	*poważny*
service		
(work)	*swoozh*-ba	*służba* (f)
(religious)	na-bo-*zhen*-stfo	*nabożeństwo* (neut)
to sew	shich	*szyć*
sex	pwech	*płeć* (f)
shade/shadow	chen	*cień* (m)
shampoo	*sham*-pon	*szampon* (m)
shape	kshtawt • *for*-ma	*kształt* (m) • *forma* (f)
to shave	*go*-leech she	*golić się*
she	*o*-na	*ona*
sheep	*of*-tsa	*owca* (f)
sheet		
(bed)	pshe-shche-*ra*-dwo	*prześcieradło* (neut)
(of paper)	*kart*-ka	*kartka* (f)
ship	*sta*-tek	*statek* (m)
shirt	ko-*shoo*-la	*koszula* (f)
shoelaces	shnoo-ro-*va*-dwa	*sznurowadła* (neut, pl)
shoes	*boo*-ti	*buty* (m, pl)
shop	sklep	*sklep* (m)
shopping	za-*koo*-pi	*zakupy* (pl)

to go shopping
eeshch na za-*koo*-pi
iść na zakupy

short		
(height)	*nees*-kee	*niski*
(length)	*kroot*-kee	*krótki*
short cut	skroot	*skrót* (m)
shortage	brak	*brak* (m)
shorts	*shor*-ti	*szorty* (pl)
shoulder	*ra*-mye	*ramię* (neut)
to shout	*kshi*-chech	*krzyczeć*
show	*po*-kas	*pokaz* (m)
to show	po-*ka*-zach	*pokazać*

Please show me on the map.
pro-she mee po-*ka*-zach na *ma*-pye
Proszę mi pokazać na mapie.

shower	*prish*-neets	*prysznic* (m)
to shut	za-*mi*-kach	*zamykać*
shy	nye-*shmya*-wi	*nieśmiały*
sick	*ho*-ri	*chory*
sickness	ho-*ro*-ba	*choroba* (f)
side	*stro*-na	*strona* (f)
sightseeing	zvye-*dza*-nye	*zwiedzanie* (neut)
sign	znak	*znak* (m)
to sign	pot-*pee*-sach she	*podpisać się*
signature	*pot*-pees	*podpis* (m)
signpost	dro-*gof*-skas	*drogowskaz* (m)
silence	*chee*-sha	*cisza* (f)
silk	*yet*-vap	*jedwab* (m)
silly	*gwoo*-pee	*głupi*
silver	*sre*-bro	*srebro* (neut)
similar	po-*dob*-ni	*podobny*
simple	*pros*-ti	*prosty*
sin	gzheh	*grzech* (m)
since (May)	ot (*ma*-ya)	*od (maja)*
to sing	*shpye*-vach	*śpiewać*
singer	pyo-*sen*-kash/ pyo-sen-*kar*-ka	*piosenkarz/ piosenkarka* (m/f)
single		
(unmarried)	ka-*va*-ler/ *pan*-na • nye-zho-*na*-ti/ nye-za-*men*-zhna	*kawaler/ panna* (m/f) • *nieżonaty/ niezamężna* (m/f)
(unique)	ye-*di*-ni	*jedyny*
single room	*po*-kooy yed-no-o-so-*bo*-vi	*pokój jednoosobowy* (m)
sister	*shos*-tra	*siostra* (f)
to sit	*she*-djech	*siedzieć*
to sit down	*oo*-shonshch	*usiąść*
size	*roz*-myar	*rozmiar* (m)
to ski	*yezh*-djeech na *nar*-tah	*jeździć na nartach*
skiing	nar-*char*-stfo	*narciarstwo* (neut)
skin	*skoo*-ra	*skóra* (f)
skirt	spood-*nee*-tsa	*spódnica* (f)
sky	*nye*-bo	*niebo* (neut)
sleep	sen	*sen* (m)
to sleep	spach	*spać*
sleeping bag	*shpee*-voor	*śpiwór* (m)
sleeping car	*va*-gon si-*pyal*-ni	*wagon sypialny* (m)
sleeping pills	*prosh*-kee na-*sen*-ne	*proszki nasenne* (m)
sleepy	*shpyon*-tsi	*śpiący*
slides (film)	*slay*-di	*slajdy* (m, pl)
slow	*vol*-ni	*wolny*
slowly	po-*vo*-lee	*powoli*
slow train	*po*-chonk o-so-*bo*-vi	*pociąg osobowy* (m)
small	*ma*-wi	*mały*
smell	*za*-pah	*zapach* (m)
to smell	*pah*-nyech	*pachnieć*
to smile	oosh-*mye*-hach she	*uśmiechać się*
smoke	dim	*dym* (m)
to smoke	*pa*-leech • za-*pa*-leech	*palić* • *zapalić*
snail	*shlee*-mak	*ślimak* (m)
snake	vonsh	*wąż* (m)
snow	shnyek	*śnieg* (m)
soap	*mi*-dwo	*mydło* (neut)
soccer	*peew*-ka *nozh*-na	*piłka nożna* (f)
social welfare	o-*pye*-ka spo-*wech*-na	*opieka społeczna* (f)
solar energy	e-*ner*-gya swo-*nech*-na	*energia słoneczna* (f)

English	Pronunciation	Polish
somebody/ someone	ktosh	*ktoś*
something	tsosh	*coś*
sometimes	*cha*-sem	*czasem*
son	sin	*syn* (m)
song	pyo-*sen*-ka	*piosenka* (f)
soon	*fkroot*-tse	*wkrótce*

I'm sorry.
pshe-*pra*-sham
Przepraszam.

English	Pronunciation	Polish
soul	*doo*-sha	*dusza* (f)
sound	djvyenk	*dźwięk* (m)
south	po-*wood*-nye	*południe* (neut)
souvenir	pa-*myont*-ka	*pamiątka* (f)
souvenir shop	sklep spa-myont-*ka*-mee	*sklep z pamiątkami* (m)
spa	oo-zdro-*vees*-ko	*uzdrowisko* (neut)
spare tyre	*ko*-wo za-pa-*so*-ve	*koło zapasowe* (neut)
to speak	*moo*-veech	*mówić*
special	spe-*tsyal*-ni	*specjalny*
speed	*prent*-koshch	*prędkość* (f)
speed limit	o-gra-nee-*che*-nye prent-*kosh*-chee	*ograniczenie prędkości* (neut)
spicy (hot)	pee-*kant*-ni	*pikantny*
spider	*pa*-yonk	*pająk* (m)
spirit (soul)	dooh	*duch* (m)
sport	sport	*sport* (m)
sportsperson	spor-*to*-vyets/ sports-*men*-ka	*sportowiec* (m)/*sportsmenka* (f)
sprain	zveeh-*nyen*-che	*zwichnięcie* (neut)
spring		
(season)	*vyos*-na	*wiosna* (f)
(coil)	spren-*zhi*-na	*sprężyna* (f)
(of water)	*zhroo*-dwo	*źródło* (neut)
square		
(shape)	*kfa*-drat	*kwadrat* (m)
(in town)	plats	*plac* (m)
(in old town)	*ri*-nek	*rynek* (m)
stadium	*sta*-dyon	*stadion* (m)
stage (in theatre)	*stse*-na	*scena* (f)
stairs	s-*ho*-di	*schody* (pl)
stairway	klat-ka	*klatka*
	sho-*do*-va	*schodowa* (f)
stamp	*zna*-chek	*znaczek* (m)
to stand	stach	*stać*
standard (quality)	*po*-zhom	*poziom* (m)
standard of living	*sto*-pa zhi-*cho*-va	*stopa życiowa* (f)
star	*gvyaz*-da	*gwiazda* (f)
start	po-*chon*-tek	*początek* (m)
to start	za-*chi*-nach	*zaczynać*
state		
(condition)	stan	*stan* (m)
(country)	*pan*-stfo	*państwo* (neut)
station (train/bus)	*sta*-tsya • *dvo*-zhets	*stacja* (f) • *dworzec* (m)
stationers	sklep pa-pyer-*nee*-chi	*sklep papierniczy* (m)
statue	*po*-sonk	*posąg* (m)
to stay		
(remain)	zos-*ta*-vach	*zostawać*
(in hotel)	za-*tshi*-mach she	*zatrzymać się*
to steal	krashch • *oo*-krashch	*kraść* • *ukraść*
steep	*stro*-mi	*stromy*
step	krok	*krok* (m)
stomach	zho-*won*-dek	*żołądek* (m)
stomachache	zho-bool *wont*-ka	*ból żołądka* (m)
stone	*ka*-myen	*kamień* (m)
to stop	za-*tshi*-mach she	*zatrzymać się*
stork	*bo*-chan	*bocian* (m)
storm	*boo*-zha	*burza* (f)
story	o-po-vya-*da*-nye	*opowiadanie* (neut)
stove	pyets	*piec* (m)
straight	*pros*-ti	*prosty*
strange	*djeev*-ni	*dziwny*

stranger	*op*-tsi • nye-zna-*yo*-mi	*obcy* (m) • *nieznajomy* (m)
stream	*stroo*-myen	*strumień* (m)
street	oo-*lee*-tsa	*ulica* (f)
strength	*shee*-wa • mots	*siła* (f) • *moc* (f)
strike	strayk	*strajk* (m)
string	*shnoo*-rek	*sznurek* (m)
to stroll	spa-tse-*ro*-vach	*spacerować*
strong	*sheel*-ni • *mots*-ni	*silny* • *mocny*
stubborn	oo-*par*-ti	*uparty*
student	*stoo*-dent/ stoo-*dent*-ka	*student/ studentka* (m/f)
studio (artist's)	pra-*tsov*-nya	*pracownia* (f)
stupid	*gwoo*-pee	*głupi*
style	stil	*styl* (m)
subtitles	na-*pee*-si	*napisy* (m)
suburb (city district)	djel-*nee*-tsa	*dzielnica* (f)
suburbs (city outskirts)	pe-ri-*fe*-rye • pshet-*myesh*-che	*peryferie* (f, pl) • *przedmieście* (neut)
subway	*me*-tro	*metro* (neut)
success	*sook*-tses	*sukces* (m)
suddenly	*na*-gle	*nagle*
to suffer	*cher*-pyech	*cierpieć*
sugar	*tsoo*-kyer	*cukier* (m)
suitcase	va-*lees*-ka	*walizka* (f)
summer	*la*-to	*lato* (neut)
sun	*swon*-tse	*słońce* (neut)
sunburnt	o-pa-*lo*-ni	*opalony*
Sunday	nye-*dje*-la	*niedziela* (f)
sunglasses	o-koo-*la*-ri swo-*nech*-ne	*okulary słoneczne* (m, pl)
sunny	swo-*nech*-ni	*słoneczny*
sunrise	fs-hoot *swon*-tsa	*wschód słońca* (m)
sunscreen	krem do o-pa-*la*-nya	*krem do opalania* (m)
sunset	*za*-hoot *swon*-tsa	*zachód słońca* (m)

Sure!
o-chi-*veesh*-che!
Oczywiście!

surface mail	*poch*-ta *zvi*-kwa	*poczta zwykła* (f)
surname	naz-*vees*-ko	*nazwisko* (neut)
surprise	nye-spo-*djan*-ka	*niespodzianka* (f)
to survive	*pshe*-zhich	*przeżyć*
swear word	pshe-*klen*-stfo	*przekleństwo* (neut)
sweater	*sfe*-ter	*sweter* (m)
sweet	*swot*-kee	*słodki*
sweets	tsoo-*kyer*-kee	*cukierki* (m, pl)
to swim	*pwi*-vach	*pływać*
swimming	pwi-*va*-nye	*pływanie* (neut)
swimming costume	*kos*-tyoom kom-pye-*lo*-vi	*kostium kąpielowy* (m)
swimming pool	*ba*-sen • pwi-*val*-nya	*basen* (m) • *pływalnia* (f)
swimsuit	*kos*-tyoom kom-pye-*lo*-vi	*kostium kąpielowy* (m)
switch	pshe-*wonch*-neek	*przełącznik* (m)
sword	myech	*miecz* (m)
synagogue	si-na-*go*-ga	*synagoga* (f)
synthetic	sin-te-*tich*-ni	*syntetyczny*
syringe	stshi-*kaf*-ka	*strzykawka* (f)

T

table (general)	stoow	*stół* (m)
(in restaurant)	*sto*-leek	*stolik* (m)
tablecloth	*o*-broos	*obrus* (m)
tablet	pas-*til*-ka	*pastylka* (f)
table tennis	*te*-nees sto-*wo*-vi	*tenis stołowy* (m)
tail	*o*-gon	*ogon* (m)
tailor	*kra*-vyets	*krawiec* (m)
to take	brach • vzhonch	*brać* • *wziąć*

to take photographs
ro-beech *zdyen*-cha
robić zdjęcia

to take time
trfach
trwać

take-away	na *vi*-nos	*na wynos*
to talk	roz-*ma*-vyach	*rozmawiać*
tall	vi-*so*-kee	*wysoki*
tampons	tam-*po*-ni	*tampony* (m)
tap	kran	*kran* (m)
taste	smak	*smak* (m)
tasty	*smach*-ni	*smaczny*
tax	po-*da*-tek	*podatek* (m)
taxi	tak-*soof*-ka	*taksówka* (f)
taxi stand	*pos*-tooy tak-*soo*-vek	*postój taksówek* (m)
tea	her-*ba*-ta	*herbata* (f)
to teach	*oo*-chich	*uczyć*
teacher	na-oo-*chi*-chel/ na-oo-chi-*chel*-ka	*nauczyciel/ nauczycielka* (m/f)
team	droo-*zhi*-na • *zes*-poow	*drużyna* (f) • *zespół* (m)
tear (crying)	wza	*łza* (f)
technique	teh-*nee*-ka	*technika* (f)
teeth	*zem*-bi	*zęby* (m, pl)
telegram	te-*le*-gram	*telegram* (m)
telephone	te-*le*-fon	*telefon* (m)
to telephone	te-le-fo-*no*-vach	*telefonować*
telephone book	*kshon*-shka te-le-fo-*neech*-na	*książka telefoniczna* (f)
television	te-le-*vee*-zya	*telewizja* (f)
to tell	po-*vye*-djech	*powiedzieć*
temperature		
(fever)	go-*ronch*-ka	*gorączka* (f)
(weather)	tem-pe-ra-*too*-ra	*temperatura* (f)
temple	shfyon-*ti*-nya	*świątynia* (f)
tenant	lo-*ka*-tor/ lo-ka-*tor*-ka	*lokator*)/ *lokatorka* (m/f)
tennis	*te*-nees	*tenis* (m)
tennis court	kort te-nee-*so*-vi	*kort tenisowy* (m)
tent	*na*-myot	*namiot* (m)
terrible	*strash*-ni • pot-*for*-ni	*straszny* • *potworny*
test	*proo*-ba	*próba* (f)
to thank	djen-*ko*-vach	*dziękować*

Thank you.
djen-*koo*-ye
Dziękuję.

theatre	*te*-atr	*teatr* (m)
theft	*kra*-djesh	*kradzież* (f)
thick	*groo*-bi	*gruby*
thief	*zwo*-djey	*złodziej* (m)
thin	*chen*-kee	*cienki*
thing	zhech	*rzecz* (f)
to think	*mish*-lech	*myśleć*
third	*tshe*-chee	*trzeci*
thirsty	spra-*gnyo*-ni	*spragniony*
thought	mishl	*myśl* (f)
throat	*gar*-dwo	*gardło* (neut)
Thursday	*chfar*-tek	*czwartek* (m)
ticket	*bee*-let	*bilet* (m)
ticket collector	kon-*tro*-ler	*kontroler* (m)
ticket office	*ka*-sa bee-le-*to*-va	*kasa biletowa* (f)
tie	*kra*-vat	*krawat* (m)
tight	*chas*-ni	*ciasny*
time	chas	*czas* (m)

What time is it?
ktoo-ra go-*djee*-na?
Która godzina?

timetable	*ros*-kwat *yaz*-di	*rozkład jazdy* (m)
tin (can)	*poosh*-ka	*puszka* (f)
tin opener	ot-*fye*-rach do *kon*-serf	*otwieracz do konserw* (m)
tip (gratuity)	na-*pee*-vek	*napiwek* (m)
tired	zmen-*cho*-ni	*zmęczony*
toad	ro-*poo*-ha	*ropucha* (f)
toast		
(bread)	*gzhan*-ka	*grzanka* (f)
(drink)	*to*-ast	*toast* (m)

tobacco	*ti*-ton	*tytoń* (m)
today	djeesh • *djee*-shay	*dziś* • *dzisiaj*
together	*ra*-zem	*razem*
toilet paper	*pa*-pyer to-a-le-*to*-vi	*papier toaletowy* (m)
toilets	to-a-*le*-ti	*toalety* (f, pl)
token (for phone)	*zhe*-ton	*żeton* (m)
tomorrow	*yoo*-tro	*jutro*

tomorrow evening
yoo-tro vye-*cho*-rem
jutro wieczorem

tomorrow morning
yoo-tro *ra*-no
jutro rano

tonight	djeesh vye-*cho*-rem	*dziś wieczorem*
too (as well)	tesh	*też*

too expensive
za *dro*-gee
za drogi

too much/many	za *doo*-zho	*za dużo*
tooth	zomp	*ząb* (m)
toothache	bool *zem*-ba	*ból zęba* (m)
toothbrush	shcho-*tech*-ka do *zem*-boof	*szczoteczka do zębów* (f)
toothpaste	*pas*-ta do *zem*-boof	*pasta do zębów* (f)
torch (flashlight)	la-*tar*-ka	*latarka* (f)
total (sum)	*soo*-ma	*suma* (f)
to touch	do-*ti*-kach	*dotykać*
tourist	too-*ris*-ta/ too-*rist*-ka	*turysta/ turystka* (m/f)
tourist information office	*byoo*-ro een-for-*ma*-tsyee too-ris-*tich*-ney	*biuro informacji turystycznej* (neut)
towel	*rench*-neek	*ręcznik* (m)
tower	*vye*-zha	*wieża* (f)
town	*mya*-sto	*miasto* (neut)
town centre	*tsen*-troom	*centrum* (neut)
town hall	*ra*-toosh	*ratusz* (m)
toy	za-*baf*-ka	*zabawka* (f)
track (path)	*shchesh*-ka	*ścieżka* (f)
trade union	*zvyon*-zek za-vo-*do*-vi	*związek zawodowy* (m)
traffic	rooh dro-*go*-vi	*ruch drogowy* (m
traffic jam	*ko*-rek	*korek* (m)
traffic lights	*shfya*-twa	*światła* (neut, pl)
trail (route)	shlak	*szlak* (m)
trailer	pshi-*che*-pa	*przyczepa* (
train	*po*-chonk	*pociąg* (m)
train station	*dvo*-zhets ko-le-*yo*-vi	*dworzec kolejowy* (m
train station (central)	*dvo*-zhets *gwoov*-ni	*dworzec główny* (m)
tram	*tram*-vay	*tramwaj* (m)
to translate	twoo-*ma*-chich • pshe-twoo-*ma*-chich	*tłumaczyć* • *przetłumaczyć*
translator	*twoo*-mach/ twoo-*mach*-ka	*tłumacz* (m)/ *tłumaczka* (
to travel	po-droo-*zho*-vach	*podróżowac*
travel agency	*byoo*-ro po-*droo*-zhi	*biuro podróży* (neut)
travel sickness	ho-*ro*-ba lo-ko-mo-*tsiy*-na	*choroba lokomocyjna*
traveller	po-*droozh*-neek/ po-droozh-*neech*-ka	*podróżnik/ podróżniczk* (m/f)
travellers cheques	*che*-kee po-*droozh*-ne	*czeki podróżne* (m
tree	*dzhe*-vo	*drzewo* (neu
trendy (person)	*mod*-ni	*modny*
trip	*po*-droosh • vi-*chech*-ka	*podróż* (f) • *wycieczka* (
trolley	*voo*-zek	*wózek* (m)
trolleybus	tro-*ley*-boos	*trolejbus* (m
trouble	*pro*-blem • *kwo*-pot	*problem* (m • *kłopot* (m)
trousers	*spod*-nye	*spodnie* (pl)
truck (lorry)	sa-*mo*-hoot chen-zha-*ro*-vi	*samochód ciężarowy* (n

true	prav-*djee*-vi	*prawdziwy*

> It's true.
> to *prav*-da
> *To prawda.*
>
> That's not true.
> to nye-*prav*-da
> *To nieprawda.*

trust	za-oo-*fa*-nye	*zaufanie* (neut)
to trust	*oo*-fach	*ufać*
truth	*prav*-da	*prawda* (f)
to try	proo-*bo*-vach	*próbować*
to try on	pshi-*mye*-zhich	*przymierzyć*
T-shirt	pot-ko-*shool*-ka	*podkoszulka* (f)
Tuesday	*fto*-rek	*wtorek* (m)
tune	me-*lo*-dya	*melodia* (f)

> Turn left/right.
> *pro*-she *skren*-cheech *fle*-vo/*fpra*-vo
> *Proszę skręcić w lewo/prawo.*

television	te-le-*vee*-zya	*telewizja* (f)
TV set	te-le-*vee*-zor	*telewizor* (m)
twice	dva *ra*-zi	*dwa razy*
twin beds	dva *woosh*-ka	*dwa łóżka*
twins	bleezh-*nyen*-ta	*bliźnięta* (pl)
type	tip	*typ* (m)
typical	ti-*po*-vi	*typowy*
tyre	o-*po*-na	*opona* (f)

U

ugly	bzhit-kee	*brzydki*
umbrella	pa-*ra*-sol	*parasol* (m)
uncle	vooy • *voo*-yek	*wuj* • *wujek* (m)
under	pot	*pod*
to understand	ro-*zoo*-myech	*rozumieć*

> Do you understand me? (m/f)
> chi pan/*pa*-nee mnye ro-*zoo*-mye?
> *Czy pan/pani mnie rozumie?*
>
> I (don't) understand.
> (nye) ro-*zoo*-myem
> *(Nie) rozumiem.*

unemployed	bez-ro-*bot*-ni	*bezrobotny*
unemployment	bez-ro-*bo*-che	*bezrobocie* (neut)
unfortunately	nye-*ste*-ti	*niestety*
unions	*zvyon*-skee	*związki* (pl)
United States	*sta*-ni zye-dno-*cho*-ne	*Stany Zjednoczone* (pl)
universe	*fsheh*-shfyat	*wszechświat* (m)
university	oo-nee-*ver*-si-tet	*uniwersytet* (m)
unleaded (petrol/gas)	(ben-*zi*-na) be-so-wo-*vyo*-va	*(benzyna) bezołowiowa* (f)
unsafe	nye-bes-*pyech*-ni	*niebezpieczny*
until (June)	do (*cher*-ftsa)	*do (czerwca)*
unusual	nye-*zvi*-kwi	*niezwykły*
up	do *goo*-ri	*do góry*
urgent	*peel*-ni	*pilny*
to use	oo-*zhi*-vach	*używać*
useful	oo-zhi-*tech*-ni	*użyteczny*
usual	*zvik*-wi	*zwykły*

V

vacant	*vol*-ni	*wolny*
vacation	va-*ka*-tsye	*wakacje* (pl)
vaccination	shche-*pye*-nye	*szczepienie* (neut)
vacuum cleaner	ot-*koo*-zhach	*odkurzacz* (m)
valid	*vazh*-ni	*ważny*
valley	do-*lee*-na	*dolina* (f)
valuable	*tsen*-ni	*cenny*
value (price)	*var*-toshch	*wartość* (f)
van	foor-go-*net*-ka	*furgonetka* (f)
vegetables	ya-*zhi*-ni	*jarzyny* (pl)
vegetarian	*ya*-rosh/ya-*rosh*-ka	*jarosz/jaroszka* (m/f)
vegetarian dishes	*da*-nya *yar*-skye	*dania jarskie* (neut, pl)
vegetation	rosh-*leen*-noshch	*roślinność* (f)

vein	*zhi*-wa	*żyła* (f)
venereal disease	ho-*ro*-ba ve-ne-*rich*-na	*choroba weneryczna* (f)
very	*bar*-dzo	*bardzo*
via	pshes	*przez*
video recorder	mag-ne-*to*-veet	*magnetowid* (m)
video tape	*tash*-ma vee-*de*-o	*taśma video* (f)
view	*vee*-dok	*widok* (m)
village	vyesh	*wieś* (f)
violin	skship-tse	*skrzypce* (pl)
virus	*vee*-roos	*wirus* (m)
visa	*vee*-za	*wiza* (f)
to visit	od-*vye*-dzach • *zvye*-dzach	*odwiedzać* • *zwiedzać*
vitamins	vee-ta-*mee*-ni	*witaminy* (f, pl)
vodka	*voot*-ka	*wódka* (f)
voice	gwos	*głos* (m)
voltage	na-*pyen*-che	*napięcie* (neut)
to vote	gwo-*so*-vach	*głosować*

W

to wait	*che*-kach • za-*che*-kach	*czekać* • *zaczekać*
waiter	*kel*-ner	*kelner* (m)
waitress	kel-*ner*-ka	*kelnerka* (f)
waiting room	po-che-*kal*-nya	*poczekalnia* (f)
wake up	*boo*-djeech she	*budzić się*
walk	*spa*-tser	*spacer* (m)
to walk	spa-tse-*ro*-vach	*spacerować*
wall		
(interior)	*shcha*-na	*ściana* (f)
(exterior)	moor	*mur* (m)
wallet	*port*-fel	*portfel* (m)
to want	hchech	*chcieć*

I want to hire a bicycle.
htse vi-po-*zhi*-chich *ro*-ver
Chcę wypożyczyć rower.

Do you want to go to the cinema?
chi htsesh pooyshch do *kee*-na?
Czy chcesz pójść do kina?

war	*voy*-na	*wojna* (f)
wardrobe	*sha*-fa	*szafa* (f)
warm	*chep*-wi	*ciepły*
to warn	os-*tshe*-gach	*ostrzegać*
Warsaw	var-*sha*-va	*Warszawa* (f)
to wash		
(clothes)	prach	*prać*
(oneself)	mich she	*myć się*
washing machine	*pral*-ka	*pralka* (f)
washing powder	*pro*-shek do *pra*-nya	*proszek do prania* (m)
watch	ze-*ga*-rek	*zegarek* (m)
to watch		
(TV)	o-*glon*-dach	*oglądać*
(guard)	peel-*no*-vach	*pilnować*
water	*vo*-da	*woda* (f)
waterfall	vo-*dos*-pat	*wodospad* (m)
waterproof		
(clothes)	nye-pshe-ma-*kal*-ni	*nieprzemakalny*
(watch)	vo-do-*shchel*-ni	*wodoszczelny*
wave	*fa*-la	*fala* (f)
way	*dro*-ga	*droga* (f)

Please show me the way to ...
pro-she mee *fska*-zach *dro*-ge do ...
Proszę mi wskazać drogę do ...

Which way?
ktoo-*ren*-di?
Którędy?

we	mi	*my*
weak	*swa*-bi	*słaby*
wealthy	bo-*ga*-ti	*bogaty*
weather	po-*go*-da	*pogoda* (f)
wedding		
(ceremony)	shloop	*ślub* (m)
(reception)	ve-*se*-le	*wesele* (neut)

English	Pronunciation	Polish
Wednesday	*shro*-da	*środa* (f)
week	*ti*-djen	*tydzień* (m)

this week
ftim ti-*god*-nyoo
w tym tygodniu

English	Pronunciation	Polish
to weigh	*va*-zhich	*ważyć*
weight	*va*-ga	*waga* (f)
welfare (social)	o-*pye*-ka spo-*wech*-na	*opieka społeczna* (f)
west	*za*-hoot	*zachód* (m)
wet	*mo*-kri	*mokry*
what	tso	*co*

What's he saying?
tso on *moo*-vee?
Co on mówi?

What's this?
tso to yest?
Co to jest?

English	Pronunciation	Polish
wheel	*ko*-wo	*koło* (neut)
wheelchair	*voo*-zek een-va-*leets*-kee	*wózek inwalidzki* (m)
when	*kye*-di	*kiedy*

When are you leaving?
kye-di vi-*yesh*-djash?
Kiedy wyjeżdżasz?

English	Pronunciation	Polish
where	gdje	*gdzie*

Where's the bank?
gdje yest bank?
Gdzie jest bank?

English	Pronunciation	Polish
which	*ktoo*-ri	*który*
white	*bya*-wi	*biały*
who	kto	*kto*

Who's coming?
kto pshi-*ho*-djee?
Kto przychodzi?

English	Pronunciation	Polish
why	dla-*che*-go	*dlaczego*

Why is the museum closed?
dla-*che*-go moo-*ze*-oom yest zam-*knyen*-te?
Dlaczego muzeum jest zamknięte?

English	Pronunciation	Polish
wide	she-*ro*-kee	*szeroki*
wife	*zho*-na	*żona* (f)
wild	*djee*-kee	*dziki*
to win	*vi*-grach	*wygrać*
wind	vyatr	*wiatr* (m)
window	*ok*-no	*okno* (neut)
window seat	*myey*-stse pshi *ok*-nye	*miejsce przy oknie* (neut)
windscreen	*pshe*-dnya *shi*-ba	*przednia szyba* (f)
wine	*vee*-no	*wino* (neut)
wing	*skshi*-dwo	*skrzydło* (neut)
winter	*zhee*-ma	*zima* (f)
wire	droot	*drut* (m)
wise	*mon*-dri	*mądry*
to wish	*zhi*-chich	*życzyć*

Best wishes.
nay-*lep*-she zhi-*che*-nya
Najlepsze życzenia.

English	Pronunciation	Polish
with	z	*z*
without	bes	*bez*
woman	ko-*bye*-ta	*kobieta* (f)
wonderful	tsoo-*dov*-ni	*cudowny*
wood	*drev*-no	*drewno* (neut)
wool	*veoo*-na	*wełna* (f)
word	*swo*-vo	*słowo* (neut)
work	*pra*-tsa	*praca* (f)
to work	pra-*tso*-vach	*pracować*
work of art	*dje*-wo *shtoo*-kee	*dzieło sztuki* (neut)
workshop	*var*-shtat	*warsztat* (m)
world	shfyat	*świat* (m)
World War II	*droo*-ga *voy*-na shfya-*to*-va	*druga wojna światowa* (f)
to worry	*mar*-tfeech she	*martwić się*
worried	zmar-*tfyo*-ni/ • za-nye-po-ko-*yo*-ni	*zmartwiony*/ • *zaniepokojony*
worse	*gor*-shi	*gorszy*
worst	nay-*gor*-shi	*najgorszy*
worth	*var*-toshch	*wartość* (f)

wound	*ra*-na	*rana* (f)
to write	*pee*-sach • na-*pee*-sach	*pisać* • *napisać*
writer	*pee*-sash pee-*sar*-ka	*pisarz/ pisarka* (m/f)
wrong	zwi	*zły*

I'm wrong. (my fault)
mo-ya *vee*-na
Moja wina.

I'm wrong. (not right)
nye mam *ra*-tsyee
Nie mam racji.

Y

yacht	yaht	*jacht* (m)
year	rok	*rok* (m)

this year
ftim *ro*-koo
w tym roku

yellow	*zhoow*-ti	*żółty*

Yes.
tak
Tak.

yesterday	*fcho*-ray	*wczoraj*

yesterday evening
fcho-ray vye-*cho*-rem
wczoraj wieczorem

yesterday morning
fcho-ray *ra*-no
wczoraj rano

yet	*yesh*-che	*jeszcze*
you (pol)	pan/*pa*-nee	*pan pani* (m/f)
young	*mwo*-di	*młody*
youth (collective)	*mwo*-djesh	*młodzież* (f)
youth hostel	sro-*nees*-ko mwo-dje-*zho*-ve	*schronisko młodzież-owe* (neut)

Z

zebra	*ze*-bra	*zebra* (f)
zero	*ze*-ro	*zero* (neut)
zoo	*zo*-o	*zoo* (neut)

POLISH – ENGLISH

The word order here is organised according to the Polish alphabet. Polish letters with diacritical marks (ą, ć, ę and so on) are treated as separate letters. The order of the letters is:

a ą b c ć d e ę f g h i j k l ł m n ń o ó p q r s ś t u v w x y z ź ż

Remember, in particular, the order of the following letters:

a before *ą*
c before *ć*
e before *ę*
l before *ł*
n before *ń*
o before *ó*
s before *ś*
z then *ź* then *ż*

A BEFORE Ą

Polish letters with diacritical marks are treated as separate letters. Remember that *a* comes before *ą*.

A

adres (m)	*a*-dres	address
alarm przeciwpożarowy (m)	*a*-larm pshe-cheef-po-zha-*ro*-vi	fire alarm
albo	*al*-bo	or
ale	*a*-le	but
aleja (f)	a-*le*-ya	avenue
amator (m)	a-*ma*-tor	amateur
ambasada (f)	am-ba-*sa*-da	embassy
ambasador (m)	am-ba-*sa*-dor	ambassador
analiza krwi (f)	a-na-*lee*-za krfee	blood test
angielski	an-*gyel*-skee	English
Anglia (f)	*an*-glya	England
antybiotyk (m)	an-ti-*byo*-tik	antibiotic
antyk (m)	*an*-tik	antique
antykwariat (m)	an-ti-*kfa*-ryat	antique shop
aparat fotograficzny (m)	a-*pa*-rat fo-to-gra-*feech*-ni	camera
aparat słuchowy (m)	a-*pa*-rat swoo-*ho*-vi	hearing aid
apteczka pierwszej pomocy (f)	ap-*tech*-ka *pyer*-fshey po-*mo*-tsi	first-aid kit
apteka (f)	ap-*te*-ka	chemist • pharmacy
architektura (f)	ar-hee-tek-*too*-ra	architecture
artykuł (m)	ar-*ti*-koow	article
artysta (m)	ar-*tis*-ta	artist (m)
artystka (f)	ar-*tist*-ka	artist (f)
aspiryna (f)	as-pee-*ri*-na	aspirin

astma (f)	*ast*-ma	asthma
atmosfera (f)	at-mos-*fe*-ra	atmosphere
autobus (m)	aw-*to*-boos	bus • coach
autokar (m)	aw-*to*-kar	coach
autostop (m)	aw-*to*-stop	hitchhiking
autostrada (f)	aw-to-*stra*-da	freeway • motorway
awaria (f)	a-*va*-rya	break down

B

babka (f)	*bap*-ka	grand-mother
bać się	bach she	to fear
bagaż (m)	*ba*-gash	luggage
bagaż podręczny (m)	*ba*-gash pod-*rench*-ni	hand luggage
balet (m)	*ba*-let	ballet
balkon (m)	*bal*-kon	balcony
bandaż (m)	*ban*-dash	bandage
bandera (f)	ban-*de*-ra	flag
bank (m)	bank	bank
banknot (m)	*ban*-knot	banknote
bankomat (m)	ban-*ko*-mat	automatic teller machine (ATM)
bar (m)	bar	bar
bardzo	*bar*-dzo	very
basen (m)	*ba*-sen	swimming pool
bateria (f)	ba-*te*-rya	battery
bawełna (f)	ba-*veoo*-na	cotton
bawić się	*ba*-veech she	to play • to have fun
bazar (m)	*ba*-zar	market
benzyna (f)	ben-*zi*-na	petrol
benzyna bezo-łowiowa (f)	ben-*zi*-na be-so-wo-*vyo*-va	unleaded petrol
bez	bes	without
bezdomny	bes-*dom*-ni	homeless
bezpiecznik (m)	bes-*pyech*-neek	fuse
bezpieczny	bes-*pyech*-ni	safe (adj)
bezpłatny	bes-*pwat*-ni	free of charge
bezpośredni	bes-posh-*red*-nee	direct
bezrobocie (neut)	bez-ro-*bo*-che	unemploy-ment
bezrobotny	bez-ro-*bot*-ni	unem-ployed
bęben (m)	*bem*-ben	drum
biały	*bya*-wi	white
biblia (f)	*bee*-blya	bible
biblioteka (f)	bee-blyo-*te*-ka	library
biedny	*byed*-ni	poor (not rich)
biegać	*bye*-gach	to run
biegły	*bye*-gwi	fluent
biegunka (f)	bye-*goon*-ka	diarrhoea
bilet (m)	*bee*-let	ticket
bilet powrotny (m)	*bee*-let po-*vrot*-ni	return ticket
bilet w jedną	*bee*-let *fyed*-nom *stro*-ne	one-way ticket
biografia (f)	byo-*gra*-fya	biography
biuro (neut)	*byoo*-ro	office
biuro informacji turystycznej (neut)	*byoo*-ro een-for-*ma*-tsyee too-ris-*tich*-ney	tourist informa-tion office
biuro podróży (neut)	*byoo*-ro po-*droo*-zhi	travel agency
biustonosz (m)	byoos-*to*-nosh	bra
biżuteria (f)	bee-zhoo-*te*-rya	jewellery
bliski	*blees*-kee	near
bliźnięta (pl)	bleezh-*nyen*-ta	twins
błąd (m)	bwont	error
błoto (neut)	*bwo*-to	mud
bochenek (m)	bo-*he*-nek	loaf
bocian (m)	*bo*-chan	stork
bogaty	bo-*ga*-ti	rich • wealthy
boks (m)	boks	boxing
boleć	*bo*-lech	to hurt
bolesny	bo-*les*-ni	painful
Boże Narodzenie (neut)	*bo*-zhe-na-ro-*dze*-nye	Christmas
Bóg (m)	book	God

DICTIONARY

ból (m)	bool	pain
ból głowy (m)	bool *gwo*-vi	headache
ból zęba (m)	bool *zem*-ba	toothache
ból żołądka (m)	bool zho-*wont*-ka	stomach ache
brać	brach	to take
brak (m)	brak	shortage
brama (f)	*bra*-ma	gate
brat (m)	brat	brother
brązowy	bron-*zo*-vi	brown
broszura (f)	bro-*shoo*-ra	brochure • leaflet
brudny	*brood*-ni	dirty • filthy
brzydki	*bzhit*-kee	ugly
budka telefoniczna (f)	*boot*-ka te-le-fo-*neech*-na	phone box
budować	boo-*do*-vach	to build
budynek (m)	boo-*di*-nek	building
budzić się	*boo*-djeech she	to wake up
budzik (m)	*boo*-djeek	alarm clock
burmistrz (m)	*boor*-meeshch	mayor
burza (f)	*boo*-zha	storm
butelka (f)	boo-*tel*-ka	bottle
buty (m, pl)	*boo*-ti	shoes • boots
być	bich	to be
być może	bich *mo*-zhe	maybe

C

całować	tsa-*wo*-vach	to kiss
cel (m)	tsel	aim • goal • target
cel podróży (m)	tsel po-*droo*-zhi	destination
cena (f)	*tse*-na	price

C BEFORE Ć

Polish letters with diacritical marks are treated as separate letters. Remember that *c* comes before *ć*.

cenny	*tsen*-ni	valuable
centralny	tsen-*tral*-ni	central
centrum (neut)	*tsen*-troom	city centre
centrum handlowe (neut)	*tsen*-troom han-*dlo*-ve	shopping centre
chcieć	hchech	to want
chleb (m)	hlep	bread
chłodnica (f)	hwod-*nee*-tsa	radiator (in car)
chłodny	*hwod*-ni	cool
chłopiec (m)	*hwo*-pyets	boy
chmura (f)	*hmoo*-ra	cloud
chodnik (m)	*hod*-neek	pavement
choroba (f)	ho-*ro*-ba	disease • illness
choroba lokomocyjna (f)	ho-*ro*-ba lo-ko-mo-*tsiy*-na	travel sickness
choroba morska (f)	ho-*ro*-ba *mor*-ska	seasickness
choroba weneryczna (f)	ho-*ro*-ba ve-ne-*rich*-na	venereal disease
chory	*ho*-ri	sick • ill
chronić	*hro*-neech	to protect

Chwileczkę.
hfee-*lech*-ke
Just a minute.

ciało (neut)	*cha*-wo	body
ciasny	*chas*-ni	tight
ciąć	chonch	to cut
ciągnąć	*chong*-nonch	to pull
ciemny	*chem*-ni	dark
cienki	*chen*-kee	thin
cień (m)	chen	shade • shadow
ciepła woda (f)	*chep*-wa *vo*-da	hot water
ciepły	*che*-pwi	warm
cierpieć	*cher*-pyech	to suffer
cierpliwy	cher-*plee*-vi	patient (adj)
cieszyć się	*che*-shich she	to enjoy
ciężki	*chen*-shkee	heavy
ciotka (f)	*chot*-ka	aunt
cisza (f)	*chee*-sha	silence
ciśnienie (neut)	cheesh-*nye*-nye	pressure

ciśnienie krwi (neut)	cheesh-*nye*-nye krfee	blood pressure
cło (neut)	tswo	customs
cmentarz (m)	*tsmen*-tash	cemetery
co	tso	what
codziennie	tso-*djen*-nye	daily • every day
cokolwiek	tso-*kol*-vyek	anything
coś	tsosh	something
córka (f)	*tsoor*-ka	daughter
cudowny	tsoo-*dov*-ni	amazing • marvellous
cudzoziemiec (m)	tsoo-dzo-*zhe*-myets	foreigner (m)
cudzoziemka (f)	tsoo-dzo-*zhem*-ka	foreigner (f)
cukier (m)	*tsoo*-kyer	sugar
cukierki (m, pl)	tsoo-*kyer*-kee	sweets
cukrzyca (f)	tsook-*shi*-tsa	diabetes
cyrk (m)	tsirk	circus
czajnik (m)	*chay*-neek	kettle
czarny	*char*-ni	black
czas (m)	chas	time
czasem	*cha*-sem	sometimes
czek (m)	chek	cheque
czekać	*che*-kach	to wait
czeki podróżne (m, pl)	*che*-kee po-*droozh*-ne	travellers cheques
czekolada (f)	che-ko-*la*-da	chocolate
czerwiec (m)	*cher*-vyets	June
czerwony	cher-*vo*-ni	red
często	*chen*-sto	often
częsty	*chen*-sti	frequent
część (f)	chenshch	part
człowiek (m)	*chwo*-vyek	human being • man
czuć (się)	chooch (she)	to feel
czułość filmu (f)	*choo*-woshch *feel*-moo	film speed
czwartek (m)	*chfar*-tek	Thursday
czynsz (m)	chinsh	rent (payment)
czysty	*chis*-ti	clean • pure
czytać	*chi*-tach	to read

Ć

ćwierć (f)	chfyerch	quarter

D

dać	dach	to give
dać łapówkę	dach wa-*poof*-ke	to bribe
daleko	da-*le*-ko	far
danie (neut)	*da*-nye	dish
danie jarskie (neut)	*da*-nye *yar*-skye	vegetarian dish
data (f)	*da*-ta	date (time)
data urodzenia (f)	*da*-ta oo-ro-*dze*-nya	date of birth
dawać	*da*-vach	to give
dawno temu	*dav*-no *te*-moo	long ago
dawny	*dav*-ni	ancient • former
decydować	de-tsi-*do*-vach	to decide
decyzja (f)	de-*tsi*-zya	decision
delikatesy (pl)	de-lee-ka-*te*-si	delicatessen
demokracja (f)	de-mo-*kra*-tsya	democracy
demonstracja (f)	de-mon-*stra*-tsya	demonstration
dentysta (m)	den-*tis*-ta	dentist (m)
dentystka (f)	den-*tist*-ka	dentist (f)
deszcz (m)	deshch	rain
dla	dla	for
dlaczego	dla-*che*-go	why
długi	*dwoo*-gee	long
długopis (m)	dwoo-*go*-pees	pen (ballpoint)
dno (neut)	dno	bottom

Dobranoc.
do-*bra*-nots
Goodnight.

dobry	*do*-bri	good

Dobry wieczór.
do-bri *vye*-choor
Good evening.

Dobrze.
do-bzhe
OK.

dochody (m, pl)	do-*ho*-di	earrings
dodatkowy	do-dat-*ko*-vi	extra (adj)
doktór (m)	*dok*-toor	doctor
dokument (m)	do-*koo*-ment	document
dokument tożsamości (m)	do-*koo*-ment tosh-sa-*mosh*-chee	identification card
dolina (f)	do-*lee*-na	valley
dom (m)	dom	house • home
dom towarowy (m)	dom to-va-*ro*-vi	department store
dorosły	do-*ros*-wi	adult
doskonały	dos-ko-*na*-wi	excellent
dostać	*dos*-tach	to get • to obtain • to receive
dostać się	*dos*-tach she	to get to
dostawa (f)	dos-*ta*-va	delivery
dosyć	*do*-sich	enough

Dość!
doshch!
Enough!

doświadczenie (neut)	dosh-fyat-*che*-nye	experience
doświadczony	dosh-fyat-*cho*-ni	experienced
dotykać	do-*ti*-kach	to touch
doustny	do-*oost*-ni	oral (drug)
dowcip (m)	*dof*-cheep	joke

Do widzenia.
do vee-*dze*-nya
Goodbye.

dowiedzieć się	do-*vye*-djech she	to find out
do wynajęcia	do vi-na-*yen*-cha	for hire • for rent
dozwolony	doz-vo-*lo*-ni	allowed • permitted
dramat (m)	*dra*-mat	drama
dramatyczny	dra-ma-*tich*-ni	dramatic
drewno (neut)	*drev*-no	wood
drobne (pl)	*drob*-ne	change (coins)
droga (f)	*dro*-ga	road • way
drogi	*dro*-gee	expensive
drogowskaz (m)	dro-*gof*-skas	signpost
druga klasa (f)	*droo*-ga *kla*-sa	second class
druga wojna światowa (f)	*droo*-ga *voy*-na shfya-*to*-va	World War II
drugi	*droo*-gee	second
drugie danie (neut)	*droo*-gye *da*-nye	main course
drut (m)	droot	wire
drużyna (f)	droo-*zhi*-na	team
drzewo (neut)	*dzhe*-vo	tree
drzwi (pl)	dzhvee	door
duch (m)	dooh	spirit (soul)
duma (f)	*doo*-ma	pride
dusza (f)	*doo*-sha	soul
dużo	*doo*-zho	many • much
duży	*doo*-zhi	large • big
dworzec (m)	*dvo*-zhets	station
dworzec autobusowy (m)	*dvo*-zhets aw-to-boo-*so*-vi	bus station
dworzec kolejowy (m)	*dvo*-zhets ko-le-*yo*-vi	train station
dym (m)	dim	smoke
dyrektor (m)	di-*rek*-tor	director • manager (m)
dyrektorka (f)	di-rek-*tor*-ka	director • manager (f)
dyskrymi nacja (f)	dis-kri-mee-*na*-tsya	discrimination
dystans (m)	*dis*-tans	distance
dywan (m)	*di*-van	carpet • rug
dziadek (m)	*dja*-dek	grandfather
dzieci (pl)	*dje*-chee	children
dziecko (neut)	*djets*-ko	child
dzielnica (f)	djel-*nee*-tsa	city district
dzieło sztuki (neut)	*dje*-wo *shtoo*-kee	work of art
dziennik (m)	*djen*-neek	daily newspaper
dziennikarka (f)	djen-nee-*kar*-ka	journalist (f)

dziennikarz (m)	djen-*nee*-kash	journalist (m)
dzień (m)	djen	day

> *Dzień dobry.*
> djen *do*-bri
> Good morning.

dziewczyna (f)	djef-*chi*-na	girl
dziękować	djen-*ko*-vach	to thank

> *Dziękuję.*
> djen-*koo*-ye
> Thank you.

dziki	*djee*-kee	wild
dzisiaj	*djee*-shay	today
dziś	djeesh	today
dziwny	*djeev*-ni	odd • strange
dzwonić	*dzvo*-neech	to call
dźwięk (m)	djvyenk	sound

E

egzamin (m)	e-*gza*-meen	exam
ekonomia (f)	e-ko-*no*-mya	economy
ekran (m)	*e*-kran	screen
elektryczność (f)	e-lek-*trich*-noshch	electricity
elektryczny	e-lek-*trich*-ni	electric
emerytowany	e-me-ri-to-*va*-ni	retired
energia (f)	e-*ner*-gya	energy
energia nuklearna (f)	e-*ner*-gya noo-kle-*ar*-na	nuclear energy

E BEFORE Ę

Polish letters with diacritical marks are treated as separate letters. Remember that e comes before ę.

energia słoneczna (f)	e-*ner*-gya swo-*nech*-na	solar energy
europejski	ew-ro-*pey*-skee	European

F

fabryka (f)	fa-*bri*-ka	factory
fajka (f)	*fay*-ka	pipe
fala (f)	*fa*-la	wave
fałszywy	faw-*shi*-vi	false • fak
fantastyczny	fan-tas-*tich*-ni	fantastic
farba (f)	*far*-ba	paint
festiwal (m)	fes-*tee*-val	festival
fikcja (f)	*feek*-tsya	fiction
film czarno-biały (m)	feelm char-no-*bya*-wi	B&W film
film fabularny (m)	feelm fa-boo-*lar*-ni	feature film
filiżanka (f)	fee-lee-*zhan*-ka	cup
fioletowy	fyo-le-*to*-vi	purple
firma (f)	*feer*-ma	company
flesz (m)	flesh	flash (for camera)
folklor (m)	*fol*-klor	folklore
fontanna (f)	fon-*tan*-na	fountain
forma (f)	*for*-ma	shape
formularz (m)	for-*moo*-lash	form
fortepian (m)	for-*te*-pyan	grand piano
fotografia (f)	fo-to-*gra*-fya	photography
fotooptyka (f)	fo-to-*op*-ti-ka	camera shop
frytki (f, pl)	*frit*-kee	chips
fryzjer (m)	*fri*-zyer	hairdresser (m)
fryzjerka (f)	fri-*zyer*-ka	hairdresser (f)
fundacja (f)	foon-*da*-tsya	foundation
furgonetka (f)	foor-go-*net*-ka	van

G

galeria sztuki (f)	ga-*le*-rya *shtoo*-kee	art gallery
gałąź (f)	*ga*-wonsh	branch (of tree)
garaż (m)	*ga*-rash	garage (for parking)

gardło (neut)	*gar*-dwo	throat
garnek (m)	*gar*-nek	pan
gaśnica (f)	gash-*nee*-tsa	fire extinguisher
gazeta (f)	ga-*ze*-ta	newspaper
gdzie	gdje	where
gej (m)	gey	gay
gęś (f)	gensh	goose
gimnastyka (f)	geem-nas-*ti*-ka	gymnastics
gitara (f)	gee-*ta*-ra	guitar
gleba (f)	*gle*-ba	soil
głęboki	gwem-*bo*-kee	deep
głodny	*gwod*-ni	hungry
głos (m)	gwos	voice
głosować	gwo-*so*-vach	to vote
głośny	*gwosh*-ni	loud
głowa (f)	*gwo*-va	head
główny	*gwoov*-ni	main
głuchy	*gwoo*-hi	deaf
głupi	*gwoo*-pee	silly • stupid
godzina (f)	go-*djee*-na	hour
godzina szczytu (f)	go-*djee*-na *shchi*-too	rush hour
godziny otwarcia	go-*djee*-ni ot-*far*-cha	opening hours
golić się	*go*-leech she	to shave
gorący	go-*ron*-tsi	hot
gorączka (f)	go-*ronch*-ka	fever
gorszy	*gor*-shi	worse
gospodarka (f)	gos-po-*dar*-ka	economy
gospodarstwo rolne (neut)	gos-po-*dar*-stfo *rol*-ne	farm
gościnność (f)	gosh-*cheen*-noshch	hospitality
gość (m)	goshch	guest
gotować	go-*to*-vach	to cook
gotowy	go-*to*-vi	ready
gotówka (f)	go-*toof*-ka	cash
góra (f)	*goo*-ra	mountain
górski	*goor*-skee	mountainous
gra (f)	gra	game
grać	grach	to play (music or games)
grafika (f)	*gra*-fee-ka	graphic art • print
gramatyka (f)	gra-*ma*-ti-ka	grammar
granica (f)	gra-*nee*-tsa	border

Gratulacje!
gra-too-*la*-tsye!
Congratulations!

grób (m)	groop	grave
gruby	*groo*-bi	fat (person) • thick
grudzień (m)	*groo*-djen	December
grupa (f)	*groo*-pa	group
grupa krwi (f)	*groo*-pa krfee	blood group
gry komputerowe (f, pl)	gri kom-poo-te-*ro*-ve	computer games
grypa (f)	*gri*-pa	flu
grzanka (f)	*gzhan*-ka	toast (bread)
grzebień (m)	*gzhe*-byen	comb
grzech (m)	gzheh	sin
grzejnik (m)	*gzhey*-neek	heater
grzyb (m)	gzhib	mushroom
gubić	*goo*-beech	to lose
guma (f)	*goo*-ma	rubber
guma do żucia (f)	*goo*-ma do *zhoo*-cha	chewing gum
guz (m)	goos	lump
guzik (m)	*goo*-zheek	button
gwałt (m)	gvawt	rape
gwiazda (f)	*gvyaz*-da	star

H

hałas (m)	*ha*-was	noise
hałaśliwy	ha-wash-*lee*-vi	noisy
hamak (m)	*ha*-mak	hammock
herbata (f)	her-*ba*-ta	tea

I

i	ee	and
igła (f)	*ee*-gwa	needle (sewing)
ilość (f)	*ee*-loshch	amount
imię (neut)	*ee*-mye	first name

informacja (f)	een-for-*ma*-tsy-a	information
inny	*een*-ni	another • different
interesujący	een-te-re-soo-*yon*-tsi	interesting
inżynier (m)	een-*zhi*-nyer	engineer
iść	eeshch	to go

J

ja	ya	I
jacht (m)	yaht	yacht
jadalnia (f)	ya-*dal*-nya	dining room
jadłospis (m)	ya-*dwos*-pees	menu
jajko (neut)	*yay*-ko	egg
jak	yak	how
jakiś	*ya*-keesh	any
jakość (f)	*ya*-koshch	quality
jarosz (m)	*ya*-rosh	vegetarian (m)
jaroszka (f)	ya-*rosh*-ka	vegetarian (f)
jarzyny (pl)	ya-*zhi*-ni	vegetables
jaskinia (f)	yas-*kee*-nya	cave
jasny	*yas*-ni	light (not dark)
jazda konna (f)	*yas*-da *kon*-na	horse riding
jechać	*ye*-hach	to go
jedwab (m)	*yet*-vap	silk
jedyny	ye-*di*-ni	unique
jedzenie (neut)	ye-*dze*-nye	food
jeleń (m)	*ye*-len	deer
jesień (f)	*ye*-shen	autumn
jeszcze	*yesh*-che	yet
jeszcze jeden	*yesh*-che *ye*-den	another (one more)
jeszcze nie	*yesh*-che nye	not yet
jeść	yeshch	to eat
jeśli	*yesh*-lee	if
jezioro (neut)	ye-*zho*-ro	lake
jeździć	*yezh*-djeech	to ride
język (m)	*yen*-zik	language
jodła (f)	*yo*-dwa	fir (tree)
jubiler (m)	yoo-*bee*-ler	jewellery shop
jutro	*yoo*-tro	tomorrow
już	yoosh	already

K

kac (m)	kats	hangover
kaczka (f)	*kach*-ka	duck
kalendarz (m)	ka-*len*-dash	calendar
kaloryfer (m)	ka-lo-*ri*-fer	radiator (in room)
kamień (m)	*ka*-myen	stone
kamizelka ratunkowa (f)	ka-mee-*zel*-ka ra-toon-*ko*-va	life jacket
kanapka (f)	ka-*nap*-ka	sandwich
kaplica (f)	ka-*plee*-tsa	chapel
kara (f)	*ka*-ra	fine (penalty)
karać	*ka*-rach	to punish
karetka pogotowia (f)	ka-*ret*-ka po-go-*to*-vya	ambulance
karta (f)	*kar*-ta	card
karta dań (f)	*kar*-ta dan	menu
karta kredytowa (f)	*kar*-ta kre-di-*to*-va	credit card
karta pokładowa (f)	*kar*-ta po-kwa-*do*-va	boarding pass
karta telefoniczna (f)	*kar*-ta te-le-fo-*neech*-na	phonecard
kartka (f)	*kart*-ka	sheet (of paper)
karty do gry (pl)	*kar*-ti do gri	playing cards
kasa biletowa (f)	*ka*-sa bee-le-*to*-va	ticket office
kaseta (f)	ka-*se*-ta	cassette
kasjer (m)	*ka*-syer	cashier (m)
kasjerka (f)	ka-*syer*-ka	cashier (f)
kask (m)	kask	helmet
kaszel (m)	*ka*-shel	cough
katedra (f)	ka-*te*-dra	cathedral
katolicki	ka-to-*leets*-kee	Catholic (adj)
katoliczka (f)	ka-to-*leech*-ka	Catholic (n, f)

katolik (m)	ka-*to*-leek	Catholic (n, m)
kawa (f)	*ka*-va	coffee
kawaler (m)	ka-*va*-ler	unmarried man
kawałek (m)	ka-*va*-wek	piece
kawiarnia (f)	ka-*vyar*-nya	cafe
każdy	*kazh*-di	each • every
kąpiel (f)	*kom*-pyel	bath
kąt (m)	kont	corner (in room)
kelner (m)	*kel*-ner	waiter
kelnerka (f)	kel-*ner*-ka	waitress
kibic (m)	*kee*-beets	fan (of a team)
kiedy	*kye*-di	when
kieliszek (m)	kye-*lee*-shek	(wine) glass
kierować	kye-*ro*-vach	to drive
kierowca (m)	kye-*rof*-tsa	driver
kierunek (m)	kye-*roo*-nek	direction
kierunkowskaz (m)	kye-roon-*kof*-skas	indicator (car)
kieszeń (f)	*kye*-shen	pocket
kilka	*keel*-ka	a few
kilku	*keel*-koo	a few
kino (neut)	*kee*-no	cinema
kiosk z gazetami (m)	kyosk sga-ze-*ta*-mee	newspaper kiosk
klasa (f)	*kla*-sa	class
klasztor (m)	*klash*-tor	convent • monastery
klatka (f)	*klat*-ka	cage
klient (m)	*klee*-yent	client (m)
klientka (f)	klee-*yen*-tka	client (f)
klimatyzowany	klee-ma-ti-zo-*va*-ni	air-conditioned
klucz (m)	klooch	key
kłamać	*kwa*-mach	to lie
kłaść	kwashch	to put
kłopot (m)	*kwo*-pot	trouble
kłódka (f)	*kwoot*-ka	padlock
kłótnia (f)	*kwoot*-nya	quarrel
kobieta (f)	ko-*bye*-ta	woman

koc (m)	kots	blanket
kochać	*ko*-hach	to love
kod pocztowy (m)	kot poch-*to*-vi	postcode
kokaina (f)	ko-ka-*ee*-na	cocaine
kolano (neut)	ko-*la*-no	knee
kolarstwo (neut)	ko-*lar*-stfo	cycling
kolega (m)	ko-*le*-ga	colleague (m)
kolej (f)	*ko*-ley	railway
kolejka (f)	ko-*ley*-ka	queue
koleżanka (f)	ko-le-*zhan*-ka	colleague (f)
kolor (m)	*ko*-lor	colour
koło (neut)	*ko*-wo	wheel
koło zapasowe (neut)	*ko*-wo za-pa-*so*-ve	spare tyre
komar (m)	*ko*-mar	mosquito
komedia (f)	ko-*me*-dya	comedy
komisariat (m)	ko-mee-*sa*-ryat	police station
kompas (m)	*kom*-pas	compass
komunia (f)	ko-*moo*-nya	communion
komunizm (m)	ko-*moo*-neezm	communism
koncert (m)	*kon*-tsert	concert
koniec (m)	*ko*-nyets	end
konieczny	ko-*nyech*-ni	necessary
konsulat (m)	kon-*soo*-lat	consulate
kontroler (m)	kon-*tro*-ler	ticket collector
koń (m)	kon	horse
kończyć	*kon*-chich	to end
koperta (f)	ko-*per*-ta	envelope
korek (m)	*ko*-rek	cork • traffic jam
korona (f)	ko-*ro*-na	crown
kort tenisowy (m)	kort te-nee-*so*-vi	tennis court
korupcja (f)	ko-*roop*-tsya	corruption
korzyść (f)	*ko*-zhishch	advantage
kostium kąpielowy (m)	*kos*-tyoom kom-pye-*lo*-vi	bathing suit
koszt (m)	kosht	cost
kosztować	kosh-*to*-vach	to cost

koszula (f)	ko-*shoo*-la	shirt
koszyk (m)	*ko*-shik	basket
kościół (m)	*kosh*-choow	church
kość (f)	koshch	bone
kot (m)	kot	cat
koza (f)	*ko*-za	goat
kradzież (f)	*kra*-djesh	theft
kraj (m)	kray	country
kran (m)	kran	tap
kraść	krashch	to steal
krawat (m)	*kra*-vat	necktie
krawiec (m)	*kra*-vyets	tailor
kredens (m)	*kre*-dens	cupboard
krem (m)	krem	cream
krem nawilżający (m)	krem na-veel-zha-*yon*-tsi	moisturiser
krew (f)	kref	blood
kroić	*kro*-eech	to cut
krok (m)	krok	step
krowa (f)	*kro*-va	cow
król (m)	krool	king
królik (m)	*kroo*-leek	rabbit
królowa (f)	kroo-*lo*-va	queen
krótki	*kroot*-kee	short
krwawić	*krfa*-veech	to bleed
krzesło (neut)	*kshe*-swo	chair
krzyczeć	*kshi*-chech	to shout
krzyż (m)	kshish	cross (religious)
ksiądz (m)	kshonts	priest
książka (f)	*kshon*-shka	book
książka telefoniczna (f)	*kshon*-shka te-le-fo-*neech*-na	phonebook
księgarnia (f)	kshen-*gar*-nya	bookshop
księżyc (m)	*kshen*-zhits	moon
kształt (m)	kshtawt	shape
kto	kto	who
ktokolwiek	kto-*kol*-vyek	anybody
ktoś	ktosh	somebody • someone
który	*ktoo*-ri	which
kubek (m)	*koo*-bek	mug
kuchnia (f)	*kooh*-nya	kitchen
kupić	*koo*-peech	to buy
kupon (m)	*koo*-pon	coupon
kupować	koo-*po*-vach	to buy
kurczak (m)	*koor*-chak	chicken
kurs (m)	koors	course
kurs językowy (m)	koors yen-zi-*ko*-vi	language course
kurs wymiany (m)	koors vi-*mya*-ni	exchange rate
kurtka (f)	*koor*-tka	jacket
kurz (m)	koosh	dust
kuszetka (f)	koo-*shet*-ka	couchette
kuzyn (m)	*koo*-zin	cousin
kuzynka (f)	koo-*zin*-ka	cousin
kwadrat (m)	*kfa*-drat	square (shape)
kwalifikacje (f, pl)	kfa-lee-fee-*ka*-tsye	qualifications
kwiaciarnia (f)	kfya-*char*-nya	florist
kwiat (m)	kfyat	flower
kwiecień (m)	*kfye*-chen	April

L

lalka (f)	*lal*-ka	doll
lampa (f)	*lam*-pa	lamp
las (m)	las	forest

L BEFORE Ł

Polish letters with diacritical marks are treated as separate letters. Remember that *l* comes before *ł*.

latać	*la*-tach	to fly
latarka (f)	la-*tar*-ka	torch (flash light)
lato (neut)	*la*-to	summer
lawina (f)	la-*vee*-na	avalanche
ląd (m)	lont	land

lecz	lech	but
lek (m)	lek	medicine (drug)
lekarka (f)	le-*kar*-ka	doctor (f)
lekarstwo (neut)	le-*kar*-stfo	medicine (drug)
lekarz (m)	*le*-kash	doctor (m)
lekcja (f)	*lek*-tsya	lesson
lekki	*lek*-kee	light (not heavy)
leniwy	le-*nee*-vi	lazy
lepszy	*lep*-shi	better
lesbijka (f)	les-*beey*-ka	lesbian
lewicowy	le-vee-*tso*-vi	left-wing (politics)
lewy	*le*-vi	left (not right)
liczyć	*lee*-chich	to count
lina (f)	*lee*-na	rope
linia (f)	*lee*-nya	line
lipiec (m)	*lee*-pyets	July
list (m)	leest	letter
list ekspresowy (m)	leest eks-pre-*so*-vi	express mail
listopad (m)	lees-*to*-pat	November
liść (m)	leeshch	leaf
lodówka (f)	lo-*doof*-ka	fridge
lody (m, pl)	*lo*-di	icecream
lokator (m)	lo-*ka*-tor	tenant (m)
lokatorka (f)	lo-ka-*tor*-ka	tenant (f)
lornetka (f)	lor-*net*-ka	binoculars
los (m)	los	luck • chance
lot (m)	lot	flight
lotnisko (neut)	lot-*nees*-ko	airport
lód (m)	loot	ice
lub	loop	or
lubić	*loo*-beech	to like
ludność (f)	*lood*-noshch	population
ludowy	loo-*do*-vi	folk
ludzie (pl)	*loo*-dje	people
luksus (m)	*look*-soos	luxury
luksusowy	look-soo-*so*-vi	luxurious
lustro (neut)	*loos*-tro	mirror
luty (m)	*loo*-ti	February

Ł

ładny	*wad*-ni	pretty • fine • nice
łagodny	wa-*god*-ni	mild
łamać	*wa*-mach	to break
łapać	*wa*-pach	to catch
łapówka (f)	wa-*poof*-ka	bribe
łatwy	*wat*-fi	easy
łazienka (f)	wa-*zhen*-ka	bathroom
łowić ryby	*wo*-veech *ri*-bi	to fish
łódź (f)	wooch	boat
łóżko (neut)	*woosh*-ko	bed
łza (f)	wza	tear (crying)

M

magazyn (m)	ma-*ga*-zin	magazine
magnetowid (m)	mag-ne-*to*-veet	video recorder
maj (m)	may	May
makijaż (m)	ma-*kee*-yash	make-up
malarka (f)	ma-*lar*-ka	painter
malarstwo (neut)	ma-*lar*-stfo	painting (the art)
malarz (m)	*ma*-lash	painter
malować	ma-*lo*-vach	to paint
mały	*ma*-wi	little • small
małżeństwo (neut)	maw-*zhen*-stfo	marriage
mama (f)	*ma*-ma	mum
mandat (m)	*man*-dat	traffic fine
mapa (f)	*ma*-pa	map
mapa drogowa (f)	*ma*-pa dro-*go*-va	road map
marka (f)	*mar*-ka	make (brand name)
marzec (m)	*ma*-zhets	March
marzyć	*ma*-zhich	to dream
masaż (m)	*ma*-sash	massage
masło (neut)	*ma*-swo	butter
martwić się	*mar*-tfeech she	to worry
maszyna (f)	ma-*shi*-na	machine

Polish	Pronunciation	English
maszynka do golenia (f)	ma-*shin*-ka do go-*le*-nya	razor
materac (m)	ma-*te*-rats	mattress
matka (f)	*mat*-ka	mother
mądry	*mon*-dri	wise
mąka (f)	*mon*-ka	flour
mąż (m)	monsh	husband
mdłości (pl)	*mdwosh*-chee	nausea
meble (m, pl)	*me*-ble	furniture
mechanik (m)	me-*ha*-neek	mechanic
mecz (m)	mech	match (sport)
meczet (m)	*me*-chet	mosque
medycyna (f)	me-di-*tsi*-na	medicine (the science)
melodia (f)	me-*lo*-dya	tune
menstruacja (f)	men-stroo-*a*-tsya	menstruation
metr (m)	metr	metre
metro (neut)	*me*-tro	subway
metryka urodzenia (f)	met-*ri*-ka oo-ro-*dze*-nya	birth certificate
mężczyzna (m)	mensh-*chiz*-na	man
mgła (f)	mgwa	mist • fog
miasto (neut)	*mya*-sto	town • city
miecz (m)	myech	sword
mieć	myech	to have
miejsce (neut)	*myey*-stse	place
miejsce przy oknie (neut)	*myey*-stse pshi *ok*-nye	window seat
miejsce urodzenia (neut)	*myey*-stse oo-ro-*dze*-nya	place of birth
miejscowy	myey-*stso*-vi	local
miesiąc (m)	*mye*-shonts	month
miesiąc miodowy (m)	*mye*-shonts myo-*do*-vi	honey moon
miesiączka (f)	mye-*shonch*-ka	period (menstruation)
mieszać	*mye*-shach	to mix
mieszkać	*myesh*-kach	to live (somewhere)
mieszkanie (neut)	myesh-*ka*-nye	apartment • flat
między	*myen*-dzi	between
międzynarodowy	myen-dzi-na-ro-*do*-vi	international
mięsień (m)	*myen*-shen	muscle
mięso (neut)	*myen*-so	meat
migrena (f)	mee-*gre*-na	migraine
milion (m)	*mee*-lyon	million
miłość (f)	*mee*-woshch	love
miły	*mee*-wi	nice
minuta (f)	mee-*noo*-ta	minute
miód (m)	myoot	honey
mleko (neut)	*mle*-ko	milk
młody	*mwo*-di	young
młodzież (f)	*mwo*-djesh	youth (collective)
młotek (m)	*mwo*-tek	hammer
mnich (m)	mneeh	monk
mniej	mnyey	less
moc (f)	mots	strength
mocny	*mots*-ni	strong
modlitwa (f)	mod-*leet*-fa	prayer
modny	*mod*-ni	fashionable • trendy
mokry	*mo*-kri	wet
moneta (f)	mo-*ne*-ta	coin
morze (neut)	*mo*-zhe	sea
most (m)	most	bridge
motocykl (m)	mo-*to*-tsikl	motorcycle
motorówka (f)	mo-to-*roof*-ka	motorboat
motyl (m)	*mo*-til	butterfly
może	*mo*-zhe	perhaps
możliwy	mozh-*lee*-vi	possible
móc	moots	can • to be able
mówić	*moo*-veech	to speak • to talk
mrożonki (f, pl)	mro-*zhon*-kee	frozen foods
mrówka (f)	*mroof*-ka	ant
mróz (m)	mroos	frost
msza (f)	msha	mass (church service)
mucha (f)	*moo*-ha	fly
mur (m)	moor	wall (outside)
muzeum (neut)	*moo*-ze-oom	museum

muzyk (m)	*moo*-zik	musician
muzyka (f)	*moo*-zi-ka	music
my	mi	we
myć się	mich she	to wash (oneself)
mydło (neut)	*mi*-dwo	soap
mysz (f)	mish	mouse
myśl (f)	mishl	thought
myśleć	*mish*-lech	to think

N BEFORE Ń

Polish letters with diacritical marks are treated as separate letters. Remember that *n* comes before *ń*.

N

na	na	on
nabiał (m)	*na*-byaw	dairy products
nabożeństwo (neut)	na-bo-*zhen*-stfo	church service
nad	nat	above
nadawca (m)	na-*daf*-tsa	sender
nadmorski	nad-*mor*-skee	seaside
nadwaga bagażu (f)	nat-*va*-ga ba-*ga*-zhoo	excess baggage
nadzieja (f)	na-*dje*-ya	hope
nagle	*na*-gle	suddenly
nagły przypadek (m)	*na*-gwi pshi-*pa*-dek	emergency
nagrobek (m)	na-*gro*-bek	tombstone
najgorszy	nay-*gor*-shi	worst

Najlepsze życzenia!
nay-*lep*-she zhi-*che*-nya!
Best wishes!

najlepszy	nay-*lep*-shi	best
nalegać	na-*le*-gach	to insist
nałóg (m)	*na*-wook	addiction
namiot (m)	*na*-myot	tent
napełnić	na-*peoo*-neech	to fill up
napięcie (neut)	na-*pyen*-che	voltage
napisać	na-*pee*-sach	to write
napiwek (m)	na-*pee*-vek	tip (gratuity)

Na pomoc!
na *po*-mots!
Help!

napój (m)	*na*-pooy	drink
naprawdę	na-*prav*-de	really
naprawić	na-*pra*-veech	to fix • to repair
naprzeciwko	na-pshe-*cheef*-ko	opposite
naprzód	*na*-pshoot	ahead
narciarstwo (neut)	nar-*char*-stfo	skiing
narkoman (m)	nar-*ko*-man	drug addict (m)
narkomanka (f)	nar-ko-*man*-ka	drug addict (f)
narkotyki (m, pl)	nar-ko-*ti*-kee	dope (drugs)
narodowość (f)	na-ro-*do*-voshch	nationality
narzeczona (f)	na-zhe-*cho*-na	fiancée • girlfriend
narzeczony (m)	na-zhe-*cho*-ni	fiancé • boyfriend
na sprzedaż	na *spshe*-dash	for sale
następny	nas-*temp*-ni	next
na szczęście	na *shchen*-shche	fortunately
naszyjnik (m)	na-*shiy*-neek	necklace
natura (f)	na-*too*-ra	nature
naturalny	na-too-*ral*-ni	natural
natychmiast	na-*tih*-myast	immediately
nauczyciel (m)	na-oo-*chi*-chel	teacher (m)
nauczycielka (f)	na-oo-chi-*chel*-ka	teacher (f)
nauka (f)	na-*oo*-ka	science
naukowiec (m)	na-oo-*ko*-vyets	scientist
nawet	*na*-vet	even (adv)
na wynos	na *vi*-nos	take-away
na zawsze	na *zaf*-she	forever

na zewnątrz	na *zev*-nonch	outside • outdoors
nazwisko (neut)	naz-*vees*-ko	surname
nic	neets	nothing

Nie.
nye
No.

niebezpieczny	nye-bes-*pyech*-ni	unsafe • dangerous
niebieski	nye-*byes*-kee	blue
niebo (neut)	*nye*-bo	sky
niedawny	nye-*dav*-ni	recent
niedziela (f)	nye-*dje*-la	Sunday
niekorzyść (f)	nye-*ko*-zhishch	disadvantage
Niemcy (pl)	*nyem*-tsi	Germany
niemiecki	nye-*myets*-kee	German (adj)
niemowlę (neut)	nye-*mov*-le	baby
niemożliwy	nye-mozh-*lee*-vi	impossible
niemy	*nye*-mi	mute
nienawidzieć	nye-na-*vee*-djech	to hate
nieparzysty	nye-pa-*zhis*-ti	odd (number)
niepełnosprawny	nye-peoo-no-*sprav*-ni	disabled
nieprzemakalny	nye-pshe-ma-*kal*-ni	waterproof (clothes)
nierówność (f)	nye-*roov*-noshch	inequality
niespodzianka (f)	nye-spo-*djan*-ka	surprise
niestety	nye-*ste*-ti	unfortunately
niestrawność (f)	nye-*strav*--noshch	indigestion
nieść	nyeshch	to carry
nieśmiały	nye-*shmya*-wi	shy
niewidomy	nye-vee-*do*-mi	blind
niewygodny	nye-vi-*god*-ni	inconvenient
niezamężna	nye-za-*men*-zhna	unmarried (woman)
niezbędny	nyes-*bend*-ni	essential
nieznajomy (m)	nye-zna-*yo*-mi	stranger
niezwykły	nye-*zvi*-kwi	unusual
nigdy	*neeg*-di	never
nikt	neekt	nobody
niski	*nees*-kee	low
niskie ciśnienie krwi	*nees*-kye cheesh-*nye*-nye krfee	low blood pressure
niszczyć	*neesh*-chich	to destroy
noc (f)	nots	night
nocleg (m)	*nots*-lek	accommodation
noga (f)	*no*-ga	leg
nos (m)	nos	nose
nosić	*no*-sheech	to carry
notatnik (m)	no-*tat*-neek	notebook • diary
Nowa Zelandia (f)	*no*-va ze-*lan*-dya	New Zealand
nowoczesny	no-vo-*ches*-ni	modern
nowy	*no*-vi	new
Nowy Rok (m)	*no*-vi rok	New Year's Day
nożyczki (pl)	no-*zhich*-kee	scissors
nóż (m)	noosh	knife
nudny	*nood*-ni	boring
numer (m)	*noo*-mer	number
numer kierunkowy (m)	*noo*-mer kye-roon-*ko*-vi	area code (phone)
numer paszportu (m)	*noo*-mer pash-*por*-too	passport number
numer telefonu (m)	*noo*-mer te-le-*fo*-noo	phone number
nurkowanie (neut)	noor-ko-*va*-nye	diving

O

o	o	about (something or someone)
obaj	*o*-bay	both
obawa (f)	o-*ba*-va	fear
obawiać się	o-*ba*-vyach she	to be afraid of

O BEFORE Ó

Polish letters with diacritical marks are treated as separate letters. Remember that o comes before ó.

obcy	*op*-tsi	foreign • strange
obiad (m)	*o*-byat	lunch • dinner
obie	*o*-bye	both
obiektyw (m)	o-*byek*-tif	lens (of camera)
oboje	o-*bo*-ye	both
obok	*o*-bok	beside • next to
obraz (m)	*o*-bras	painting (picture)
obrus (m)	*o*-broos	tablecloth
obszar (m)	*op*-shar	area
obywatelstwo (neut)	o-bi-va-*tel*-stfo	citizenship
oczywisty	o-chi-*vees*-ti	obvious
oczywiście	o-chi-*veesh*-che	certainly • of course

Oczywiście.
o-chi-*veesh*-che
Sure.

od	ot	since • from
odbicie (neut)	ot-*bee*-che	reflection (in mirror)
odbiór bagażu (m)	*ot*-byoor ba-*ga*-zhoo	baggage claim
oddychać	ot-*di*-hach	to breathe
oddział (m)	*ot*-djaw	branch (of institution)
odjazd (m)	*ot*-yast	departure
odjeżdżać	ot-*yesh*-djach	to depart • to leave
odkrywać	ot-*kri*-vach	to discover
odkurzacz (m)	ot-*koo*-zhach	vacuum cleaner
odległy	ot-*le*-gwi	remote • distant
odlot (m)	*ot*-lot	departure (of plane)
odmówić	ot-*moo*-veech	to refuse
odpoczynek (m)	ot-po-*chi*-nek	rest (relaxation)
odpoczywać	ot-po-*chi*-vach	to relax • to rest
odpowiadać	ot-po-*vya*-dach	to answer
odpowiedź (f)	ot-*po*-vyech	answer
odprawa celna (f)	ot-*pra*-va *tsel*-na	customs control
odprawa paszportowa (f)	ot-*pra*-va pash-por-*to*-va	passport control
odważny	ot-*vazh*-ni	brave
odwiedzać	od-*vye*-dzach	to visit
odwołać	ot-*vo*-wach	to cancel
odzież (f)	*o*-djesh	clothes
odżywka dla niemowląt (f)	od-*zhif*-ka dla nye-*mov*-lont	baby food
ogień (m)	*o*-gyen	fire (flames)
oglądać	o-*glon*-dach	to watch
ognisko (neut)	og-*nees*-ko	fire (campfire)
ogon (m)	*o*-gon	tail
ogólny	o-*gool*-ni	general
ograniczenie (neut)	o-gra-nee-*che*-nye	restriction
ograniczenie prędkości	o-gra-nee-*che*-nye prent-*kosh*-chee	speed limit
ogrodnictwo (neut)	o-grod-*neets*-tfo	gardening
ogród (m)	*o*-groot	garden
ogrzewanie (neut)	o-gzhe-*va*-nye	heating
ojciec (m)	*oy*-chets	father
okno (neut)	*ok*-no	window
oko (neut)	*o*-ko	eye
okolica (f)	o-ko-*lee*-tsa	neighbourhood
około	o-*ko*-wo	approximately • about

okrągły	o-*kron*-gwi	round
okres (m)	*o*-kres	period (of time)
okropny	o-*krop*-ni	awful • horrible
okulary (m, pl)	o-koo-*la*-ri	glasses
okulary słoneczne (m, pl)	o-koo-*la*-ri swo-*nech*-ne	sunglasses
olej (m)	*o*-ley	oil (cooking)
olimpiada (f)	o-leem-*pya*-da	Olympic Games
oliwa (f)	o-*lee*-va	olive oil
ołówek (m)	o-*woo*-vek	pencil
on	on	he
ona	*o*-na	she
opalony	o-pa-*lo*-ni	sunburnt
opera (f)	*o*-pe-ra	opera (pefor-mance or house)
operacja (f)	o-pe-*ra*-tsya	operation
opieka (f)	o-*pye*-ka	care • protection
opieka społeczna (f)	o-*pye*-ka spo-*wech*-na	social welfare
opiekować się	o-pye-*ko*-vach she	to look after
opinia (f)	o-*pee*-nya	opinion
opłata (f)	o-*pwa*-ta	charge • fee
opłata lotniskowa (f)	o-*pwa*-ta lot-nees-*ko*-va	airport tax
opłata pocztowa (f)	o-*pwa*-ta poch-*to*-va	postage
opona (f)	o-*po*-na	tyre
opowiadanie (neut)	o-po-vya-*da*-nye	story
opóźnienie (neut)	o-poozh-*nye*-nye	delay
oprócz	*o*-prooch	except
organizować	or-ga-nee-*zo*-vach	to organise
orkiestra (f)	or-*kyes*-tra	orchestra
osoba (f)	o-*so*-ba	person
osobny	o-*sob*-ni	separate
osobowość (f)	o-so-*bo*-voshch	personality
ostatni	os-*tat*-nee	last
ostatnio	os-*tat*-nyo	recently
ostrożny	os-*trozh*-ni	careful
ostrzegać	os-*tshe*-gach	to warn
oszczędzać	osh-*chen*-dzach	to save (money)
oszustwo (neut)	o-*shoos*-tfo	cheat
ośrodek (m)	osh-*ro*-dek	centre (institution)
oświata (f)	osh-*fya*-ta	education
otwarcie (neut)	ot-*far*-che	opening
otwarty	ot-*far*-ti	open
otwieracz do butelek (m)	ot-*fye*-rach do boo-*te*-lek	bottle opener
otwieracz do konserw (m)	ot-*fye*-rach do *kon*-serf	can opener
otwierać	ot-*fye*-rach	to open
otworzyć	ot-*fo*-zhich	to open
owad (m)	*o*-vat	insect
owca (f)	*of*-tsa	sheep
owoce (pl)	o-*vo*-tse	fruit

P

pachnieć	*pah*-nyech	to smell
pacjent (m)	*pa*-tsyent	patient (m)
pacjentka (f)	pa-*tsyen*-tka	patient (f)
paczka (f)	*pach*-ka	package • parcel • packet (of cigarettes)
pająk (m)	*pa*-yonk	spider
pakować	pa-*ko*-vach	to pack
palec (m)	*pa*-lets	finger
palić	*pa*-leech	to smoke

> *Pali się!*
> *pa*-lee she!
> Fire!

pałac (m)	*pa*-wats	palace
pamiątka (f)	pa-*myon*-tka	souvenir
pamiętać	pa-*myen*-tach	to remember
pamiętnik (m)	pa-*myent*-neek	diary

Polish	Pronunciation	English
pan (m)	pan	Mr • Sir • you (m,pol)
pani (f)	*pa*-nee	Mrs • Madam • you (f, pol)
panna (f)	*pan*-na	Miss
państwo (neut)	*pan*-stfo	country
papier (m)	*pa*-pyer	paper
papieros (m)	pa-*pye*-ros	cigarette
papier toaletowy (m)	*pa*-pyer to-a-le-*to*-vi	toilet paper
Papież (m)	*pa*-pyesh	Pope
para (f)	*pa*-ra	couple • pair
parasol (m)	pa-*ra*-sol	umbrella
parę	*pa*-re	a couple of
park (m)	park	park
parking (m)	*par*-keenk	parking lot • carpark
park narodowy (m)	park na-ro-*do*-vi	national park
parkować	par-*ko*-vach	to park
parlament (m)	par-*la*-ment	parliament
parter (m)	*par*-ter	ground floor
partia (f)	*par*-tya	party (politics)
parzysty	pa-*zhis*-ti	even (number)
pasażer (m)	pa-*sa*-zher	passenger (m)
pasażerka (f)	pa-sa-*zher*-ka	passenger (f)
pasek klinowy (m)	*pa*-sek klee-*no*-vi	fan belt
pasmo górskie (neut)	*pas*-mo *goor*-skye	mountain range
pasować	pa-*so*-vach	to fit
pasta do zębów (f)	*pas*-ta do *zem*-boof	toothpaste
pastylka (f)	pas-*til*-ka	tablet • pill
pasy bezpieczeństwa (m, pl)	*pa*-si bes-pye-*chen*-stfa	seatbelts
paszport (m)	*pash*-port	passport
patrzeć	*pat*-shech	to look
październik (m)	pazh-*djer*-neek	October
pchać	phach	to push
pchła (f)	phwa	flea
pełny	*pew*-ni	full
pensja (f)	*pen*-sya	salary
pensjonat (m)	pen-*syo*-nat	guesthouse
peron (m)	*pe*-ron	platform (train)
peryferie (f, pl)	pe-ri-*fe*-rye	city outskirts
pianino (neut)	pya-*nee*-no	piano
piasek (m)	*pya*-sek	sand
piątek (m)	*pyon*-tek	Friday
pić	peech	to drink
piec (m)	pyets	stove
piekarnia (f)	pye-*kar*-nya	bakery
pielęgniarka (f)	pye-leng-*nyar*-ka	nurse (f)
pielęgniarz (m)	pye-*leng*-nyash	nurse (m)
pielgrzym (m)	*pyel*-gzhim	pilgrim
pielgrzymka (f)	pyel-*gzhim*-ka	pilgrimage
pieluszka (f)	pye-*loosh*-ka	nappy
pieniądze (m, pl)	pye-*nyon*-dze	money
pieprz (m)	pyepsh	pepper
pierś (f)	pyersh	chest (body part)
pierścionek (m)	pyer-*shcho*-nek	ring (on finger)
pierwsza klasa (f)	*pyer*-fsha *kla*-sa	first class
pierwsza pomoc (f)	*pyer*-fsha *po*-mots	first aid
pierwszy	*pyer*-fshi	first
pies (m)	pyes	dog
pies przewodnik (m)	pyes pshe-*vod*-neek	guidedog
pieszy	*pye*-shi	pedestrian (adj/n)
piękny	*pyen*-kni	beautiful
piętro (neut)	*pyen*-tro	floor (storey)
pigułka antykoncepcyjna (f)	pee-*goow*-ka an-ti-kon-tsep-*tsiy*-na	the Pill
pijany	pee-*ya*-ni	drunk

pikantny	pee-*kant*-ni	spicy (hot)
pilnować	peel-*no*-vach	to guard
pilny	*peel*-ni	urgent
piłka (f)	*peew*-ka	ball
piłka nożna (f)	*peew*-ka *nozh*-na	soccer
piosenka (f)	pyo-*sen*-ka	song
piosenkarka (f)	pyo-sen-*kar*-ka	singer (f)
piosenkarz (m)	pyo-*sen*-kash	singer (m)
pióro (neut)	*pyoo*-ro	pen
pisać	*pee*-sach	to write
pisarka (f)	pee-*sar*-ka	writer (f)
pisarz (m)	*pee*-sash	writer (m)
piwnica (f)	peev-*nee*-tsa	cellar
plac (m)	plats	square (in town)
plac zabaw (m)	plats *za*-baf	playground
plakat (m)	*pla*-kat	poster
planeta (f)	pla-*ne*-ta	planet
plaża (f)	*pla*-zha	beach
plecak (m)	*ple*-tsak	backpack
plecy (pl)	*ple*-tsi	back (body)
płacić	*pwa*-cheech	to pay
płakać	*pwa*-kach	to cry
płaski	*pwas*-kee	flat • plain
płaszcz (m)	pwashch	coat
płeć (f)	pwech	sex
płot (m)	pwot	fence
płuca (neut, pl)	*pwoo*-tsa	lungs
płyta (f)	*pwi*-ta	record (LP)
płyta kompaktowa (f)	*pwi*-ta kom-pak-*to*-va	compact disc (CD)
pływać	*pwi*-vach	to swim
pływalnia (f)	pwi-*val*-nya	swimming pool
pływanie (neut)	pwi-*va*-nye	swimming
po	po	after
pocałunek (m)	po-tsa-*woo*-nek	kiss
pochmurny	poh-*moor*-ni	cloudy
pociąg (m)	*po*-chonk	train
pociąg ekspresowy (m)	*po*-chonk eks-pre-*so*-vi	express train
pociąg osobowy (m)	*po*-chonk o-so-*bo*-vi	slow train
pociąg pospieszny (m)	*po*-chonk pos-*pyesh*-ni	fast train
poczekalnia (f)	po-che-*kal*-nya	waiting room
poczta (f)	*poch*-ta	mail • post-office
poczta główna (f)	*poch*-ta *gwoov*-na	main post office
poczta lotnicza (f)	*poch*-ta lot-*nee*-cha	airmail
poczta polecona (f)	*poch*-ta po-le-*tso*-na	registered mail
poczta zwykła (f)	*poch*-ta *zvi*-kwa	surface mail
pocztówka (f)	poch-*toof*-ka	postcard
pod	pot	below • under
podać	*po*-dach	to serve
podatek (m)	po-*da*-tek	tax
podatek dochodowy (m)	po-*da*-tek do-ho-*do*-vi	income tax
podczas	*pot*-chas	during
podkoszulka (f)	pot-ko-*shool*-ka	T-shirt
podłoga (f)	po-*dwo*-ga	floor (of room)
podobny	po-*dob*-ni	similar
podpaski higieniczne (f, pl)	pot-*pas*-kee hee-gye-*neech*-ne	sanitary napkins
podpis (m)	*pot*-pees	signature
podpisać się	pot-*pee*-sach she	to sign
podróż (f)	*po*-droosh	journey • trip
podróżniczka (f)	po-droozh-*neech*-ka	traveller (f)
podróżnik (m)	po-*droozh*-neek	traveller (m)
podróżować	po-droo-*zho*-vach	to travel
podstawowy	pot-sta-*vo*-vi	essential
poduszka (f)	po-*doosh*-ka	pillow
podwójny	pod-*vooy*-ni	double
podziwiać	po-*djee*-vyach	to admire
poezja (f)	po-*e*-zya	poetry

pogoda (f)	po-*go*-da	weather
pogrzeb (m)	*pog*-zhep	funeral
pojechać	po-*ye*-hach	to go
pojemnik na śmieci (m)	po-*yem*-neek na *shmye*-chee	rubbish bin
pojutrze	po-*yoot*-she	day after tomorrow
pokaz (m)	*po*-kas	show
pokazać	po-*ka*-zach	to show
pokład (m)	*po*-kwat	deck (of ship)
pokój (m)	*po*-kooy	peace • room
pokój dwu-osobowy (m)	*po*-kooy dvoo-o-so-*bo*-vi	double room
pokój jednoo-sobowy (m)	*po*-kooy yed-no-o-so-*bo*-vi	single room
pokwitowanie (neut)	pok-fee-to-*va*-nye	receipt (left lugg-age or laundry)
Polacy (pl)	po-*la*-tsi	Poles
Polak (m)	*po*-lak	Pole
pole (neut)	*po*-le	field
polecać	po-*le*-tsach	to recom-mend
polecieć	po-*le*-chech	to fly
policja (f)	po-*lee*-tsya	police
policjant (m)	po-lee-tsyant	police officer (m)
policjantka (f)	po-lee-*tsyan*-tka	police officer (f)
polityka (f)	po-*lee*-ti-ka	politics
Polka (f)	*pol*-ka	Pole
Polska (f)	*pol*-ska	Poland
polski	*pol*-skee	Polish
połączenie (neut)	po-won-*che*-nye	connection
połowa	po-wo-va	half
położenie (neut)	po-wo-*zhe*-nye	location
położyć	po-*wo*-zhich	to put
południe (neut)	po-*wood*-nye	south • midday
pomagać	po-*ma*-gach	to help
pomarańcza (f)	po-ma-*ran*-cha	orange
pomnik (m)	*pom*-neek	monument
pomoc (f)	*po*-mots	help • aid
pomocny	po-*mots*-ni	helpful

Pomocy!
po-*mo*-tsi!
Help!

pomóc	*po*-moots	to help
pompa (f)	*pom*-pa	pump
pomyłka (f)	po-*miw*-ka	mistake
pomysł (m)	*po*-misw	idea
poniedziałek (m)	po-nye-*dja*-wek	Monday
ponieważ	po-*nye*-vash	because
poniżej	po-*nee*-zhey	below
popielniczka (f)	po-pyel-*neech*-ka	ashtray
popołudnie (neut)	po-po-*wood*-nye	afternoon

po południu
po po-*wood*-nyoo
in the afternoon

popularny	po-poo-*lar*-ni	popular
porada (f)	po-*ra*-da	advice
poronienie (neut)	po-ro-*nye*-nye	miscar-riage
port (m)	port	port • harbour
portfel (m)	*port*-fel	wallet
porządek (m)	po-*zhon*-dek	order
posąg (m)	*po*-sonk	statue
posiłek (m)	po-*shee*-wek	meal
posterunek policji (m)	pos-te-*roo*-nek po-*lee*-tsyee	police station
postój taksówek (m)	*pos*-tooy tak-*soo*-vek	taxi stand
potrzebować	pot-she-*bo*-vach	to need
potwierdzić	pot-*fyer*-djeech	to confirm
potworny	pot-*for*-ni	terrible
poważny	po-*vazh*-ni	serious
powiedzieć	po-*vye*-djech	to tell
powieść (f)	*po*-vyeshch	novel (book)

P

powietrze (neut)	po-*vyet*-she	air
powłoczka (f)	po-*vwoch*-ka	pillowcase

Powodzenia!
po-vo-*dze*-nya!
Good luck!

powoli	po-*vo*-lee	slowly
powód (m)	*po*-voot	reason • cause
powódź (f)	*po*-vooch	flood
powrót (m)	*po*-vroot	return
powszechny	pof-*sheh*-ni	common • general
powtórzyć	pof-*too*-zhich	to repeat
poziom (m)	*po*-zhom	standard • level
pozwalać	poz-*va*-lach	to allow • to permit
pozwolenie (neut)	poz-vo-*le*-nye	permission
pożar (m)	*po*-zhar	fire (emergency)

Pożar!
po-zhar!
Fire!

pożyczać	po-*zhi*-chach	to borrow • to lend
pójść	pooyshch	to go
pół	poow	half
północ (f)	*poow*-nots	north • midnight
później	*poozh*-nyey	later
późno	*poozh*-no	late
praca (f)	*pra*-tsa	work • job
praca biurowa (f)	*pra*-tsa byoo-*ro*-va	office work
pracodawca (m)	pra-tso-*daf*-tsa	employer (m)
pracodawczyni (f)	pra-tso-daf-*chi*-nee	employer (f)
pracować	pra-*tso*-vach	to work
pracownia (f)	pra-*tsov*-nya	studio (artist's)
pracowniczka (f)	pra-tsov-*neech*-ka	employee (f)
pracownik (m)	pra-*tsov*-neek	employee (m)
prać	prach	to wash (clothes)
pralka (f)	*pral*-ka	washing machine
pralnia (f)	*pral*-nya	laundry
pralnia chemiczna (f)	*pral*-nya he-*meech*-na	drycleaner
prawda (f)	*prav*-da	truth
prawdopodobnie	prav-do-po-*dob*-nye	probably
prawdziwy	prav-*djee*-vi	true • real • genuine
prawicowy	pra-vee-*tso*-vi	right-wing (politics)
prawidłowy	pra-vee-*dwo*-vi	right (correct)
prawie	*pra*-vye	almost
prawniczka (f)	prav-*neech*-ka	lawyer (f)
prawnik (m)	*prav*-neek	lawyer (m)
prawny	*prav*-ni	legal
prawo (neut)	*pra*-vo	law
prawodawstwo (neut)	pra-vo-*das*-tfo	legislation
prawo jazdy (neut)	*pra*-vo *yaz*-di	driving licence
prawy	*pra*-vi	right (not left)
prąd (m)	pront	current
premier (m)	*pre*-myer	prime minister
prezent (m)	*pre*-zent	present • gift
prezydent (m)	pre-*zi*-dent	president
prędkość (f)	*prent*-koshch	speed
problem (m)	*pro*-blem	problem • trouble
procent (m)	*pro*-tsent	percent
program (m)	*pro*-gram	program
project (m)	*pro*-yekt	design • project
prom (m)	prom	ferry
propozycja (f)	pro-po-*zi*-tsya	proposal
prosić	*pro*-sheech	to ask (for something)

DICTIONARY

prosty	*pros*-ti	straight • simple
proszek do prania (m)	*pro*-shek do *pra*-nya	washing powder

> *Proszę.*
> *pro*-she
> Please.

proszki nasenne (m, pl)	*prosh*-kee na-*sen*-ne	sleeping pills
protest (m)	*pro*-test	protest
protestować	pro-tes-*to*-vach	to protest
prowadzić	pro-*va*-djeech	to drive • to lead
próba (f)	*proo*-ba	test
próbować	proo-*bo*-vach	to try
prysznic (m)	*prish*-neets	shower
prywatny	pri-*vat*-ni	private
prywatyzacja (f)	pri-va-ti-*za*-tsya	privatisation
przebaczyć	pshe-*ba*-chich	to forgive
przechowalnia bagażu (f)	pshe-ho-*val*-nya ba-*ga*-zhoo	left luggage office
przeciętny	pshe-*chent*-ni	average
przeciwko	pshe-*cheef*-ko	against
przeciwny	pshe-*cheev*-ni	opposite
przeczytać	pshe-*chi*-tach	to read
przed	pshet	before • in front of
przedłużacz (m)	pshe-*dwoo*-zhach	extension cable
przedmieście (neut)	pshet-*myesh*-che	city outskirts
przednia szyba (f)	*pshe*-dnya *shi*-ba	windscreen
przedsiębiorstwo (neut)	pshet-shem-*byor*-stfo	company
przedstawienie (neut)	pshet-sta-*vye*-nye	performance
przedszkole (neut)	pshet-*shko*-le	kindergarten
przedwczoraj	pshet-*fcho*-ray	day before yesterday
przegląd (m)	*pshe*-glont	review
przejście dla pieszych (neut)	*pshey*-shche dla *pye*-shih	pedestrian crossing
przekleństwo (neut)	pshe-*klen*-stfo	swearword
przełącznik (m)	pshe-*wonch*-neek	switch
przełęcz (f)	*pshe*-wench	pass (in mountains)
przemysł (m)	*pshe*-misw	industry
przemysłowy	pshe-mi-*swo*-vi	industrial

> *Przepraszam.*
> pshe-*pra*-sham
> I'm sorry. • Excuse me.

przerwa (f)	*psher*-va	intermission
przerywanie ciąży	pshe-ri-*va*-nye *chon*-zhi	abortion
przeszłość (f)	*pshesh*-woshch	past (history)
przeszły	*pshesh*-wi	past (adj)
prześcieradło (neut)	pshe-shche-*ra*-dwo	bedsheet
przetłumaczyć	pshe-twoo-*ma*-chich	to translate
przewodniczka (f)	pshe-vod-*neech*-ka	guide (f) (person)
przewodnik (m)	pshe-*vod*-neek	guide (m) (person/guidebook)
przez	pshes	via
przeziębienie (neut)	pshe-zhem-*bye*-nye	cold
przeżyć	*pshe*-zhich	to survive
przód (m)	pshoot	front
przybliżony	pshi-blee-*zho*-ni	approximate
przychodzić	pshi-*ho*-djeech	to come
przyczepa (f)	pshi-*che*-pa	caravan • trailer

przygotować	pshi-go-*to*-vach	to prepare
przyjaciel (m)	pshi-*ya*-chel	friend (m)
przyjaciółka (f)	pshi-ya-*choow*-ka	friend (f)
przyjazd (m)	*pshi*-yast	arrival
przyjechać	pshi-*ye*-hach	to arrive
przyjemność (f)	pshi-*yem*-noshch	pleasure
przyjemny	pshi-*yem*-ni	pleasant • enjoyable
przyjęcie (neut)	pshi-*yen*-che	party (fiesta)
przyjmować	pshiy-*mo*-vach	to accept
przyjść	pshiyshch	to come
przykład (m)	*pshi*-kwat	example
przylot (m)	*pshi*-lot	arrival (of plane)
przymierzyć	pshi-*mye*-zhich	to try on
przynieść	*pshi*-nyeshch	to bring
przynosić	pshi-*no*-sheech	to bring
przyrzekać	pshi-*zhe*-kach	to promise
przystanek autobusowy (m)	pshis-*ta*-nek aw-to-boo-*so*-vi	bus stop
przystojny	pshis-*toy*-ni	handsome
przyszłość (f)	*pshish*-woshch	future
przyszły	*pshish*-wi	next (in time)
przyznawać	pshi-*zna*-vach	to admit
ptak (m)	ptak	bird
pudełko (neut)	poo-*deoo*-ko	box
punkt (m)	poonkt	point
punkt kontroli (m)	poonkt kon-*tro*-lee	checkpoint
pusty	*poos*-ti	empty
pustynia (f)	poos-*ti*-nya	desert
puszka (f)	*poosh*-ka	can • tin
pytać	*pi*-tach	to ask (a question)
pytanie (neut)	pi-*ta*-nye	question • query

R

rabować	ra-*bo*-vach	to rob
rachunek (m)	ra-*hoo*-nek	receipt (for purchased goods) • bill
raczej	*ra*-chey	rather
rakieta (f)	ra-*kye*-ta	racquet (for tennis) • rocket (missile or spacecraft)
rama (f)	*ra*-ma	frame
ramię (neut)	*ra*-mye	arm • shoulder
rana (f)	*ra*-na	injury • wound
randka (f)	*ran*-tka	date (appointment)
ranny	*ran*-ni	injured
rano (neut)	*ra*-no	morning
rasa (f)	*ra*-sa	race (ancestry)
rasizm (m)	*ra*-sheezm	racism
ratować	ra-*to*-vach	to save (rescue)
ratownik (m)	ra-*tov*-neek	lifeguard

Ratunku!
ra-*toon*-koo!
Help!

ratusz (m)	*ra*-toosh	town hall
raz	ras	once • one time
razem	*ra*-zem	together
recepcja (f)	re-*tsep*-tsya	reception
recepta (f)	re-*tsep*-ta	prescription
redaktor (m)	re-*dak*-tor	editor (m)
redaktorka (f)	re-dak-*tor*-ka	editor (f)
refleksja (f)	re-*flek*-sya	reflection (thinking)
regionalny	re-gyo-*nal*-ni	regional
religia (f)	re-*lee*-gya	religion
religijny	re-lee-*geey*-ni	religious

Polish	Pronunciation	English
rencista (m)	ren-*chees*-ta	pensioner (m)
rencistka (f)	ren-*cheest*-ka	pensioner (f)
republika (f)	re-poo-*blee*-ka	republic
restauracja (f)	res-ta-oo-*ra*-tsya	restaurant
reszta (f)	*resh*-ta	rest (what's left) • change (coins)
rezerwacja (f)	re-zer-*va*-tsya	reservation • booking
rezerwować	re-zer-*vo*-vach	to book
reżyser (m)	re-*zhi*-ser	film director (m)
reżyserka (f)	re-zhi-*ser*-ka	film director (f)
ręcznik (m)	*rench*-neek	towel
robić	*ro*-beech	to do • to make
robić zdjęcia	*ro*-beech *zdyen*-cha	to take photographs
robotnica (f)	ro-bot-*nee*-tsa	manual worker (f)
robotnik (m)	ro-*bot*-neek	manual worker (m)
rodzaj (m)	*ro*-dzay	kind • type
rodzice (m, pl)	ro-*djee*-tse	parents
rodzina (f)	ro-*djee*-na	family
rok (m)	rok	year
rolnictwo (neut)	rol-*neets*-tfo	agriculture
rolnik (m)	*rol*-neek	farmer
romans (m)	*ro*-mans	romance
rondo (neut)	*ron*-do	roundabout
ropa naftowa (f)	*ro*-pa naf-*to*-va	crude oil
rosnąć	*ros*-nonch	to grow
roślina (f)	rosh-*lee*-na	plant
roślinność (f)	rosh-*leen*-noshch	vegetation
rower (m)	*ro*-ver	bicycle
rower górski (m)	*ro*-ver *goor*-skee	mountain bike
rower wyścigowy (m)	*ro*-ver vish-chee-*go*-vi	racing bike
rozkład jazdy (m)	*ros*-kwat *yaz*-di	timetable
rozmawiać	roz-*ma*-vyach	to talk
rozmiar (m)	*roz*-myar	size
rozmowa (f)	roz-*mo*-va	talk • call
rozmowa międzymiastowa (f)	roz-*mo*-va myen-dzi-myas-*to*-va	long-distance call
rozmówki (f, pl)	roz-*moof*-kee	phrasebook
rozpoznać	ros-*poz*-nach	to recognise (identify)
rozrywka (f)	roz-*rif*-ka	entertainment
rozsądny	ros-*sond*-ni	reasonable
rozum (m)	*ro*-zoom	mind
rozumieć	ro-*zoo*-myech	to understand
rozwolnienie (neut)	roz-vol-*nye*-nye	diarrhoea
rozwój (m)	*roz*-vooy	development
róg (m)	rook	corner (of street)
równina (f)	roov-*nee*-na	plain (flat area)
równość (f)	*roov*-noshch	equality
równy	*roov*-ni	equal
różnica (f)	roozh-*nee*-tsa	difference
różowy	roo-*zho*-vi	pink
ruch (m)	rooh	movement
ruch drogowy (m)	rooh dro-*go*-vi	traffic
ruchliwy	rooh-*lee*-vi	busy (street)
ruiny (f, pl)	roo-*ee*-ni	ruins
rura (f)	*roo*-ra	pipe (for water)
ruszać	*roo*-shach	to move
ryba (f)	*ri*-ba	fish
rynek (m)	*ri*-nek	old town square
rytm (m)	ritm	rhythm
ryzyko (neut)	ri-*zi*-ko	risk

ryzykowny	ri-zi-*kov*-ni	risky
rzadki	*zhat*-kee	rare (uncommon)
rząd (m)	zhont	government
rzecz (f)	zhech	thing
rzeka (f)	*zhe*-ka	river
rzemiosło (neut)	zhe-*myo*-swo	craft
rzeźba (f)	*zhezh*-ba	sculpture

S

sałatka (f)	sa-*wat*-ka	salad
sam/sama	sam/*sa*-ma	alone
samica (f)	sa-*mee*-tsa	female animal
samochód (m)	sa-*mo*-hoot	car
samochód ciężarowy (m)	sa-*mo*-hoot chen-zha-*ro*-vi	truck • lorry

S BEFORE Ś

Polish letters with diacritical marks are treated as separate letters. Remember that *s* comes before *ś*.

samolot (m)	sa-*mo*-lot	aeroplane
samoobsługa (f)	sa-mo-op-*swoo*-ga	self-service
samotny	sa-*mot*-ni	lonely
sąd (m)	sont	court (legal)
sądzić	*son*-djeech	to judge
scena (f)	*stse*-na	stage (in theatre)
scenariusz (m)	stse-*na*-ryoosh	film script
schody (pl)	*s-ho*-di	stairs
schronisko górskie (neut)	sro-*nees*-ko *goor*-skye	mountain refuge
schronisko młodzieżowe (neut)	sro-*nees*-ko mwo-dje-*zho*-ve	youth hostel
scyzoryk (m)	stsi-*zo*-rik	penknife
sekretarka (f)	se-kre-*tar*-ka	secretary
sekunda (f)	se-*koon*-da	second
sen (m)	sen	sleep • dream
ser (m)	ser	cheese
serce (neut)	*ser*-tse	heart
sędzia (m)	*sen*-dja	judge
siatka (f)	*shat*-ka	net
siedzenie (neut)	she-*dze*-nye	seat
siedzieć	*she*-djech	to sit
sierpień (m)	*sher*-pyen	August
silnik (m)	*sheel*-neek	engine
silny	*sheel*-ni	strong
siła (f)	*shee*-wa	strength
siostra (f)	*shos*-tra	sister
skakać	*ska*-kach	to jump
skaleczenie (neut)	ska-le-*che*-nye	cut • wound
skała (f)	*ska*-wa	rock
skażenie (neut)	ska-*zhe*-nye	pollution
sklep (m)	sklep	shop • store
sklep mięsny (m)	sklep *myen*-sni	butcher (shop)
sklep odzieżowy (m)	sklep o-dje-*zho*-vi	clothing store
sklep owocowo-warzywny (m)	sklep o-vo-*tso*-vo va-*zhiv*-ni	greengrocer
sklep papierniczy (m)	sklep pa-pyer-*nee*-chi	stationers
sklep rybny (m)	sklep *rib*-ni	fishmonger
sklep spożywczy (m)	sklep spo-*zhif*-chi	gocery store
sklep z pamiątkami (m)	sklep spa-myont-*ka*-mee	souvenir shop
skoczyć	*sko*-chich	to jump
skóra (f)	*skoo*-ra	skin • leather
skrót (m)	skroot	short cut
skrzydło (neut)	*skshi*-dwo	wing

Polish	Pronunciation	English
skrzynka pocztowa (f)	skshin-ka poch-to-va	letter box
skrzypce (pl)	skship-tse	violin
skrzyżowanie (neut)	skshi-zho-va-nye	intersection
slajdy (m, pl)	slay-di	slides (film)
słaby	swa-bi	weak
sławny	swav-ni	famous
słodki	swot-kee	sweet
słoik (m)	swo-eek	jar
słoneczny	swo-nech-ni	sunny
słońce (neut)	swon-tse	sun
słownik (m)	swov-neek	dictionary
słowo (neut)	swo-vo	word
słuchać	swoo-hach	to listen
słuchawki (f, pl)	swoo-haf-kee	headphones
służba (f)	swoozh-ba	service
służba wojskowa (f)	swoozh-ba voy-sko-va	military service
słyszeć	swi-shech	to hear

Smacznego!
smach-ne-go!
Bon appetit!

Polish	Pronunciation	English
smaczny	smach-ni	tasty
smak (m)	smak	taste • flavour
smażony	sma-zho-ni	fried
smoczek (m)	smo-chek	dummy • pacifier
smutny	smoot-ni	sad
sobota (f)	so-bo-ta	Saturday
sok (m)	sok	juice
sok owocowy (m)	sok o-vo-tso-vi	fruit juice
sosna (f)	sos-na	pine (tree)
sól (f)	sool	salt
spacer (m)	spa-tser	walk
spacerować	spa-tse-ro-vach	to walk
spać	spach	to sleep
specjalny	spe-tsyal-ni	special
spieszyć się	spye-shich she	to hurry
spodnie (pl)	spod-nye	trousers
spodziewać się	spo-dje-vach she	to expect
spokojny	spo-koy-ni	quiet
sport (m)	sport	sport
sportowiec (m)	spor-to-vyets	sportsman
sportsmenka (f)	sports-men-ka	sports woman
spotkać	spot-kach	to meet
spotkanie (neut)	spot-ka-nye	meeting • appointment
spotykać	spo-ti-kach	to meet
spowiedź (f)	spo-vyech	confession (religious)
spódnica (f)	spood-nee-tsa	skirt
spóźnić się	spoozh-neech she	to miss (be late)
spragniony	spra-gnyo-ni	thirsty
sprawa (f)	spra-va	issue
sprawdzać	sprav-dzach	to check
sprawiedliwość (f)	spra-vye-dlee-voshch	justice
sprężyna (f)	spren-zhi-na	spring (coil)
sprzątanie (neut)	spshon-ta-nye	cleaning
sprzedać	spshe-dach	to sell
sprzedawać	spshe-da-vach	to sell
sprzedaż (f)	spshe-dash	sale
sprzęt (m)	spshent	equipment
srebro (neut)	sre-bro	silver
stacja (f)	sta-tsya	station
stacja benzynowa (f)	sta-tsya ben-zi-no-va	petrol (gas) station
stacja kolejowa (f)	sta-tsya ko-le-yo-va	train station
stać	stach	to stand
stać się	stach she	to become
stadion (m)	sta-dyon	stadium
stały	sta-wi	permanent
stan (m)	stan	state • condition
stan cywilny (m)	stan tsi-veel-ni	marital status
Stany Zjednoczone (pl)	sta-ni zye-dno-cho-ne	United States
stare miasto (neut)	sta-re mya-sto	old town
starożytny	sta-ro-zhit-ni	ancient

stary	*sta*-ri	old
statek (m)	*sta*-tek	ship
stawać się	*sta*-vach she	to become
sto	sto	hundred
stolik (m)	*sto*-leek	table (in restaurant)
stopa (f)	*sto*-pa	foot
stopa życiowa (f)	*sto*-pa zhi-*cho*-va	standard of living
stopień (m)	*sto*-pyen	degree
stół (m)	stoow	table
strach (m)	strah	fear
strajk (m)	strayk	strike
straszny	*strash*-ni	terrible
strata (f)	*stra*-ta	loss
strażak (m)	*stra*-zhak	fire fighter
straż pożarna (neut)	strash po-*zhar*-na	fire brigade
strefa wolnocłowa (f)	*stre*-fa vol-no-*tswo*-va	duty-free zone
stromy	*stro*-mi	steep
strona (f)	*stro*-na	page/side
strumień (m)	*stroo*-myen	stream
strzykawka (f)	stshi-*kaf*-ka	syringe
strzyżenie (neut)	stshi-*zhe*-nye	haircut
student (m)	*stoo*-dent	student (m)
studentka (f)	stoo-*dent*-ka	student (f)
styczeń (m)	*sti*-chen	January
styl (m)	stil	style
sukces (m)	*sook*-tses	success
sukienka (f)	soo-*kyen*-ka	dress
suma (f)	*soo*-ma	total (sum)
suszyć	*soo*-shich	to dry
sweter (m)	*sfe*-ter	jumper • sweater
swędzenie (neut)	sfen-*dze*-nye	itch
Sylwester (m)	sil-*ves*-ter	New Year's Eve
syn (m)	sin	son
synagoga (f)	si-na-*go*-ga	synagogue
syntetyczny	sin-te-*tich*-ni	synthetic
sypialnia (f)	si-*pyal*-nya	bedroom
szachownica (f)	sha-hov-*nee*-tsa	chess board

szachy (m, pl)	*sha*-hi	chess
szacunek (m)	sha-*tsoo*-nek	respect
szafa (f)	*sha*-fa	wardrobe cupboard
szalony	sha-*lo*-ni	mad • crazy
szampan (m)	*sham*-pan	champagne
szampon (m)	*sham*-pon	shampoo
szary	*sha*-ri	grey
szatnia (f)	*shat*-nya	cloak room
szczegół (m)	*shche*-goow	detail
szczepienie (neut)	shche-*pye*-nye	vaccination
szczenię (neut)	*shche*-nye	puppy
szczęście (neut)	*shchen*-shche	luck

> *Szczęśliwej podróży!*
> shchen-*shlee*-vey po-*droo*-zhi!
> Bon voyage!

szczęśliwy	shchen-*shlee*-vi	happy • lucky
szczoteczka do zębów (f)	shcho-*tech*-ka do *zem*-boof	toothbrush
szczotka (f)	*shchot*-ka	brush
szczotka do włosów (f)	*shchot*-ka do *vwo*-soof	hairbrush
szczur (m)	shchoor	rat
szczyt (m)	shchit	peak • summit
szeroki	she-*ro*-kee	wide
szklanka (f)	*shklan*-ka	glass (for water or tea)
szkła kontaktowe (neut, pl)	shkwa kon-tak-*to*-ve	contact lenses
szkło (neut)	shkwo	glass (material)
szkoła (f)	*shko*-wa	school
szkoła wyższa (f)	*shko*-wa *vish*-sha	high school
szlak (m)	shlak	trail • route
szminka (f)	*shmeen*-ka	lipstick
sznurek (m)	*shnoo*-rek	string

Polish	Pronunciation	English
sznurowadła (neut, pl)	shnoo-ro-*va*-dwa	shoelaces
szorty (pl)	*shor*-ti	shorts
szosa (f)	*sho*-sa	road • highway
szpital (m)	*shpee*-tal	hospital
sztuka (f)	*shtoo*-ka	art
sztuka ludowa (f)	*shtoo*-ka loo-*do*-va	folk art
sztuka teatralna (f)	*shtoo*-ka te-a-*tral*-na	play (theatre)
szukać	*shoo*-kach	to look for
szybki	*ship*-kee	fast • quick
szyć	shich	to sew
szyja (f)	*shi*-ya	neck
szynka (f)	*shin*-ka	ham

Ś

Polish	Pronunciation	English
ściana (f)	*shcha*-na	wall (inside)
ścieżka (f)	*shchesh*-ka	footpath
śliczny	*shleech*-ni	lovely
ślimak (m)	*shlee*-mak	snail
ślub (m)	shloop	wedding (ceremony)
śmiać się	shmyach she	to laugh
śmiech (m)	shmyeh	laugh
śmieci (m, pl)	*shmye*-chee	rubbish • garbage
śmierć (f)	shmerch	death
śniadanie (neut)	shnya-*da*-nye	breakfast
śnić	shneech	to dream
śnieg (m)	shnyek	snow
śpiący	*shpyon*-tsi	sleepy
śpiewać	*shpye*-vach	to sing
śpiwór (m)	*shpee*-voor	sleeping bag
średni	*shred*-ni	medium
środa (f)	*shro*-da	Wednesday
środek (m)	*shro*-dek	middle • medium
środek antykoncepcyjny (m)	*shro*-dek an-ti-kon-tsep-*tsiy*-ni	contraceptive
środek przeciwbólowy (m)	*shro*-dek pshe-cheef-boo-*lo*-vi	painkiller
środek przeczyszczający (m)	*shro*-dek pshe-chish-cha-*yon*-tsi	laxative
środowisko (neut)	shro-do-*vees*-ko	environment
śrubokręt (m)	shroo-*bo*-krent	screwdriver
świat (m)	shfyat	world
światło (neut)	*shfya*-two	light
światłomierz (m)	shfya-*two*-myesh	lightmeter
świątynia (f)	shfyon-*ti*-nya	temple
świeca (f)	*shfye*-tsa	candle
świetny	*shwyet*-ni	brilliant
świeży	*shfye*-zhi	fresh
święto (m)	*shfyen*-to	holiday
święto państwowe (neut)	*shfyen*-to pan-*stfo*-ve	public holiday
święty	*shfyen*-ti	holy • saint
świnia (f)	*shfee*-nya	pig
świt (m)	shfeet	dawn

T

Tak.
tak
Yes.

Polish	Pronunciation	English
taksówka (f)	tak-*soof*-ka	taxi • cab
także	*tak*-zhe	also
talerz (m)	*ta*-lesh	plate
talia (f)	*ta*-lya	deck of cards
tampony (m, pl)	tam-*po*-ni	tampons
tani	*ta*-nee	cheap
taniec (m)	*ta*-nyets	dance
tańczyć	*tan*-chich	to dance
targ (m)	tark	market
targi (m,pl)	*tar*-gee	trade fair
taryfa (f)	ta-*ri*-fa	fare • tariff
taśma video (f)	*tash*-ma vee-*de*-o	video tape

tata (m)	*ta*-ta	dad
teatr (m)	*te*-atr	theatre
technika (f)	teh-*nee*-ka	technique
telefon (m)	te-*le*-fon	telephone
telefon komórkowy (m)	te-*le*-fon ko-moor-*ko*-vi	mobile phone
telefonować	te-le-fo-*no*-vach	to telephone
telewizja (f)	te-le-*vee*-zya	television
telewizor (m)	te-le-*vee*-zor	TV set
temperatura (f)	tem-pe-ra-*too*-ra	temperature
tenis (m)	*te*-nees	tennis
tenis stołowy (m)	*te*-nees sto-*wo*-vi	table tennis
teraz	*te*-ras	now
teściowa (f)	tesh-*cho*-va	mother-in-law
teść (m)	teshch	father-in-law
też	tesh	also • too
tlen (m)	tlen	oxygen
tłumacz (m)	*twoo*-mach	translator (m)
tłumaczka (f)	twoo-*mach*-ka	translator (f)
tłumaczyć	twoo-*ma*-chich	to translate
tłusty	*twoos*-ti	fat (meat)
toaleta publiczna (f)	to-a-*le*-ta poo-*bleech*-na	public toilet
toalety (f, pl)	to-a-*le*-ti	toilets
toast (m)	*to*-ast	toast (drink)
torba (f)	*tor*-ba	bag
torebka (f)	to-*rep*-ka	handbag
tramwaj (m)	*tram*-vay	tram
trasa (f)	*tra*-sa	route
trasa podróży (f)	*tra*-sa po-*droo*-zhi	itinerary
trawa (f)	*tra*-va	grass
trawnik (m)	*trav*-neek	lawn
trochę	*tro*-he	a little (amount)
trolejbus (m)	tro-*ley*-boos	trolleybus
trudny	*trood*-ni	difficult
trwać	trfach	to last • to take time
trzeci	*tshe*-chee	third
trzęsienie ziemi (neut)	tshen-*she*-nye *zhe*-mee	earthquake
trzymać	*tshi*-mach	to keep
tu	too	here
turysta (m)	too-*ris*-ta	tourist (m)
turystka (f)	too-*rist*-ka	tourist (f)
tutaj	*too*-tay	here
tuzin (m)	*too*-zheen	dozen
twardy	*tfar*-di	hard (not soft)
twarz (f)	tfash	face
tydzień (m)	*ti*-djen	week
tylko	*til*-ko	only
typ (m)	tip	type
typowy	ti-*po*-vi	typical
tytoń (m)	*ti*-ton	tobacco

U

ubezpieczenie (neut)	oo-bes-pye-*che*-nye	insurance
ubierać się	oo-*bye*-rach she	to dress
ubranie (neut)	oo-*bra*-nye	clothing
ucho (neut)	*oo*-ho	ear
uchodźca (m)	oo-*hoch*-tsa	refugee
uczciwy	ooch-*chee*-vi	honest
uczucie (neut)	oo-*choo*-che	feeling
uczulenie (neut)	oo-choo-*le*-nye	allergy
uczyć	*oo*-chich	to teach
uczyć się	*oo*-chich she	to learn
ufać	*oo*-fach	to trust
ugryzienie (neut)	oo-gri-*zhe*-nye	bite (dog)
ukarać	oo-*ka*-rach	to punish
ukąszenie (neut)	oo-kon-*she*-nye	bite (insect)
ukraść	*oo*-krashch	to steal
ulepszać	oo-*lep*-shach	to improve

Polish	Pronunciation	English
ulica (f)	oo-*lee*-tsa	street
ulubiony	oo-loo-*byo*-ni	favourite
umierać	oo-*mye*-rach	to die
Unia Europejska (f)	*oo*-nya ew-ro-*pey*-ska	European Union
uniwersytet (m)	oo-nee-*ver*-si-tet	university
upadać	oo-*pa*-dach	to fall
upał (m)	*oo*-paw	heat
uparty	oo-*par*-ti	stubborn
uprzejmy	oo-*pshey*-mi	polite
uratować	oo-ra-*to*-vach	to save (rescue)
urodziny (pl)	oo-ro-*djee*-ni	birthday
urlop (m)	*oor*-lop	holidays • leave
urwisko (neut)	oor-*vees*-ko	cliff
usiąść	*oo*-shonshch	to sit down
usłyszeć	oo-*swi*-shech	to hear
usta (pl)	*oos*-ta	mouth
uśmiechać się	oosh-*mye*-hach she	to smile
uzdrowisko (neut)	oo-zdro-*vees*-ko	spa
uznać	*ooz*-nach	to recognise (acknowledge)
użyteczny	oo-zhi-*tech*-ni	useful
używać	oo-*zhi*-vach	to use
używany	oo-zhi-*va*-ni	second-hand

W

Polish	Pronunciation	English
wada (f)	*va*-da	fault (something's)
wadliwy	vad-*lee*-vi	faulty
waga (f)	*va*-ga	weight
wagon (m)	*va*-gon	car • carriage
wagon restauracyjny (m)	*va*-gon res-ta-oo-ra-*tsiy*-ni	dining car
wagon sypialny (m)	*va*-gon si-*pyal*-ni	sleeping car
wakacje (pl)	va-*ka*-tsye	holidays • vacation
walczyć	*val*-chich	to fight
walizka (f)	va-*lees*-ka	suitcase
walka (f)	*val*-ka	fight
waluta (f)	va-*loo*-ta	currency
Warszawa (f)	var-*sha*-va	Warsaw
warsztat (m)	*var*-shtat	workshop
warsztat samochodowy (m)	*var*-shtat sa-mo-ho-*do*-vi	garage (mechanic)
wartość (f)	*var*-toshch	value
ważny	*vazh*-ni	valid • important
ważyć	*va*-zhich	to weigh
wąski	*von*-skee	narrow
wąsy (m, pl)	*von*-si	moustache
wątroba (f)	von-*tro*-ba	liver
wąż (m)	vonsh	snake
wchodzić	*fho*-djeech	to enter
w ciąży	*fchon*-zhi	pregnant
wcześnie	*fchesh*-nye	early
wczoraj	*fcho*-ray	yesterday
wdzięczny	*vdjench*-ni	grateful
wejść	veyshch	to enter
wełna (f)	*veoo*-na	wool
wentylator (m)	ven-ti-*la*-tor	fan
wesele (neut)	ve-*se*-le	wedding (reception)
wewnątrz	*vev*-nonch	inside
wewnętrzny	vev-*nench*-ni	extension (phone)
wędkarstwo (neut)	vent-*kar*-stfo	fishing (hobby)
wędrować	ven-*dro*-vach	to hike
wędrówki piesze	ven-*droof*-kee *pye*-she	hiking
wiadomości (f, pl)	vya-do-*mosh*-chee	news
wiadomość (f)	vya-*do*-moshch	message
wiadro (neut)	*vya*-dro	bucket
wiatr (m)	vyatr	wind
widok (m)	*vee*-dok	view
widzieć	*vee*-djech	to see

Polish	Pronunciation	English
wieczór (m)	*vye*-choor	evening
wiedzieć	*vye*-djech	to know
wiek (m)	vyek	age • century
Wielka Brytania (f)	*vyel*-ka bri-*ta*-nya	Great Britain
Wielkanoc (f)	vyel-*ka*-nots	Easter
Wielki Post (m)	*vyel*-kee post	Lent
wieś (f)	vyesh	village
wieża (f)	*vye*-zha	tower
więcej	*vyen*-tsey	more
większość (f)	*vyenk*-shoshch	majority
więzienie (neut)	vyen-*zhe*-nye	prison • jail
Wigilia (f)	vee-*gee*-lya	Christmas Eve
wina (f)	*vee*-na	fault (someone's)
winda (f)	*veen*-da	elevator • lift
winny	*veen*-ni	guilty
wino (neut)	*vee*-no	wine
winogrono (m)	vee-no-*gro*-no	grape
wiosna (f)	*vyos*-na	spring (season)
wirus (m)	*vee*-roos	virus
witaminy (f, pl)	vee-ta-*mee*-ni	vitamins
wiza (f)	*vee*-za	visa
wizyta (f)	vee-*zi*-ta	appointment (with doctor)
wkrótce	*fkroot*-tse	soon
władza (f)	*vwa*-dza	power • authority
włamanie (neut)	vwa-*ma*-nye	break-in
własność (f)	*vwas*-noshch	property
właściciel (m)	vwash-*chee*-chel	owner (m)
właścicielka (f)	vwash-chee-*chel*-ka	owner (f)
włączać	*vwon*-chach	to include
włosy (m, pl)	*vwo*-si	hair
wnuczka (f)	*vnooch*-ka	granddaughter
wnuk (m)	vnook	grandson
woda (f)	*vo*-da	water
woda mineralna (f)	*vo*-da mee-ne-*ral*-na	mineral water
woda pitna (f)	*vo*-da *peet*-na	drinking water
wodospad (m)	vo-*dos*-pat	waterfall
wodoszczelny	vo-do-*shchel*-ni	waterproof
wojna (f)	*voy*-na	war
woleć	*vo*-lech	to prefer
wolny	*vol*-ni	slow (not fast) • free (not bound) • vacant
wołać	*vo*-wach	to call
wódka (f)	*voot*-ka	vodka
wózek (m)	*voo*-zek	trolley
wózek inwalidzki (m)	*voo*-zek een-va-*leets*-kee	wheelchair
wracać	*vra*-tsach	to return
wrócić	*vroo*-cheech	to return
wrzesień (m)	*vzhe*-shen	September
wschód (m)	fs-hoot	east
wschód słońca (m)	fs-hoot *swon*-tsa	sunrise
wspaniały	fspa-*nya*-wi	great
wspinaczka (f)	fspee-*nach*-ka	climbing
wspinaczka górska (f)	fspee-*nach*-ka *goor*-ska	mountaineering
wspinaczka skalna (f)	*fspee*-nach-ka *skal*-na	rock climbing
wspinać się	*fspee*-nach she	to scale • to climb
wspominać	fspo-*mee*-nach	to recall • to mention
wspólny	*fspool*-ni	common
współczesny	fspoow-*ches*-ni	contemporary
wstać	fstach	to get up (from bed)
wstęp (m)	fstemp	admission
wszechświat (m)	*fsheh*-shfyat	universe

wszędzie	*fshen*-dje	everywhere
wszy (f, pl)	fshi	lice
wszyscy	*fshis*-tsi	everyone
wszystko	*fshis*-tko	every thing
wśród	fshroot	among
wtorek (m)	*fto*-rek	Tuesday
wtyczka (f)	*ftich*-ka	plug (electric)
wuj/wujek (m)	vooy/*voo*-yek	uncle
wybierać	vi-*bye*-rach	to choose • to elect
wybory (m, pl)	vi-*bo*-ri	elections
wybrać	*vi*-brach	to choose • to elect
wybrzeże (neut)	vi-*bzhe*-zhe	coast
wycieczka (f)	vi-*chech*-ka	excursion • trip
wycieczka z przewodnikiem (f)	vi-*chech*-ka spshe-vod-*nee*-kyem	guided tour
wygodny	vi-*god*-ni	comfortable
wygrać	*vi*-grach	to win
wyjaśnić	vi-*yash*-neech	to explain
wyjeżdżać	vi-*yesh*-djach	to leave (depart)
wyjście	*viy*-shche	emergency
wyjście awaryjne (neut)	*viy*-shche a-va-*riy*-ne	emergency exit
wyjście bezpieczeństwa	*viy*-shche bes-pye-*chen*-stfa	emergency exit
wymiana (f)	vi-*mya*-na	exchange
wymieniać	vi-*mye*-nyach	to exchange (money)
wynajem samochodów (m)	vi-*na*-yem sa-mo-*ho*-doof	car rental
wynajmować	vi-nay-*mo*-vach	to rent • to hire
wypadek (m)	vi-*pa*-dek	accident
wypadek drogowy (m)	vi-*pa*-dek dro-*go*-vi	road accident
wypełnić	vi-*peoo*-neech	to fill in
wypić	*vi*-peech	to drink
wyrok (m)	*vi*-rok	sentence (court's verdict)
wysłać	*vi*-swach	to send
wysoki	vi-*so*-kee	high • tall
wysokość (f)	vi-*so*-koshch	altitude
wyspa (f)	*vis*-pa	island
wystawa (f)	vis-*ta*-va	exhibition
wysypka (f)	vi-*sip*-ka	rash
wyścig (m)	*vish*-cheek	race (sport)
wywiad (m)	*vi*-vyat	interview
wywołanie filmu (neut)	vi-vo-*wa*-nye *feel*-moo	film processing
wzgórze (neut)	*vzgoo*-zhe	hill
wziąć	vzhonch	to take

Z

z	z	with
za	za	behind
zabawa (f)	za-*ba*-va	party • fiesta • fun
zabawka (f)	za-*baf*-ka	toy

Z BEFORE Ź BEFORE Ż

Polish letters with diacritical marks are treated as separate letters. Remember that z comes before ź, which is followed by ż.

zabić	*za*-beech	to kill
zachód (m)	*za*-hoot	west
zachód słońca (m)	*za*-hoot *swon*-tsa	sunset
zaczekać	za-*che*-kach	to wait
zaczynać	za-*chi*-nach	to begin
zadzwonić	za-*dzvo*-neech	to call (by phone)
zagranicą	za-gra-*nee*-tsom	abroad

Z

zagraniczny	za-gra-*neech*-ni	foreign (from abroad)
zajęty	za-*yen*-ti	busy • occupied • engaged
zakłopotanie (neut)	za-kwo-po-*ta*-nye	embarrassment
zakłopotany	za-kwo-po-*ta*-ni	embarassed
zakonnica (f)	za-kon-*nee*-tsa	nun
zakończyć	za-*kon*-chich	to end • to complete
zakupy (pl)	za-*koo*-pi	shopping
zakurzony	za-koo-*zho*-ni	dusty
zaliczka (f)	za-*leech*-ka	advance payment
załamany	za-wa-*ma*-ni	broken
załatwić	za-*wat*-feech	to fix (arrange)
zamek (m)	*za*-mek	castle • lock
zamiar (m)	*za*-myar	intention
zamiast	*za*-myast	instead of
zamknąć	*zam*-knonch	to close
zamknięty	zam-*knyen*-ti	closed
zamówić	za-*moo*-veech	to order (in restaurant)
zamówienie (neut)	za-moo-*vye*-nye	order (request)
zamykać	za-*mi*-kach	to close • to shut
zamykać na klucz	za-*mi*-kach na klooch	to lock
zamrażać	za-*mra*-zhach	to freeze
zamrażarka (f)	za-mra-*zhar*-ka	freezer
zanieczyszczenie (neut)	za-nye-chish-*che*-nye	pollution
zaniepokojony	za-nye-po-ko-*yo*-ni	worried
zapach (m)	*za*-pah	smell
zapalić	za-*pa*-leech	to smoke
zapalniczka (f)	za-pal-*neech*-ka	cigarette lighter
zapałki (f, pl)	za-*paw*-kee	matches
zapłacić	za-*pwa*-cheech	to pay
zapłata (f)	za-*pwa*-ta	payment
zapobiegać	za-po-*bye*-gach	to prevent
zapobieganie ciąży (neut)	za-po-bye-*ga*-nye *chon*-zhi	contraception
zapominać	za-po-*mee*-nach	to forget
zapomnieć	za-*pom*-nyech	to forget
zapraszać	za-*pra*-shach	to invite
zaprosić	za-*pro*-sheech	to invite
zaproszenie (neut)	za-*pro*-she-nye	invitation
zapytać	za-*pi*-tach	to ask (a question)
zarabiać	za-*ra*-byach	to earn
zarezerwować	za-re-zer-*vo*-vach	to reserve • to book
zaręczony	za-ren-*cho*-ni	engaged (betrothed)
zarobki (m, pl)	za-*rop*-kee	earrings
zasiłek (m)	za-*shee*-wek	dole
zastrzyk (m)	*zas*-tshik	injection
zasypka dla niemowląt (f)	za-*sip*-ka dla nye-*mov*-lont	baby powder
zatłoczony	za-two-*cho*-ni	crowded
zatrucie pokarmowe (neut)	za-*troo*-che po-kar-*mo*-ve	food poisoning
zatrudnienie (neut)	za-trood-*nye*-nye	employment
zatrzymać (się)	za-*tshi*-mach (she)	to stop
zatwardzenie (f)	zat-far-*dze*-nye	constipation
zaufanie (neut)	za-oo-*fa*-nye	trust • confidence
zawody (pl)	za-*vo*-di	games (sport)
zawód (m)	*za*-voot	profession • occupation
zawsze	*zaf*-she	always
zazdrosny	zaz-*dros*-ni	jealous
ząb (m)	zomp	tooth
zdalne sterowanie (neut)	*zdal*-ne ste-ro-*va*-nye	remote control

DICTIONARY

Polish	Pronunciation	English
zdanie (neut)	*zda*-nye	sentence (grammatical)
zdechły	*zdeh*-wi	dead (animal)
zdjęcie (neut)	*zdyen*-che	photo
zdrowie (neut)	*zdro*-vye	health
zdrowy	*zdro*-vi	healthy
zebranie (neut)	ze-*bra*-nye	meeting
zegar (m)	*ze*-gar	clock
zegarek (m)	ze-*ga*-rek	watch
zepsuć się	*zep*-sooch she	to break down
zero (neut)	*ze*-ro	zero
zespół (m)	*zes*-poow	group • band • team
zewnętrzny	zev-*nench*-ni	outside
zęby (m, pl)	*zem*-bi	teeth
zgadzać się	*zga*-dzach she	to agree

Zgoda.
zgo-da
Agreed.

Polish	Pronunciation	English
zguba (f)	*zgoo*-ba	loss
zgubić	*zgoo*-beech	to lose
zielony	zhe-*lo*-ni	green
ziemia (f)	*zhe*-mya	Earth
zima (f)	*zhee*-ma	winter
zimna woda (f)	*zheem*-na *vo*-da	cold water
zimny	*zheem*-ni	cold
zioło (neut)	*zho*-wo	herb
złamanie (neut)	zwa-*ma*-nye	fracture
złapać	*zwa*-pach	to catch
złodziej (m)	*zwo*-djey	thief
złodziej kieszonkowy (m)	*zwo*-djey kye-shon-*ko*-vi	pickpocket
złoto (neut)	*zwo*-to	gold
zły	zwi	wrong • bad • angry
zmarły	*zmar*-wi	dead (person)
zmartwiony	zmar-*tfyo*-ni	worried
zmęczony	zmen-*cho*-ni	tired
zmieniać	*zmye*-nyach	to change
zmierzch (m)	zmyeshh	dusk
znaczek (m)	*zna*-chek	stamp
znaczyć	*zna*-chich	to mean • to mark
znać	znach	to know (someone)
znak (m)	znak	sign
znak drogowy (m)	znak dro-*go*-vi	road sign
znaleźć	*zna*-leshch	to find
znikać	*znee*-kach	to disappear
zniszczyć	*zneesh*-chich	to destroy
zniżka (f)	*zneesh*-ka	discount
znowu	*zno*-voo	again
znudzony	znoo-*dzo*-ni	bored
zobaczyć	zo-*ba*-chich	to see
zoo (neut)	*zo*-o	zoo
zostać	*zos*-tach	to stay (remain)
zostawać	zos-*ta*-vach	to stay (remain)
zostawiać	zos-*ta*-vyach	to leave (behind)
zrobić	*zro*-beech	to do • to make
zwariowany	zva-ryo-*va*-ni	mad • crazy
związek (m)	*zvyon*-zek	relationship • union
związek zawodowy (m)	*zvyon*-zek za-vo-*do*-vi	trade union
zwichnięcie (neut)	zveeh-*nyen*-che	sprain
zwiedzać	*zvye*-dzach	to visit
zwiedzanie (neut)	zvye-*dza*-nye	sightseeing
zwierzę (neut)	*zvye*-zhe	animal
zwyczajny	zvi-*chay*-ni	ordinary
zwykły	*zvik*-wi	usual
zysk (m)	zisk	profit

Ź

źródło (neut)	*zhroo*-dwo	spring (of water)

Ż

żaden	*zha*-den	none • neither
żaglówka (f)	zha-*gloof*-ka	sailing boat
żałować	zha-*wo*-vach	to regret
żarówka (f)	zha-*roof*-ka	light bulb
żart (m)	zhart	joke
żartować	zhar-*to*-vach	to joke
żebraczka (f)	zhe-*brach*-ka	beggar (f)
żebrak (m)	*zhe*-brak	beggar (m)
żeglarstwo (neut)	zhe-*glar*-stfo	sailing
żelazko (neut)	zhe-*las*-ko	iron (for clothes)
żeton (m)	*zhe*-ton	token (for phone)
żołądek (m)	zho-*won*-dek	stomach
żona (f)	*zho*-na	wife
żółty	*zhoow*-ti	yellow
życie (neut)	*zhi*-che	life
życzliwy	zhich-*lee*-vi	friendly
życzyć	*zhi*-chich	to wish
żyć	zhich	to live (life)
żyd (m)	zhit	Jew
żydowski	zhi-*dof*-skee	Jewish
żydówka (f)	zhi-*doof*-ka	Jew
żyletka (f)	zhi-*let*-ka	razor blade
żyła (f)	*zhi*-wa	vein
żywność (f)	*zhiv*-noshch	food

INDEX

INDEX

SPIS TREŚCI

COMPLETE LIST OF LONELY PLANET BOOKS

AFRICA Africa on a shoestring • Cairo • Cape Town • East Africa • Egypt • Ethiopia, Eritrea & Djibouti • The Gambia & Senegal • Healthy Travel Africa • Kenya • Malawi • Morocco • Mozambique • Read This First: Africa • South Africa, Lesotho & Swaziland • Southern Africa • Southern Africa Road Atlas • Tanzania, Zanzibar & Pemba • Trekking in East Africa • Tunisia • Watching Wildlife East Africa • Watching Wildlife Southern Africa • West Africa • World Food Morocco • Zimbabwe, Botswana & Namibia

AUSTRALIA & THE PACIFIC Aboriginal Australia & the Torres Strait Islands • Auckland • Australia • Australia Road Atlas • Bushwalking in Australia • Cycling Australia • Cycling New Zealand • Fiji • Healthy Travel Australia, NZ and the Pacific • Islands of Australia's Great Barrier Reef • Melbourne • Micronesia • New Caledonia • New South Wales & the ACT • New Zealand • Northern Territory • Outback Australia • Out to Eat – Melbourne • Out to Eat – Sydney • Papua New Guinea • Queensland • Rarotonga & the Cook Islands • Samoa • Solomon Islands • South Australia • South Pacific • Sydney • Sydney Condensed • Tahiti & French Polynesia • Tasmania • Tonga • Tramping in New Zealand • Vanuatu • Victoria • Walking in Australia • Watching Wildlife Australia • Western Australia

CENTRAL AMERICA & THE CARIBBEAN Bahamas, Turks & Caicos • Baja California • Bermuda • Central America on a shoestring • Costa Rica • Cuba • Dominican Republic & Haiti • Eastern Caribbean • Guatemala • Guatemala, Belize & Yucatán: La Ruta Maya • Havana • Healthy Travel Central & South America • Jamaica • Mexico • Mexico City • Panama • Puerto Rico • Read This First: Central & South America • World Food Mexico • Yucatán

EUROPE Amsterdam • Amsterdam Condensed • Andalucía • Austria • Barcelona • Belgium & Luxembourg • Berlin • Britain • Brussels, Bruges & Antwerp • Budapest • Canary Islands • Central Europe •Copenhagen • Corfu & the Ionians • Corsica • Crete • Crete Condensed • Croatia • Cycling Britain • Cycling France • Cyprus • Czech & Slovak Republics • Denmark • Dublin • Eastern Europe • Edinburgh • England • Estonia, Latvia & Lithuania • Europe on a shoestring • Finland • Florence • France • Frankfurt Condensed • Georgia, Armenia & Azerbaijan • Germany • Greece • Greek Islands • Hungary • Iceland, Greenland & the Faroe Islands • Ireland • Istanbul • Italy • Krakow • Lisbon • The Loire • London • London Condensed • Madrid • Malta • Mediterranean Europe • Milan, Turin & Genoa • Moscow • Mozambique • Munich • The Netherlands • Normandy • Norway • Out to Eat – London • Paris • Paris Condensed • Poland • Portugal • Prague • Provence & the Côte d'Azur • Read This First: Europe • Rhodes & the Dodecanese • Romania & Moldova • Rome • Rome Condensed • Russia, Ukraine & Belarus • Scandinavian & Baltic Europe • Scotland • Sicily • Slovenia • South-West France • Spain • St Petersburg • Sweden • Switzerland • Trekking in Spain • Tuscany • Venice • Vienna • Walking in Britain • Walking in France • Walking in Ireland • Walking in Italy • Walking in Spain • Walking in Switzerland • Western Europe • World Food France • World Food Ireland • World Food Italy • World Food Spain

COMPLETE LIST OF LONELY PLANET BOOKS

INDIAN SUBCONTINENT Bangladesh • Bhutan • Delhi • Goa • Healthy Travel Asia & India • India • Indian Himalaya • Karakoram Highway • Kerala • Mumbai (Bombay) • Nepal • Pakistan • Rajasthan • Read This First: Asia & India • South India • Sri Lanka • Tibet • Trekking in the Indian Himalaya • Trekking in the Karakoram & Hindukush • Trekking in the Nepal Himalaya

ISLANDS OF THE INDIAN OCEAN Madagascar &Comoros • Maldives • Mauritius, Réunion & Seychelles

MIDDLE EAST & CENTRAL ASIA Bahrain, Kuwait & Qatar • Central Asia • Dubai • Iran • Israel & the Palestinian Territories • Istanbul • Istanbul to Cairo on a Shoestring • Istanbul to Kathmandu • Jerusalem • Jordan • Lebanon • Middle East • Oman & the United Arab Emirates • Syria • Turkey • World Food Turkey • Yemen

NORTH AMERICA Alaska • Boston • Boston Condensed • British Colombia • California & Nevada • California Condensed • Canada • Chicago • Deep South • Florida • Great Lakes • Hawaii • Hiking in Alaska • Hiking in the USA • Honolulu • Las Vegas • Los Angeles • Louisiana & The Deep South • Miami • Montreal • New England • New Orleans • New York City • New York City Condensed • New York, New Jersey & Pennsylvania • Oahu • Out to Eat – San Francisco • Pacific Northwest • Puerto Rico • Rocky Mountains • San Francisco • San Francisco Map • Seattle • Southwest • Texas • Toronto • USA • Vancouver • Virginia & the Capital Region • Washington DC • World Food Deep South, USA • World Food New Orleans

NORTH-EAST ASIA Beijing • China • Hiking in Japan • Hong Kong • Hong Kong Condensed • Hong Kong, Macau & Guangzhou • Japan • Korea • Kyoto • Mongolia • Seoul • Shanghai • South-West China • Taiwan • Tokyo • World Food – Hong Kong

SOUTH AMERICA Argentina, Uruguay & Paraguay • Bolivia • Brazil • Buenos Aires • Chile & Easter Island • Colombia • Ecuador & the Galapagos Islands • Healthy Travel Central & South America • Peru • Read This First: Central & South America • Rio de Janeiro • Santiago • South America on a shoestring • Santiago • Trekking in the Patagonian Andes • Venezuela

SOUTH-EAST ASIA Bali & Lombok • Bangkok • Cambodia • Hanoi • Healthy Travel Asia & India • Ho Chi Minh City • Indonesia • Indonesia's Eastern Islands • Jakarta • Java • Laos • Malaysia, Singapore & Brunei • Myanmar (Burma) • Philippines • Read This First: Asia & India • Singapore • South-East Asia on a shoestring • Thailand • Thailand's Islands & Beaches • Thailand, Vietnam, Laos & Cambodia Road Atlas • Vietnam • World Food Thailand • World Food Vietnam

Also available; Journeys travel literature, illustrated pictorials, calendars, diaries, Lonely Planet maps and videos. For more information on these series and for the complete range of Lonely Planet products and services, visit our website at **www.lonelyplanet.com**.

LONELY PLANET

Series Description

travel guidebooks	in depth coverage with background and recommendations download selected guidebook Upgrades at www.lonelyplanet.com
shoestring guides	for travellers with more time than money
condensed guides	highlights the best a destination has to offer
citySync	digital city guides for Palm TM OS
outdoor guides	walking, cycling, diving and watching wildlife
phrasebooks	don't just stand there, say something!
city maps and road atlases	essential navigation tools
world food	for people who live to eat, drink and travel
out to eat	a city's best places to eat and drink
read this first	invaluable pre-departure guides
healthy travel	practical advice for staying well on the road
journeys	travel stories for armchair explorers
pictorials	lavishly illustrated pictorial books
ekno	low cost international phonecard with e-services
TV series and videos	on the road docos
web site	for chat, Upgrades and destination facts
lonely planet images	on line photo library

LONELY PLANET OFFICES

Australia
Locked Bag 1, Footscray,
Victoria 3011
☎ 03 8379 8000
fax 03 8379 8111
email: talk2us@lonelyplanet.com.au

USA
150 Linden St, Oakland,
CA 94607
☎ 510 893 8555
TOLL FREE: 800 275 8555
fax 510 893 8572
email: info@lonelyplanet.com

UK
10a Spring Place,
London NW5 3BH
☎ 020 7428 4800
fax 020 7428 4828
email: go@lonelyplanet.co.uk

France
1 rue du Dahomey,
75011 Paris
☎ 01 55 25 33 00
fax 01 55 25 33 01
email: bip@lonelyplanet.fr
website: www.lonelyplanet.fr

World Wide Web: www.lonelyplanet.com *or* AOL keyword: lp
Lonely Planet Images: lpi@lonelyplanet.com.au